088.7
STO

W9-ABG-846

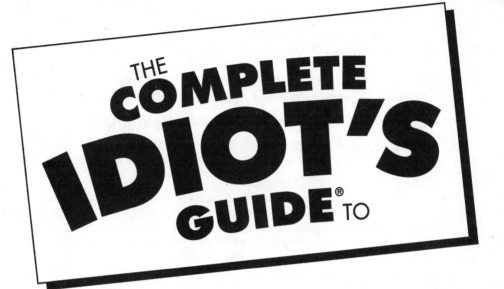

THE COMPLETE IDIOT'S GUIDE® TO

Beanie Babies

by Holly Stowe and Carol Turkington

051997

alpha books

A Division of Macmillan General Reference
A Simon & Schuster Macmillan Company
1633 Broadway, New York, NY 10019-6785

FAIRHOPE PUBLIC LIBRARY
161 N. SECTION ST.
FAIRHOPE, AL 36532

For Kara Kennedy, Elise Landau, Elizabeth Arnold, Rachel Boscov, Emma McCaskey, Cimmie Binning, Miranda Dillon, Cassie Duignan, Cassie Kasun, Julia Flood, Sarah Gawn, Betsy Herr, Fiona Johan, Maggie Kegel, Laura Boles, Kaitlyn Lukehart, Becca Rast, Emily Weida, Katie McMahon, Deanna Ross, Ariel Levine, Kate Roosa, Phoebe Fasulo, Kristin Connor, Brittany Formica, Anastasia Roda, and Katie Miller

Copyright © 1998 Holly Stowe and Carol Turkington

THIS PUBLICATION HAS NOT BEEN PREPARED, APPROVED, ENDORSED, OR AUTHORIZED BY TY INC., THE CREATOR AND MANUFACTURER OF BEANIE BABIES PLUSH TOYS.

All rights reserved. No part of this book shall be reproduced, stored in a retrieval system, or transmitted by any means, electronic, mechanical, photocopying, recording, or otherwise, without written permission from the publisher. Beanie Babies and the Ty name and logo are registered trademarks of Ty Inc. For information, address Alpha Books, 1633 Broadway, 7th Floor, New York, NY 10019-6785.

THE COMPLETE IDIOT'S GUIDE To & Design is a registered trademark of Prentice-Hall, Inc.

Note: This publication contains the opinions and ideas of its authors. It is intended to provide helpful and informative material on the subject matter covered. It is sold with the understanding that the author and publisher are not engaged in rendering personal professional services in the publication. If the reader requires personal assistance or advice, a competent professional should be consulted.

The authors and publisher specifically disclaim any responsibility for any liability, loss or risk, personal or otherwise, which is incurred or claimed as a consequence, directly or indirectly, of the use and application of any of the contents of this publication.

Macmillan Publishing books may be purchased for business or sales promotional use. For information please write: Special Markets Department, Macmillan Publishing USA, 1633 Broadway, New York, NY 10019.

International Standard Book Number: 0-02-863077-7
Library of Congress Catalog Card Number: 98-88316

01 00 99   8 7 6 5 4 3 2 1

Interpretation of the printing code: the rightmost number of the first series of numbers is the year of the book's printing; the rightmost number of the second series of numbers is the number of the book's printing. For example, a printing code of 99-1 shows that the first printing occurred in 1999.

Printed in the United States of America

Alpha Development Team

Publisher
Kathy Nebenhaus

Editorial Director
Gary M. Krebs

Managing Editor
Bob Shuman

Marketing Brand Manager
Felice Primeau

Senior Editor
Nancy Mikhail

Editor
Jessica Faust

Development Editors
Phil Kitchel
Amy Zavatto

Assistant Editor
Maureen Horn

Production Team

Development Editors
Lynn Northrup
Matthew X. Kiernan

Production Editor
Lori Cates

Cover Designer
Mike Freeland

Photo Editor
Richard H. Fox

Cover Photographs
Steffany Rubin Photography

Interior Photos
Chad Hill, Metaphor Photography
Holly Stowe

Illustrator
Jody P. Schaeffer

Designer
Ruth Lewis

Indexer
Lisa Stumpf

Layout/Proofreading
Melissa Auciello-Brogan, Angela Calvert, Mary Hunt

Contents at a Glance

Contents

10 Birds of a Feather   117

11 Bow-Wowing the Critics   137

12 Creepy-Crawlers   157

13 Unbearably Cute   173

14 It's a Jungle Out There   195

Appendices

Foreword

Beanie Babies are truly one of the great inventions of the 20th century. Five years ago, no one could have predicted that these happy, soft, cuddly animals filled with plastic pellets—complete with a name, poem, and birth date—would have caused such a nationwide and worldwide sensation. These simple toys have caught the imagination of collectors like nothing before. Almost overnight, "Beanie Baby" became a household word.

A unique aspect of Beanie Babies is that they cross all boundaries. There is no "average" Beanie collector. Men, women, and children of all ages and professions collect them. From doctors, teachers, and lawyers to moms, dads, grandparents, and school-children, Beanie Babies have, in effect, become a glue that binds people together in a common interest. That's a pretty deep and complicated phenomenon created by such a simple toy.

I get asked all the time: "When will people stop buying Beanie Babies? Isn't this just a fad?" People have asked those questions for the past three years, believing that Beanie Babies are just a passing fad like Tickle-Me-Elmo and other flashes in the pan. I always respond, "Beanie Babies are here to stay." There are many factors that determine the future of a collectible. Beanie Babies rank high in every category: They have a proven track record; they're both a toy and a collectible; Ty piques collector interest with regular retirements and new releases; and Beanie Babies are a high-quality item with a low retail cost. Beanie Babies are everything a classic collectible should be.

With that said, don't be afraid to start collecting Beanie Babies today. The best way to start is to first know as much as you can about collecting Beanie Babies. Don't start by throwing money at every Beanie that happens your way. Learn the ins and outs of this great hobby from people who've "been there, done that." That's where *The Complete Idiot's Guide® to Beanie Babies* enters the equation. Holly Stowe and Carol Turkington share their experience and knowledge in this outstanding presentation for beginning Beanie Baby collectors (there's some good stuff for us seasoned collectors, as well).

The guide traces the history of Beanies, then takes an in-depth look at sports promotion Beanies, the Teddys, Princess, holiday-related Beanies, McDonald's Teenie Beanies, and so on. The authors examine each Beanie Baby within a unique "Family Album" setting: "Here Kitty, Kitty..." for cats, "Birds of a Feather" for birds, and so on. The book is loaded with collecting advice, plus buying, selling, and trading tips. There are sections devoted to identifying hangtags and tush tags; how to care for, dress, and display Beanies; and how to spot fakes. There are numerous Beanie checklists and listings of Web sites and publications. *The Complete Idiot's Guide® to Beanie Babies* is an indispensable guide for new collectors who want to get their feet wet in Beanie Babies. It has all the information you'll need to know from the people in the know.

—Shawn Brecka, author of *The Bean Family Album* and *The Bean Family Pocket Guide*, and editor-at-large for *Beans!* magazine (Tuff Stuff Publications).

Introduction

This book is divided into five parts, designed to help you learn everything there is to know about Beanies, from hangtags to tush tags and everything in between. Along the way, you'll read about many of the rumors, gaffes, and ups and downs these little furry creatures have encountered on the road to superstardom.

By the time you've made your way through *The Complete Idiot's Guide to Beanie Babies*, you'll know what to look for in a Beanie Baby, and how to buy, trade, care for, display, and use your Beanies. You'll learn how to spot a counterfeit and which Beanies are more valuable than their close cousins—and why.

Part 1, "Welcome to the Wonderful World of Beanies," explores just what a Beanie is—what they are, where they come from, how it all began, what makes them such a hot commodity, what turned the critters into the biggest toy craze ever—and whether the boom will one day go bust.

Part 2, "Oh, the Places We've Been," gets down to the Beanie-gritty with details about the special origins of some of the more unusual Beanies. You'll learn about the incredible phenomenon of the sports-associated giveaways and how the toys are beefing up attendance at national sporting events around the country. Then there are the heartwarming stories of ways that Beanies are giving a helping paw to charities of every size and stripe, from the regal (the Diana, Princess of Wales Memorial Fund), to the Special Olympics, to local community raffles of a small hospital or private school.

Part 3, "Family Album," is where you can obtain basic information about each and every individual Beanie Baby. You'll get the vital statistics: tag number, birthdate, retirement date, and a description of each Beanie. Numerous informational boxes in the margins provide extra nuggets of information. You'll also find photos of each and every Beanie. Unlike most other books, our Beanies are divided into groups by category (fish, dogs, cats, and so on) in order to illustrate to the reader how each individual Beanie Baby fits into the Beanie Baby family.

Part 4, "A Little Something Special," is the place to go if you want some in-depth information on hangtags—what they mean and how to figure out which generation you've got. This is also the place to go to track down those mistakes, and to find out if a misnamed tag, missing leg, or upside-down flag makes your Beanie more or less valuable—or just the same as his "normal" cousins! But owning a Beanie is more than just figuring out what's wrong with the ones you've got. There is a world of accessories out there, and this is the spot to learn more about them. From beds to berets, from charms to chokers, look here to find out how to have the best-dressed Beanie in town.

Part 5, "Keeping an Eye on Things," tells you everything you need to know about getting what you want, keeping what you have safe, cleaning what you've gotten dirty, and insuring what you don't want to lose! We've also collected all the buying, selling, and trading hints you could wish for.

If that's not enough, you can check out Appendix A (checklists of every Beanie organized by birthday, style number, release, and retirement, along with a promotional Beanies checklist); Appendix B (further reading), or C (Web sites). And while you're at it, check out the many checklists and lists of birthdays that we've included for each of the bears.

And yet, there's more! This book also has lots of informational boxes to help you learn more about Beanies. These boxes contain interesting tidbits that are sure to catch your eye. Here's what you'll see:

Beanie Tails

In these boxes you'll find anecdotes and stories behind the Beanies that provide you with a little peek behind the scenes.

On the Sly

The warnings in these boxes will help you become a more knowledgeable collector and help you avoid counterfeits and other mistakes that could cost you big money.

Get the Scoop

These boxes contain insider tips and hints to help you earn your B.B.A. (Bachelor's of Beanie Arts). This is where we provide you with all the extra details you never knew you didn't know!

Baby Talk

If there's a term you don't understand in connection with Beanie Babies, look for the answer in these boxes.

CAVEAT: This book is not sponsored, affiliated, or endorsed by Ty, Inc. in any way. Beanie Babies™ and the TY name and logo are registered trademarks of Ty, Inc.

Acknowledgments

So many people. So little time. It's kind of been the way of this whole project, actually.

Huge thanks to Mollie McMillan, research assistant, Beanie wrangler, go-fer, fellow hunter of Teenies, who did her best (probably unsuccessfully) to help me maintain my sanity; and her daughter, Morgan, for her great ideas, Beanie wrangling, loan of Spike the real green iguana for the pictures, and just being great. I would not have been able to do this had Mollie not been willing to go hunt things down for me.

Ditto to Carol Turkington who came in on this at the last minute not knowing what she was getting into. She threw herself into this body and soul. Her guidance and patience has been that of a saint.

Thanks also go to:

Our acquisitions editor, Jessica Faust, who had the enormous task of keeping this whole thing from flying out of control.

Chad Hill of Metaphor Photography for being willing and able to fit a zillion pictures into his busy schedule and allowing crazed women into his studio with several hundred stuffed toys.

Mike Holdeman of Village Collectibles in Indianapolis for loaning us his newly arrived Cubby and many of the props and locations for our pictures; as well as his great staff, Judy, Lisa, Pam, Joy, Ted, and Jeremy.

Vicky Krupka, Counterfeit Queen, who was the one who got me started writing about Beanies; and Sara Nelson, Beanie Mom, who got me into this project in the first place.

The Beckys, Becky Phillips and Becky Estenssoro, for their friendship and the tickets to the Cubs' games even when Wrigley Field in May felt more like Soldier Field in January.

The Kvetches (whom I'll list alphabetically) and their children: Andrea (who found me my blank-tagged Bernie); Ann (who gave up her pretense of disinterest when she sent me the NYPD sweatsuit); April (for whom it's been a tough year); Bob ("We educate for a living"); Cindy (who pretends to only collect "holiday" Beanies and is making up new holidays for the rest); Diane (Beanie Herder); Dianne ("Resistence is futile"); Dixie (B.H.E. who helped me complete my 14 May releases); Em (Bh.D. and finder of Princess and Erin); Lynda (almost a D.V.M.!!); Lynn (who learned the hard way that one should not remove Teenie Twigs from his plastic bag); Mark (protector and defender of Righty and other elephants); Mary (pal to Bessie, Daisy, Tabasco, and Snort); and Robin (truck pulls are not better than Beanies, especially Doby).

Dianne Moumousis and Ashley Williamson for finding my Britannia and beloved Humphrey for me and for their patience and trust; and to Lu Venia, the best Beanie doctor around.

Paula Hood and her terrific staff at Blue Diamond, Torre, Jerry, and Rodney, for going the extra mile.

Phil Shaw for 15 years of friendship and level-headed advice with a little gossip for good measure.

Jeannie and John Ruther at Northstar Motorsports for their lifetime of friendship.

The chemists in my life, Marty Hulce and Bob Schmidt, who helped explain the difference between PE and PVC pellets to me so I could pass that wisdom on.

My kids, Chloe, Winter, and especially Yuno, my doofy boy dog recently diagnosed with cancer, who were left much to their own devices over the last weeks.

My nieces, Laura, who still seems to think I'm "cool" in spite of my Beanies; Gretchen, who at 12, shares my passion for Beanies and reminds me of the joy of being young; and, of course, their parents, Heather and Bob, for raising wonderful kids.

And most of all, thanks to my Mom and Dad, both owners of Beanies themselves, for understanding the attraction to these little critters, and their love and whole-hearted support for this project and every part of my life.

Trademarks

Certain terms mentioned in this book that are known to be claimed as trademarks or service marks by the authors have been appropriately indicated. The authors and publisher do not attest to the accuracy of this information. Use of a term in this book should not be regarded as affecting the validity of any trademark or service mark.

The Ty name and logo are registered trademarks of Ty, Inc.

Beanie Babies is a registered trademark of Ty, Inc.

Beanie Baby names and Teenie Beanies are registered trademarks of Ty, Inc.

Part 1

Welcome to the Wonderful World of Beanies

Maybe you're the proud possessor of an entire complete collection of Beanie Babies—or maybe you're just starting out with one or two of the little critters. Chances are, you've seen the near-riots as Beanie fanatics grapple for the latest shipments. Maybe you've seen the calendars, books, magazines, furniture, clothing, trade shows, chat shows, CD-ROMS—or one of the other million and one products linked to Beanies. Wondering what it's all about?

Read on to find out more about Beanies, how the whole craze started, the secrets of its success, and whether these Beanies are going to retain their value into the second millennium and beyond!

What Are These "Beanies"?

Welcome to *The Complete Idiot's Guide to Beanie Babies*!

What do you get when you take about a square foot of plush fabric, some fiberfill stuffing, a bunch of small plastic beads, string, thread, paper, and a boatload of creative ideas combined with marketing genius? You get a national craze that's spreading world-wide: *Beanie Babies*.

I'll never forget the day I ran into my first Beanie Baby, piled in neat baskets at a local card store. There they were, peering gaily out from their shelves, a riot of colors in plush and curls. They were so unusually well crafted with uncannily expressive faces, I couldn't stop myself. I bought one. And another. And another. I didn't get out of the store that day without a handful, and I've found it almost impossible to pass up subsequent displays without buying at least one. Who could resist something named Smoochy staring at you with goofy pop eyes and floppy yellow flippers?

If you're like most folks, you've already succumbed to their furry, floppy charm. Maybe you've already got a collection going, or you have a child who does. By the time you've completed your trek through this book, you'll be armed with everything you need to know about Beanies. You will be able to amaze friends and astound relatives with your command of the Beanie lingo. You'll probably even be able to name many of the Beanies by heart. And you'll have fun doing it!

Why Would I Want to Collect Beanies?

There really is something magical about these toys, something that goes beyond the affordable retail price. They're well-made. They provoke the imagination. They're cuddly. They're non-violent. In short, they're a parent's dream toy.

Except it's not just kids who are flocking to the stores to stock up. Adults seem to melt when face to face with the gentle charm of Humphrey the camel or the irresistible face of Smoochy the frog. People are so enthusiastic about these critters that whole networks of Beanie mavens have sprouted up in villages, towns, and on the Internet! Yes, there are people who are "into" Beanies for purely financial interests, but true collectors share their passion openly and create bonds of friendship that carry on into other parts of their lives.

You can buy Beanies anonymously through the mail or via Internet sites, but most people seem to prefer gathering at local stores or flea markets to swap experiences, collect tips, and trade their favorite Beanie rumors. You'll find young kids, teenagers, mothers, fathers, grandparents, businesspeople, and, yes—even an occasional biker, sheepishly pocketing a Beanie or two. No matter what group you fit into, you won't be alone in your passion for Beanies.

Get the Scoop

Collect Beanies because you like them, not because you can make some money. That way, even if their popularity goes the way of the Hula Hoop, you aren't stuck with something you don't really care about.

That First Beanie

Everyone has a different story about how they got started and why they keep on collecting. Many became addicted thanks to their kids, who brought Beanies home after finding they could buy them out of their own pocket money without having to ask Mom or Dad for a loan. And with each new *Teenie Beanie* promotion at McDonald's, a whole new parcel of collectors has jumped on the Beanie bandwagon, traveling from one McDonald's to the next in a continuing quest to snag the next Teenie in the series before they sell out.

Beanie Tails

Beanies first became popular in the Chicago area (Ty's home office). From there, the popularity mushroomed until it became a nationwide craze. Now Beaniemania has crossed the borders, gaining popularity in Canada and the United Kingdom, thanks to releases like Maple and Britannia.

My own addiction to Beanies started in the fall of 1996 when my father was hospitalized after emergency surgery. One day, I stopped at a little Hallmark shop not far from my parents' house in suburban Chicago to pick up a few balloons to try to brighten up his room. On the door was a sign that proclaimed, simply, "Beanie Babies." Not having lived in the area for about 26 years, I had no idea what a Beanie Baby was. I found out—quickly!

Stacked in neat little baskets were about 25 different varieties of small, plush beanbag animals. Although this may be hard to fathom today, given the typical Beanie feeding frenzy, I was the only one standing there at the time. I bought three for my father's hospital room (Curly, Righty, and Chocolate), and several more for myself, including Tank, Twigs, and Squealer. When I got to the hospital, I set them up on a shelf below the TV facing the foot of my father's bed where he could see them. One of the nurses entered the room and excitedly said, "Oh! Beanie Babies!" Every time I walked into his room, the Beanies were sitting in different positions. My dad was bedridden, so I knew it had to be the nurses who were playing with them. I could understand it—I played with them, too!

Get the Scoop

Only five Beanies diverge from the soft-and-smooth formula. These are covered in a slightly sculptured nappy plush: Curly the bear, Scottie the Scottish terrier, Fleece the lamb, and Tuffy the terrier. Gigi the poodle is the only Beanie covered in both the smooth and napped plush.

Stuff It!

Part of the attraction of a Beanie Baby is its simplicity: There are no moving parts, no batteries to buy, no tough, cheap plastic parts. With a Beanie, what you see is pretty much what you get. Each one is covered with a short plush fabric, and most are soft and smooth. The plush comes in a wide range of colors and patterns, including spots, stripes, and—probably the most popular—a tie-dye fabric that results in one-of-a-kind pastels, rainbows, blues, browns, and jewel tones.

Get the Scoop

Garcia, Peace, Erin, and Glory are the only new-faced bears that don't sport ribbons around their necks, although the 1997 Teddy has a red scarf in place of a ribbon. None of the old-faced bears have ribbons.

Beanies are born with a variety of plastic eyes and noses in black, brown, and even fuzzy pink, with tiny molded nostrils. Some Beanies are accented by felt (such as Lucky the ladybug's feet) or very short plush, like the legs on Pinky the flamingo. You'll find some with soft fake fur, like Roary the lion's mane. Whiskers on many of the critters are various colors of string, (usually black, pink, or white).

Sometimes the accents match the color of the Beanie (like Radar the bat's feet), but sometimes they're used to set off surrounding parts of the Beanie, such as Stretch the ostrich's "necklace" of white fur. Many of the bears and rabbits have color-coordinated ribbons tied in a bow around their necks. Batty the bat is the only Beanie with Velcro accents on his wing tips.

What Makes Them So Special?

Anyone who has ever picked up a Beanie has usually ended up playing with it. What makes Beanies truly irresistible is their floppiness. Even though their features (like the heads of the bears) are fairly firm, their bodies are partially filled with small plastic pellets made of either polyvinylchloride (PVC) or polyethelene (PE). PVC is the same material you'll find in new plumbing fixtures; PE is used to make softer plastic containers like milk jugs. Ty switched from PVC to PE in late 1997, probably because while PE is more expensive, it's better for the environment and it's less likely to deteriorate over time.

Wanna Buy a Beanie Wannabe?

You'll find lots of Beanie wannabes on the market these days—stuffed beanbag toys that often are remarkably similar (almost identical) to the true Ty Beanie Baby. Called "bean pals," "plush beanbags" or "beanbag toys," among other things, they represent attempts by other toymakers to cash in on the Beanie Baby craze. While perfectly acceptable stuffed toys, they often lack that curious whimsical appearance of true Ty Beanies.

It's not too hard to tell the difference between the real thing and a "wannabeanie" Check out the tags that should be attached to each toy. You'll find everything you need to know about the tags in a later chapter, but if an original Beanie Baby is what you're after, look for the red heart with the white "Ty" on the front of it.

The Starting Line

You'll be happy to know it's not too late to get in on the Beanie Baby craze. The first thing you'll need is a Beanie Baby checklist. (You'll find a master checklist on the tearcard at the front of this book.) The checklist will help you keep track of the Beanies you have. You can also use the individual checklists on each "profile" page to track how much you paid and where you bought a particular Beanie. Current Beanies should cost between $5 and $7 from a Ty retailer. It may take you some time to find some of the "hard to find" Beanie Babies, but with some patience and luck, you'll be able to track down every current Beanie there is.

Where's the Beanie?

Once you've got your checklist, it's time to start scouting around for authorized Ty retailers. You can find lots of collectibles stores that will sell them at higher prices, but their stock often comes from "secondary market" dealers who've already snatched up current Beanies from authorized retailers. The collectible stores pay more than the retail price for these Beanies, which means that YOU will end up paying even more than that.

What you want to do is omit the middleman. By not patronizing secondary markets for current Beanies, Beanie resellers lose their customer base and will end up leaving the currents on the shelves for the real collector—you!

A Good Place to Start

A good place to start looking for Beanies are Hallmark stores and small shops that usually still sell the toys at the going retail price of $5 to $7. You can also try looking in hospital gift shops (these are nice because the profits usually go to the hospital!) or hotel and airport gift shops (expect to pay a little more here).

Make up a call list of the stores you've found that you like and call them regularly—but remember to be polite when you ask if the store has any Beanies in stock. You want to develop a good relationship with retailers, not alienate them by getting pushy when they seem slow in stocking the latest releases. If you remain unflappable, you may find yourself getting some consideration that rude customers won't. It's perfectly appropriate to ask "Do you have any new Beanies?," but don't expect a rundown of exactly which ones they have. If they carry Beanies, you know they're already busy! It also helps if you buy other things at the store besides Beanies. Odds are you'll need to buy an occasional birthday card or other gift item—shop there and build up a good relationship.

Once you've found a couple of stores you like that carry Beanies, you'll meet other collectors there, too. They may be willing to share with you the names of other "favorite" Beanie retailers. Networking helps!

Stalking the Wild Retirees

Retired Beanies may be a little harder to find. Some stores will carry retired Beanies that they've bought from collectors or traded for other Beanies, but your best bet may be a local Beanie show. Besides offering all sorts of retired critters, a Beanie show will give you a chance to talk to other collectors and see all sorts of retired characters. Track down local Beanie shows via classified ads in your local paper, and don't over-

Get the Scoop

Before you start collecting Beanie Babies, read, read, read!! The more you know before you buy, the less likely you are to pay too much or be fooled by one of the many counterfeit Beanies.

look the "Collectibles" or "Antiques" sections! Beanie magazines (such as *Beanie Mania*) also list upcoming local shows.

> ## The Least You Need to Know
>
> ➤ Collect Beanies because you like them, not just because they're popular.
>
> ➤ A checklist will help you keep track of what Beanies you have and what you paid for them.
>
> ➤ Make a list of your favorite authorized retailers and call them regularly.
>
> ➤ Be a good customer: Be polite and patient!
>
> ➤ Check your local newspaper for listings of Beanie shows.
>
> ➤ Read! Read! Read! The more you know, the better collector you'll be.

A Beanie Is Born!

It may seem like there's never been anything like them, before or since—but in fact, beanbag dolls are not a new invention. They've been around, in one form or another, for quite a long time—but it took someone with an eye for whimsy and a flair for marketing to parlay a few plastic beans, a scrap of pretty cloth, and a couple of plastic eyeballs into an all-time toy phenomenon.

That someone was H. Ty Warner, owner of Ty, Inc., and inventor of the Beanie Baby in 1993. He's been riding the crest of a marketing phenomenon ever since.

How It All Began

As all great inventions are, the idea behind Beanie Babies is startling in its simplicity: Take a simple, well-made toy with bright, attractive colors. Make it cuddly and cute, and add a name, a poem, a birth date, and a personality. Price them so every child can afford at least one.

Now make it just a bit impossible to buy, and retire them when they've been on sale for a few months. What do you have? Something that everybody wants but can't find, and the more they can't find it, the more they'll want it.

The genius behind the beanbag toys, Ty Warner, is a 1962 Kalamazoo College grad who parlayed his degree into a job with Dakin selling stuffed animals to gift shops in Illinois. It wasn't long before he'd learned the lesson of a lifetime, he told *Forbes* magazine in 1996: It's better to have lots of small accounts in little shops than one or two behemoths in big discount stores.

Get the Scoop

Forbes magazine estimates that Ty sold 100 million Beanies in 1996.

He left Dakin in 1980 and came up with his own line of soft, poseable, full-sized Himalayan cats, which were sold at the low retail price of $10 to $20 (more about this later!). He's never looked back (but odds are the folks at Dakin were sorry they lost him).

Eventually, he saw a larger market for less expensive versions of these toys. Ty introduced his Beanie Baby in 1993 at a toy trade fair.

Get the Scoop

The first two Beanies to be retired from the original nine were Splash and Flash, who went to the Beanie stalk in the sky in May of 1997.

The Original Nine were first sold in January 1994, and included Cubbie the bear, Legs the frog, Patti the platypus, Spot the dog (the one without a spot), Squealer the pig, Flash the dolphin, Splash the whale, Chocolate the moose, and Punchers the lobster. They sold respectably, and additional designs were marketed later that year. They didn't really take off—and we mean *take off*—until Christmas 1996. Some experts think that kids started getting the little animals in Christmas stockings that year, toted them to school, and the rest was history.

The Original Nine.

Today, Ty is notoriously unreachable, more reclusive than J.D. Salinger and Greta Garbo rolled into one—which only serves to add to his mystique. He doesn't give interviews, he doesn't release his company's phone number, and he doesn't seem to spend his money on any sort of big-ticket ad promos or PR campaigns. You won't find him hawking his wares on the shopping channel, or spilling his guts on Jay Leno. Yet there is probably no one in the developed world who doesn't know his name—or the names of at least 10 of his Beanie offspring.

What Do Kids Want?

A large part of his success seems to be that, to an incredible degree, this Pied Piper of Plush, this 50-something toy man with the gentle smile and elfin eyes, seems to understand what makes kids tick. Here's a guy who isn't afraid to stand up to the retail shops (without which he'd be left with a pile of unsold beanbags) and lay it on the line: They don't charge more than a kid can spend ($5 or $6) or he'll pull the plush plug.

Period.

You have to admire a guy like that.

Birthdays

For some reason, the idea that each animal has its own birth date fascinates kids. They spend hours poring over calendars, laboriously writing down their Beanies' birthdays, entering them into notebooks, comparing notes online with their friends. Perhaps a birthday makes the little creatures real to these kids. Perhaps they just like details. Whatever it is, it works.

Poems

No one seems to know why, but the poems are part of the toy's attraction, too. Even kids who balk at learning the times tables or the chief exports of Brazil can turn around and belt out every single Beanie poem in their collection. By heart.

Thrill of the Hunt

It's like an Easter egg hunt that never stops, a treasure hunt with new surprises behind each tree, a real chance at grabbing the brass ring on the carousel. Kids never know when they go into an unfamiliar store if they might find a hidden cache of Beanies, and it keeps fueling the urge to try.

Even adults admit to a little thrill of satisfaction when they enter an unknown store and stumble into a hidden pile of Ty toys.

In a dreary grownup world of stress and instability, who can resist the serendipitous joy of following a string and finding a pony attached to the other end?

To Market(ing) to Market(ing)

But the success of Beanies is not based just on the fact that Ty seems to know what kids like. It's also based on a brilliant marketing strategy.

Boutique Sales

Ty avoids large discount markets such as Toys 'R' Us and WalMart in favor of small, quirky, out-of-the-way gift stores. When a toy is hard to get, everybody wants it. If it's lying out there in a heap on the shelves like day-old bread, who's gonna care?

Limits

There's a limit of how many Beanies the company will sell to any one store in any one month. This just about guarantees standing-room-only crowds when a shipment finally rumbles in. It creates excitement, it generates news—and nobody has to spend a dime on advertising. A full-page ad in the *New York Times* doesn't carry the impact of the wildfire power of positive word of mouth.

Beanie Tails

If a store orders Erin bears but they're out of stock at Ty when the order comes through, the Erin order is cancelled. The store owner takes his lumps and sits around waiting to try his luck again the next month.

New Styles

Because Ty knows that familiarity breeds boredom, three or four times a year a new batch of Beanies is born. This means that collectors, kids, and Beanie lovers alike are always anxiously awaiting the new styles to come rolling off the line.

A cottage industry of prognosticators has grown up around this event, with lots of people betting on which animals might appear, which country might be honored. Rumors can fly faster than a plague of locusts on a Midwestern wheat field, but who can tell what new creatures Ty is going to produce?

➤ A katydid named Kate?

➤ A llama named Louise?

➤ A rabbit named Bill?

➤ A bear honoring Kuala Lumpur?

No one really knows—but try to guess. It's part of the fun!

Retirements

Hand in hand with introductions is the requirement that certain Beanies must periodically head off into retirement, in much the same way that Disney pulls its popular videos off the shelves after a certain time. In both cases, consumers are warned: Limited time! Soon to be retired! We walk around with a retirement date hanging over our heads, and we're afraid if we don't buy now, we'll miss the Beanie boat. So we buy. And buy. And buy!

The reasoning goes: The harder something is to find, the more you're going to want it, and it certainly seems to work that way. It's sort of like truffles: Who would think that a crinkly black fungus that has to be dug up by large pink pigs would be worth *anything*?

If you could grow a truffle in your garden along with the rutabagas and the raspberries, an entire porcine industry in France would be out of business. But truffles are rare, and it's that very evanescence that makes them so desirable.

Ever since January 1995, Ty has been yanking Beanies into retirement, and folks have been trying to figure out which ones will be next. The guessing game is partly financial—if you knew ahead of time which ones would be retired, you could stock up and theoretically make a financial killing.

But it's impossible to guess, because Ty doesn't seem to follow any retirement rule. He doesn't mandate that his Beanies retire when they reach age 65, or fail to get enough votes, or just become expensive to make. Some people have joked that perhaps Ty chooses retirees by throwing Beanies into the air and choosing whichever lands on the ground first.

Always wanting to keep collectors on their toes, Ty chose an unusual method of retiring Beanies in September 1998. Rather than retiring a bunch of Beanies at one time, he spread the retirement out over a period of days. Some days no Beanies would retire. Some days several would bite the Beanie dust. Collectors can't wait to see what Ty will do next time! "Newbeans" are due out next, but no word as of when this book went to print.

Get the Scoop

Any time a Beanie giveaway is promoted for one national sports program or another, tickets start flying out the door. Headlines are made. Desire flames into frenzy—and it hasn't cost a dime.

Promotional Wizardry

In any case, the company doesn't seem to be content to rest on its laurels. Promotional events around the country are a guaranteed way to jump-start a flagging fad—and like so much about the Beanie phenomenon, when Beanies are promoted, everybody wins.

Whether its sports events or the hugely successful Teenie Beanie giveaways with McDonald's Happy Meals, special promotions can move meals, sell stadium seats—and raise lots and *lots* of money for charity.

Universal Attraction

Finally, one of the things that seem to make Beanies so attractive to so many people is the fact that they are universal in appeal. Almost anyone can find at least one Beanie that seems designed especially for him- or herself.

Ty does this in many ways. First, the birthdays: no matter how old or crusty we are, every one of us has a birthday. If Ty makes enough Beanies, eventually there could be a toy for every date on the calendar—and people seem to enjoy finding a Beanie who shares their birth date.

Next, if you think about it, most people collect *something*. It might not be a world-class grouping of fine 18th-century Hepplewhite chairs—maybe it's just a box of matches you've been picking up from watering holes around the country. Prince Charles collects toilet seats and antique outhouses.

Maybe you just like a "theme": Pears. Pigs. Roosters. Horses. Whatever you collect, whatever your theme, odds are there's a Beanie that might fit in with your creation. If you collect rooster figures, get a Strut. If polar bears are your totem animal, there's Chilly. Maybe you're a fan of astrology: If you're a Scorpio, you'll want Stinger the scorpion.

By now, you can see that this is taking Ty, Inc. straight to the bank without passing Go or collecting $200.

Ten Minutes of Fame

Ty appears to have learned a very valuable lesson: By deliberately refusing to court the media, he adds to the mystique of his company and his product. When all too many celebrities are all too eager to hawk their products on every TV show and radio gig, Ty remains elusive.

Beanie Tails

His company is making lots of profits, but Ty doesn't appear to spend money on public relations or advertising. Even his company phone number is unlisted, and if you call his company's number as listed in directory assistance, you'll get a fax machine. Some say even company representatives have trouble communicating with the home office.

Success

The success of Beanie Babies is driven by consumer demand, clever marketing, and enthusiastic promotion by a wide variety of players in the secondary markets.

In addition, Ty has made it very clear that it believes in selling the toys to children at a low rate, not to adult collectors at inflated prices. High prices come from adults (and some kids) trading in secondary markets. On its Web site, the company admits that it can't control these secondary markets—adults will be adults, after all.

What the company does control are its retail store customers—and Ty has vowed to stop selling its Beanies to any store who knowingly sells to a secondary market dealer, who diverts the toys, or who sells on consignment.

"We take pride in creating and distributing a nonviolent, creative toy," the company explains on its Web site (**www.ty.com**). "It is upsetting and intolerable to us when the 'short term greed' of some of our customers takes over."

Laurels Never Rest

It's true that Ty, Inc., produces those wonderful Beanies—but the company is involved in much more than just a bunch of bean-filled, poem-toting little creatures. They've also created several other lines of toys: Ty Plush, Attic Treasures, and Pillow Pals.

Ty Plush

The highly successful Ty company was built on plush—Himalayan cat and kitten plush to be exact. In 1986, Ty created the large, understuffed kitties so lifelike you almost expect them to purr.

It wasn't long before the cats were joined by other animals, including the same sort of creatures you'll find in the Beanie aisle. Just like with its Beanies, Ty periodically retires its plush animals and introduces new ones throughout the year.

Attic Treasures Collection

For those nostalgia buffs out there, you may be interested to find out that Ty also offers a collection of jointed dogs, cats, farm creatures, and jungle critters, invented in 1992 and released a year later.

Like other Ty products, they all have Ty swing tags and undergo changes. They were known as Ty Collectibles from 1995 through 1997. While they didn't start out wearing clothes, today you'll find them attired in a wide variety of outfits.

Get the Scoop

For lots of details on Ty Plush, Attic Treasures, and Pillow Pals, visit **www.beaniephenomenon.com.**

Pillow Pals

If you've got a baby and you're yearning to let your child cuddle a Ty product, reach for the Pillow Pals—they have embroidered-only eyes and mouths, so there aren't any dangerous add-ons to choke a small child.

They look sort of like a Beanie Teenager, with many similar styles, and they also go through retirements and new introductions.

There's also an active secondary market for many of these pals, in part because so many of them look like their Beanie counterparts. Lots of collectors like to buy both and match up the Pals with the Beanies.

The Least You Need to Know

➤ Beanie Babies were born in 1993 and show no sign of fading away.

➤ Ty, Inc.'s success is based on limited availability, boutique sales, retirements, and canny promotions.

➤ Beanie Babies were designed to be bought by kids, not collectors.

Part 2
Oh, the Places We've Been

Yes, they're all special, but some are more special than others. And we're here to tell you why! Beanie Babies have been used to promote everything from sports teams to political parties, from small-town fund-raisers to internationally known charities such as the Special Olympics and the Diana, Princess of Wales Memorial Fund.

But Beanie Babies go out into the world not just to raise money, but as sort of goodwill ambassabears, causing chaos on an international basis. Read all about it, as the Beanies conquer the hearts of Canada, Britain, and Ireland.

Chapter 3

Take Me Out to the Ballgame

In This Chapter

➤ Learn how the Chicago Cubs started a trend

➤ Who's the only Beanie to ever have her regular hangtag temporarily replaced by a special one?

➤ Find out which Beanie is in residence in Cooperstown, New York

Beanie Baby Promotion Day: It's the nation's biggest craze! When sports clubs team up with Ty to offer special Beanie Baby giveaways, the response is stronger than a line drive to first base. Kids camp out at stadiums to make sure they get a place in line… collectors line up to tempt kids with buyouts…it's big business, and expected to get even bigger. At these events, a certain number of fans (most set age restrictions) receive an official Beanie Baby along with the commemorative card. (It's the card that makes the Beanie even more valuable.)

What could be better than spending a lovely spring afternoon with the sun shining, a light breeze, popcorn in one hand and a soda in the other, watching your favorite baseball team take on the rival?

I'll tell you what can be better—any game with a Beanie Baby promotion, that's what!

Baseball 'n' Beanies

In what's been the most incredible tool yet to lure young fans into ballparks around the nation, baseball franchises are finding out that if they want to pack their stands, all they have to do is pack some cartons (well, LOTS of cartons) with Beanie Babies and give 'em away at the door to their young fans. Turns out, a Beanie Baby is more popular at baseball games than a hot dog—and a lot less messy!

Beanie Tails

In May I took my niece and a friend of hers to Wrigley Field for the Chicago Cubs Beanie Baby Day. The Cubs were giving out Daisy the cow with a special Harry Caray commemorative tag to kids who attended the game. My nieces were very understanding—they agreed to fork over the little fluffy cow to their aunt. I was to get first dibs on Daisy, and if both nieces snagged a cow, the second Daisy was going to go to my mother, a 70-something Beanie collector.

Instead, we got lucky and ended up with *three* "Harry Caray" Daisys, so my niece also lucked out. Her friend went home with an armload of other Beanies she didn't have in her collection. Unfortunately, the weather was cold—"I-can-see-my-breath" cold! The wind whipped across the field and right up the stands into our faces. The girls huddled under a Cubs stadium blanket. In my excitement to get into line (a mere three hours before the gates opened), I left my jacket in the car. But it was okay. It was more than okay—it was *great!* I not only got to spend time with my niece and see my favorite team, I was the proud owner of a Harry Caray Daisy. Life was good. Cold, but good.

Cubs in First!

Those of you who know even the least little bit about baseball probably know the saga (and curse) of the Chicago Cubs. The Cubs haven't made it to the World Series since 1945 (even though they did make the playoffs a couple of times in the 1980s). They haven't won a World Series since 1908. Still, Cubs fans are as loyal a crowd as you would ever want to meet. Year after year they come to the Cubs' field of dreams, and year after year, those dreams are unfulfilled.

Get the Scoop

Until the May 18, 1997 Cubs Beanie promotion, the only previous Beanie promotion had been the first McDonald's Teenie Beanie Baby series only a month before. And guess who threw out the first ball: Ty Warner, Beanie Baby creator!

But in 1997, the Cubs happened on a brainstorm, thanks to John McDonough, Cubs' marketing vice-president, and his daughter, a Beanie collector. McDonough negotiated a promotional deal with Ty to hand out 10,000 Cubbie-the-bear Beanie Babies along with a commemorative card to fans age 13 and under.

At the time, the Beanies had only been used as a promo-tion with the McDonald's Happy Meal. Initially, rumor has it that Ty wasn't so sure it wanted to go along—until the club emphasized that the Beanies would go to kids, who often lose out when frenzied collectors start scrambling for the toys.

As soon as the two giveaways were announced, the sports world went wild. The first game was a quick sellout, with more than 37,000 tickets sold. The rest, as they say, was Beanie Baby history: The Cubs' excursion into Beanie Baby giveaways became the first of what has quickly become a Beanie tradition—professional sports commemorative Beanies. The "Opening Day" Cubbie is one of the most valuable professional sports commemorative Beanies you can get.

Get the Scoop

Cubbie was retired prior to any other Ty-sponsored sports promotions. As a result, the Chicago Cubs are the only team to have ever used Cubbie as a promotional Beanie.

Back to School Beanie

The Cubs obviously knew a good thing when they saw it. They repeated the Beanie promotion on Sept. 6, 1997, with a "Back to School" Cubbie. Just like its May twin, the second Cubbie promotion was also a great success—fans lined up along the street hours before the gates opened. By then, Beanie fever had spread nationwide. With Beanie shipments to retailers few and far between, collectors were already desperate to get their Beanie fix. The "Back to School" Cubbie helped fill the void for many—and helped fill the stadium for the Cubs.

Hats Off to Convention Cubbie

During the Cubs' annual convention in January 1998, Cubbie made one final promotional appearance even though he had recently retired. At the convention, 100 lucky attendees won a "Convention Cubbie." Needless to say, with such a limited edition, these special Beanies and their commemorative cards are not easy to come by. Which means that their value goes over the fence faster than a fly ball at a Cubs' game!

Holy Cow!!

Harry Caray began broadcasting major league baseball games in 1945 for the St. Louis Cardinals. The first game he called was the Cards' opening day game, coincidentally played against the Cubs. After a quarter of a century broadcasting for the Cards' followed by a year with the A's, Caray moved to Chicago where he called White Sox games for 11 seasons. In 1982, Harry shifted his baseball devotion to the north side of the city where he became a Cubs legend, replacing retiring Jack Brickhouse who had broadcast games for the Cubs since 1948. Like Brickhouse before him, Harry became known for catch phrases and leading the fans in a 7th inning stretch rendition of "Take Me Out to the Ball Game." Over the years, Harry also became famous for his pet phrase, "Holy Cow!!"

Soon it was time for the Cubs to join with Ty to create their third Beanie Baby promotion—but Cubbie had already been retired. Which Beanie should they pick? Harry was included in the plans for the promotion, and he approved Daisy the cow (she was not yet retired at that time) as the Beanie of choice not only because of his own trademark war cry, but also because Harry's mother's name was Daisy.

Get the Scoop

Inducted in 1989 into the broadcaster's wing of the Baseball Hall of Fame, Cubs broadcaster Harry Caray and his similarly honored predecessor Jack Brickhouse both passed away in 1998.

It all seemed so perfect, until Harry collapsed during a Valentine's Day dinner with his wife. He died February 18, 1998, without ever seeing the Daisy the cow promotion come to life.

In Harry's memory, Ty did something it's never done with any other Beanie before or since: In addition to the now-traditional commemorative card handed out with promotional Beanies, Ty and the Cubs organization got together and designed a special tag for the Daisy Beanies that were to be given out.

Get the Scoop

The same caricature that's printed on the inside front of the Harry Caray Daisy's hangtag is seen on patches sewn onto the right sleeves of the Cubs players' uniforms this season.

Although the front and back of the hangtag remained the same, the inside front of the tag was printed with a caricature of Harry Caray. On the inside back of the hangtag where the Beanie's name, birthday, and poem are normally printed, a special poem was written to honor Harry.

Though thousands of Beanie collectors, young and old, came away from the game happy, Cubs fans couldn't echo Harry's famed "Cubs win!!" The Cubs lost the game 8-5. It was the first Beanie professional sports promo loss.

A Perfect Beanie for a Perfect Game

Just two weeks after the Cubs' Harry Caray Daisy giveaway, the New York Yankees held their own Beanie Baby promotion on May 17, using the ever-popular Valentino the bear. It was Valentino's debut as a promotional Beanie.

In Yankee Stadium, in front of a full house of close to 50,000 Beanie and Yankee fans, southpaw pitcher David Wells pitched a perfect game against the Minnesota Twins. To give you an idea of how rare a perfect game is, in the entire history of major league baseball (more than 100 years), only 15 perfect games have ever been pitched. Wells is one of only 13 pitchers to have pitched one. Coincidence? Beanie lovers don't think so!

After the game, the cap that Wells wore during the game was donated to the Baseball Hall of Fame in Cooperstown, New York, for the "year's highlights" exhibit. Soon after, Valentino—with his commemorative card and a ticket stub—joined the display.

According to an Associated Press article, Hall of Fame spokesperson Jeff Idelson stated that promotional items are not generally put on display, but that due to the "unusual coincidence" of Valentino's presence at the game and his effect on the game's "incredible" attendance, the Hall made an exception for the popular toy. (It has to make you wonder who gave up a perfect Valentino!)

Glory—An All-Star Beanie

The May 17 perfect game wasn't the last experience David Wells had with a very special Beanie sports promotion. Wells was named as the starting pitcher for the American League in the July 7 All-Star game held in Denver.

Much to the delight of ticket-holders, on June 26 (just 10 days before the game), Ty announced that the newly released star-spangled Glory the bear would be given out to fans at the game in conjunction with the Major League Baseball Players Association and Major League Baseball.

Unlike previous promotions, *every* fan, not just children, would receive Glory and his commemorative card honoring children and youth baseball. Considering that Glory had just barely made an appearance at retailers by game time, the giveaway prompted a frenzy of wheeling and dealing as Beanie collectors and dealers tried to get their hands on this rare bear.

Tickets to the game had long been sold out, so collectors and dealers found themselves lining the streets making offers to fans for the bears. According to newspaper reports, one dealer reportedly spent $15,000 in cash and ended up with 150 of the prized bears to take back home for resale. Other game attendees knew that selling their bespeckled bears might get them in serious trouble with their kids, so they refused to part with them—except for the one poor soul who finally gave in when offered $200 for his Glory and commemorative card. The next day he was in a local store that specializes in collectible bears looking to repurchase an All-Star Glory at any cost in order to save his marriage.

Get the Scoop

Yankee Stadium's Beanie Day on August 9 drew the largest crowd they'd had since opening day (55,911), and the 10th largest since the stadium had opened after remodeling in 1976.

The Beanie Beanwagon

Not to be outdone, the Chicago White Sox jumped on the Beanie Baby beanwagon July 12, earning the biggest attendance of the season (32,929)—and nearly double the number of kids who normally appear—for their Blizzard the tiger promotion.

The same day, the New York Mets struck pay dirt with Batty the bat in Shea Stadium, winging in their largest crowd that year as they gave away Batty and a commemorative card to kids 14 and under. They had such a great time that the Mets went ahead and set up another giveaway for August 22.

Then came the Minnesota Twins with their own Beanie Baby promotion July 31, 1998. This time, the giveaway was Lucky the ladybug. The Twins decided which Beanie they would give away by taking a public survey, with the choices being Mystic the unicorn, Nanook the husky, and Lucky. Lucky came from behind with votes made after her May 1 retirement.

They were followed in short order by giveaways in Oakland, which drew the sixth-largest regular season crowd ever (48,241); and Houston, which gave away 20,000 beanies to the largest-ever crowd in Astrodome history (52,199).

A Basket(ball) Full of Beanies

At first, only Major League Baseball cared a hill of beans for Beanie Babies, but it didn't take other major sports teams long to wake up and smell the coffee (beans)! Just after the Cubs' Convention in January, the National Basketball Association started their own ride on the fast train to sellout crowds. There were six NBA Beanie promotions in the spring of 1998.

The whole NBA Beanie Baby idea was kicked off by the Philadelphia 76ers, who gave away 5,000 Baldy the eagle Beanie Babies along with laminated, numbered commemorative cards to young fans who attended the January 17, 1998 game. It took a few months for other teams to catch onto the trend, but catch on they did, just as other Major League Baseball teams followed the Cubs' lead into the 1998 season.

The Indiana Pacers found a way to pique interest even more than it already was by making an agreement with Ty to not announce which Beanie would be given away for their April 2, 1998 game. The rumors flew, and collectors wondered if perhaps a new Beanie would be released for the game. Even better, they whispered that maybe Velvet the panther, retired since October 1997, would be the giveaway to tie in with the Pacers' panther mascot.

As it turned out, there was no new Beanie Baby and no re-released Velvet. Instead, the Pacers used the theme "Strut your stuff!" and featured the still hard-to-find Strut the rooster. The promotion was a hit!

Just three days after the Pacers promo, the Cleveland Cavaliers came through with their own Bongo promotion. The highlight of the evening was a surprise for fans, courtesy of Ty, which had sent along several Erin the bear Beanies along with Bongo. The Erin Beanies were distributed to a few lucky fans by random draw of seat numbers.

Get the Scoop

The San Antonio Spurs were the only NBA team to do two Beanie promotions during the 1998 season. Curly the bear was the Beanie of choice on the 27th of April. Two days later, they gave away Pinky the flamingo.

What's Good for the Gander Is Good for the Goose

Although Dave Lowery, the Cavaliers' marketing director, was a little disappointed in the response to the Bongo promo, he still knew that Beanies were a good thing when it came to promotions and began working with Ty for the organization's women's NBA (WNBA) team, the Rockers. The Rockers' August 15 promo followed the Pacers' lead, and the Beanie giveaway-to-be wasn't announced ahead of the game. Fans were tantalized with hints: "You'll like him beary much."

When the day of the promo dawned, the first 2,000 lucky children into the stadium were given the ever-popular Curly the bear. Fan response to the Rockers promo was greater than expected, and several young fans left disappointed. But because Beanie promotions garner a lot of attention, and assuming Beanies stay as popular as they are now, it looks like they'll be given away next year as well.

Three other WNBA teams also sponsored Beanie promotions during their summer season. The first giveaway promotion of a woman's pro basketball team came along June 15 with the Charlotte Sting. Unfortunately, the Sting lost in front of a crowd of over 6,000 fans. (While 6,000 fans may seem like a drop in the stadium bucket, the young WNBA league is just starting out—so actually, it was quite a good showing.)

The Washington Mystics, like the Toronto MLB team, have a built-in Beanie promo thanks to their outstanding choice of team name. As a result, on July 11 they hitched up Mystic the unicorn to draw in young fans to their game. Later in the month, Detroit's WNBA team the Shock shocked fans with their Mel the koala Beanie promotion.

Beanie Tails

Other major league sports have discovered that they can boost their ticket sales by joining forces with Ty and offering their own Beanie Baby promotions. The truth of the matter is that many of the ticket holders don't actually stay to watch the game (which has to be a little demoralizing to the teams). Today, major league sports are major league businesses, and a ticket sold is money in the bank for them.

FAIRHOPE PUBLIC LIBRARY

ie Babies Kick Off!

meanwhile, the effect of Beanie promotions on ticket sales hadn't gone unnoticed in the ranks of the NFL. The Dallas Cowboys stepped into the Beaniemania frenzy with a September 6 giveaway of Chocolate the moose. With Chocolate almost assuredly on the "short list" of retirement choices, fans rushed to gather this first of the NFL promotions to add to their collections.

The Chicago Bears have taken a little different route with their Beanie promotion. Though I'm sure we'll see them with their own version of Beanie Baby Days at Soldier Field, the organization's official fan club also has a children's club. During the summer of 1998, the Bears offered a choice of Blackie the bear and a commemorative card, or a fan club T-shirt, to any child 12 and under who paid $10 to join the fan club. The Bears noted that there were only 20,000 Blackies available.

At least two NHL teams will also be offering Beanies to young fans in the hopes of both increasing ticket sales and garnering interest for the future of their organizations. The Boston Bruins gave away Blackie for their October 12, 1998 game, and the St. Louis Blues, obviously learning from their neighborhood team, the St. Louis Cardinals, planned promotions on November 24, 1998 and March 22, 1999—the first of the 1999 promos to be announced.

The Least You Need to Know

➤ The Chicago Cubs gave away Cubbie on May 18, 1997— the very first professional sports Beanie promotion.

➤ The Chicago Cubs honored late announcer Harry Caray with a specially tagged Daisy the cow on May 3, 1998.

➤ On May 17, 1998, the Yankees' Valentino the bear promo made it into the Baseball Hall of Fame in honor of David Wells' having pitched a perfect game that day.

➤ Glory was given out to every fan regardless of age at the July 7, 1998 All-Star game in Denver.

➤ Future sports promotions involving Beanie giveaways include Major League Baseball, the men's and women's National Basketball Associations, the National Hockey League, and the National Football League.

Chapter 4

Going for the Gold

In This Chapter

➤ Check out Ty's memorial to Princess Diana

➤ Discover just how "special" Maple can be

➤ Learn how non-profit organizations can hike their income by using Beanies

➤ Discover Beanies on Broadway

➤ Find out how to be selective about picking and choosing Beanie promotions

➤ Read what Ty has to say about promotional Beanies

They're small, they're cute, and they're highly desirable—and Ty's Beanie Babies make an ideal way for nonprofit organizations to "go for the gold" and boost donations while promoting their causes.

Of course, not all of the fund-raiser Beanies are used to raise funds for non-profit organizations. Some of them are used to promote a company or product (much like the Beanie giveaways at professional sports games, which we discussed in Chapter 3).

In any case, Beanie Babies are big news on the promotional circuit for both large and small organizations—some groups so small most people outside their immediate area have never heard of them. In fact, many individual store owners have taken to using more popular current Beanies (such as Erin and Glory), to raise money for local charities in their own communities, selling raffle tickets for $1 each for the chance to win a prized Beanie, or the right to buy one at the price of any other current Beanie. Private schools are finding that auctioning a basket of Beanies—or just one highly desirable toy—can bring in big dollars.

Princess: A Farewell Tribute

Hauntingly beautiful in royal purple with a simple white rose etched over her heart, the Princess bear was an instant sellout when Ty announced her birth two days before Halloween 1997, just two months after the death of Diana, Princess of Wales. Snapped up by eager auctioneers on the Internet shortly thereafter, her cost rose astronomically—as if she were a limited edition rather than a newly released $5 or $6 stuffed bear. People were even pre-paying huge sums of money since Princess wasn't shipped for about six weeks after the announcement of her appearance. Collectors assume that 1998 will be her retirement year; no one but Ty knows for sure.

Like many of the Beanie Babies, the Princess bear has value not just to collectors of Beanie Babies and bears in general, but also to the people around the world who collect Princess Diana memorabilia.

With the one-year anniversary of her death, interest in anything related to Princess Diana has burgeoned. Books, magazines, key chains, trading cards, lapel pins, and Beanie Babies...if it has the word "princess" on it, it sells, retail shops report.

Beanie Tails

Experts say that the incredibly rich color of the first-issue Princess bear is produced from a special dye that has been used since ancient times, extracted from a species of sea snails. During the reign of Nero, this color was restricted to the dyeing of the emperor's cloth.

The People's Princess

After the death of the beautiful British princess, Ty Warner decided to honor Diana's memory—and make a significant donation to her memorial foundation—with a Beanie. Since Ty isn't talking, no one knows exactly what prompted the gesture.

What *is* known is that the folks at the British memorial fund are plenty picky about what gets approved. The memorial foundation, including members of the Princess' family and her trusted former butler, had been set up after her death to accept donations and channel the huge flood of money into her favorite charities.

It sounds like a good idea—but right from the beginning, the foundation has fended off one controversy after another. Given the adoration in which Princess Diana was held, soon almost no product was deemed suitable to carry the official imprimatur of the foundation.

Smarting from criticism about plastering Princess Diana's logo (her signature) on such prosaic products as margarine tubs, the foundation has struck out against unauthorized use of the Princess' name or image.

To begin with, they have brought suit against some prestigious companies for exploiting her name—including the Franklin Mint itself, which had created an unapproved Princess Diana doll. The memorial fund has also sent "cease and desist" orders to more than 50 companies it felt were selling tacky products and producing unauthorized souvenirs worldwide.

Among the hundreds of ideas the fund rejected on the grounds of poor taste include a toilet brush, air freshener, toilet seat, a bumper sticker reading "Bye bye Di," seat belts, a car breakdown kit, and a colonic irrigation kit. The fund says it's fighting for a British trademark of Diana's image, to block commercial exploitation.

Wisely, the Ty company sought approval from the memorial fund before going ahead with their design honoring the Princess. Moreover, the Princess bear refrains from actually using Diana's likeness or her name anywhere in connection with the product.

As of August 21, 1998, the Princess bear was one of only seven products the foundation had approved. (The other products include a candleholder, candle, stamps, a tribute compact disk, and two enamel boxes.) Approved products carry the fund's trademark (Diana's signature). The fact that the bear was approved, however, didn't stop some people from objecting.

British tabloids report that members of the Princess' family objected to some of the seven items the fund did approve—including the Princess bear. There was nothing the family could do to prevent the production, however, since the fund had given its approval to Ty.

Beanie Tails

According to reports, the original foundation contract with Ty expired March 31, 1998. At this point, Ty had the option of paying for the use of the new Diana logo (her signature in purple), or to redesign the tags and/or the Beanie itself. Several British newspapers have reported that the foundation has approved the new tag for the Princess bear, even though Diana's family does not approve.

Get the Scoop

Depending on the profit actually earned from the sale of each Princess bear produced, collectors estimate that Ty must have sold between 1,002,425 to 1,152,213 Princess bears in the first quarter of 1998!

Profits for the Princess

Like her lovely namesake, it was clear from the beginning that the Princess Beanie Baby had her heart in the right place. Because Ty pledged to donate ALL of the profits from the bear's sale to the memorial foundation, many people followed Ty's example, refusing to buy or sell the bear at inflated secondary prices that would not directly benefit her foundation.

When Donation Day arrived at 1 p.m. on May 14, 1998, at the Dorchester Hotel in London, Ty representatives Michael Kinzler and Patricia Roche presented a check for first-quarter profits of $2,004,850 to Paul Burrell, Princess Diana's former butler (now fund-raising and events manager for the memorial fund).

Alphabet Soup (PVS vs. PE)

When the Princess bear became available in stores in December 1997, she arrived wearing two different tush tags identifying to all that she was available with both "PVC pellets" and "PE pellets." This confused many people. What were these alphabet soup pellets, and why were they inside their Beanie Baby?

PVC stands for polyvinyl chloride—the stuff that gets turned into plastic pipes. PE is a different sort of plastic resin called polyethylene, used in things like milk jugs and food storage containers. It's thought that Ty made the change because PE pellets are more environmentally friendly than PVC pellets.

The two tush tags describing the pellets were different, all right, but they were not separate versions (one earlier, one later). Instead, they are both first-issue to describe the two different kinds of pellets used. Many collectors will pay a premium for the PVC-tagged Princess bears, believing that they are older. While they really aren't any older, they are probably more rare since Ty was switching over to PE pellets just about the time Princess was released.

Get the Scoop

If you would like to make a donation to the Diana, Princess of Wales Memorial Fund, you may send a check (in U.S. dollars) to the Fleet Bank, P.O. Box 30596, Hartford, CT 06150.

How Valuable Is She?

It's always tough to assign a value to any of the Beanies, since costs fluctuate depending on what part of the country you live in and each Beanie's retirement status. However, right from the start, the Princess bear was really something special.

Because the Princess bear was created to honor the late Princess, scores of Princess Diana fans clamored for the toy. Before she actually appeared, she was being presold over the Internet for between $400 to $600 in the first week of December 1997. It's still expected that on the secondary market, she'll bring in royal sums of between $50 to $150.

A Very Special Maple

One of the best-known of the promotional Beanies is Maple the Canadian bear, who helps promote the Special Olympics founded by Eunice Kennedy Shriver in the summer of 1968. The Special Olympics, in promoting a program of athletic training and competition for developmentally disabled kids, gives these athletes a forum where they can excel while showing the world that the mentally retarded can achieve remarkable goals. The group has brought together volunteers, athletes, and families in a community of support and love.

The first Special Olympics Games were held in Chicago at Soldier Field on July 20, 1968; over the next 30 years, the ranks have swelled to include more than a million athletes in all 50 states and 150 foreign countries. One of these countries is Canada, home to Maple the bear.

When it comes to holding fund-raisers, nobody does it better in Canada than the Sports Celebrities Festival (SCF). The group presents yearly fund-raising breakfasts, dinners, auctions, and golf tournaments throughout the country in an effort to raise money for charity. Founded in 1983, the Festival is now one of Canada's largest fund-raising organizations.

When it came time to promote the Special Olympics in Canada, fund-raisers were looking for something special to help promote the organization. As a result, Ty Canada joined with the Sports Celebrities Festival in 1997 to offer a Special Olympics Beanie that would be used to raise money for the Special Olympics.

What they came up with was a Special Olympics Maple the Bear. This new Special Olympics Ambassabear would be exactly the same as the regular Beanie Baby Maple we all know and love—except for an extra swing tag. This tag is imprinted with the Sports Celebrities Festival logo on the front and the motto of the Special Olympians on the back: "Let me win, but if I cannot win, let me be brave in the attempt."

As part of the promotion, these Special Maples were sold during the last week of August at the Canadian National Exposition for $10 (Cdn) each. The remaining Maples were available during the SCF's year-end annual event—"Sports Celebrities Festival Day"—held in December.

This special day included a breakfast (where a limited number of special Maples were available), or a dinner/auction/telethon. As well-known

Get the Scoop

If you have Internet access, you can find out more about the Sports Celebrities Festival and the Special Olympics at their Web site: **http://www.sportscelebritiesfestival.ca/**.

entertainers performed during the telethon, phone pledges were taken by sports celebrities; for a $300 pledge you could take home your very own Special Maple.

The Sports Celebrities Festival Day during which Special Olympics Maple and many other highly desirable collectibles were auctioned was awarded "Best Festival" and "Best Event for a Charitable Organization" at the 1997 Canadian Event Industry Awards. It also made a lot of money for the Special Olympics.

Beanie Tails

Although the exact number of Special Olympics Maples sold is unknown, most folks believe it's somewhere around 5,000. (Some have reported as many as 20,000, but the Sports Celebrity Festival spokespeople aren't talking.) Whatever the details, it's clear that this beary special bear earned more than $100,000 for the Special Olympics in Canada!

There are a couple of notable things about the placement of the swing tag that you probably should know before you go looking for a Special Olympics Maple to add to your collection. The extra tag is usually attached to the left ear (the same ear as the Ty heart tag), but some were attached to the right ear instead. Moreover, the connector is clear plastic as opposed to the red plastic used on the last two years' worth of Beanies.

Don't be concerned if the tag isn't connected through the prepunched hole, however. Company designers found that the prepunched hole at the top of the tag was too close to the edge and had a tendency to tear through, so the tag was moved to poke through the left edge as you look at it.

Beanie Tails

Are these white bears starting a trend? The 1998 Special Olympics Beanie Baby is Valentino, which will be available at select events held throughout the year in all 10 Canadian provinces. He'll also be available during the end-of-year Sports Celebrities Festival Day on December 2, 1998, to breakfast attendees and for a donation during the televised black-tie dinner and auction.

Don't expect it to be easy to track down a Special Olympics Maple, however. Maple is naturally scarce in the United States as it is, and since so much time has passed since the Special Olympics Maple was sold, you may end up paying a lot to add him to your collection. The Special Olympics Maple is one of the most valuable of all the promotional Beanies.

Toys for Tots—Beanies for Collectors

You may think of the holiday season as a time of cheer and celebration, but odds are, kids think of it as a time for presents—and who can blame them! But for millions of children living in poverty, the winter holiday season is a time of emptiness and longing.

It was a problem that haunted Major Bill Hendricks of the U.S. Marine Corps Reserve, who in 1947 came up with the idea of collecting toys to distribute to the needy children of Los Angeles. By the next year, the program went national—and over the next 50 years, more than 213 million toys have been distributed to more than 116 million children.

In his private life, Major Hendricks was the publicity director for Warner Brothers, where his on-the-job contacts helped him reel in the support of many celebrities. In fact, the Toys for Tots logo and the first nationally used poster were designed by none other than Walt Disney himself.

To celebrate the 50th anniversary of Toys for Tots, the foundation that oversees the program decided that they could raise money by offering a specially tagged Valentino the bear and certificate of authenticity. Although the promotion was not co-sponsored by Ty, because of the popularity of Valentino and the nature of the limited edition, the Toys for Tots Valentino sold out quickly, even priced at $165. (Remember, the money went to a great cause. The Marine Toys for Tots Foundation's ratio of program to support costs in 1997 was a whopping 95:5!)

Valentino sports a second round tag bearing the 50th Anniversary Toys for Tots logo. The edition was limited to 5,500, and each Valentino's tag and certificate of authenticity is numbered. Interestingly, the tag also states that this is "Series 1," so keep your eyes peeled for subsequent Beanie promotions from the Toys for Tots.

Get the Scoop

More and more promotional Beanies are offered with certificates of authenticity or commemorative cards. With many Beanies being counterfeited, the certificates and cards are one more way you can tell you're buying a legitimate promotional Beanie.

Heart-to-Heart Valentino

Imagine what it would feel like to learn that your unborn child will have a life-threatening heart defect. It happened to Joe and Christine Aurelio, when she gave birth in April 1997 to a son, Austin, who lived for only two weeks. Although Joe and Christine grieved deeply for their child, they turned their grief into a foundation to benefit the Hope Children's Hospital, whose staff and doctors had cared so well for the Aurelios during their darkest days. Through the Heart to Heart Foundation, the hospital has received medical equipment and other items it might not have otherwise been able to provide to its tiny patients.

In the spring of 1998, the Aurelios joined forces with the Michael Bolton Foundation for their final event, a celebrity charity softball game. The Michael Bolton Foundation raises money for women and children in crisis and has its own softball team, The Bolton Bombers. The Aurelios gathered celebrities to make up their own softball team to compete against the Bombers, including Steve Kerr from the Bulls, former Chicago Bear Mike Singletary, the Cubs' great Milt Pappas, ex-Yankee Ron Santo, Jr., and several players from the "ghost" team in the Oscar-winning movie, *Field of Dreams*.

A thousand Valentinos (chosen because of its embroidered heart) were donated and offered for sale during the game for $150 (and after the game on the **BeanieMom.com** Web site). The Heart-to-Heart Valentinos came with a special tag designed like a softball, and each tag was numbered. Best of all, every tag was autographed by one of four of the celebrities playing that day; singer Michael Bolton, singer Richard Marx, Michael Singletary, or Steve Kerr. The bears were placed in a display box before being sent to their new homes.

The Heart to Heart Foundation is closing its doors with this successful promotion, but it's with good reason. Christine and Joe are expecting a baby to be born this fall and will be dedicating themselves to parenthood.

The Year of the Tiger

If you happen to be visiting Toronto, you might want to make a stop at the Art House, a gift and collectibles store, to see if you can grab a tiger by the tail. The Art House created their own fund-raiser Beanie early in 1998 to help benefit the Asian senior community in the Toronto area. Ty Canada agreed to sell quantities of the then-current Stripes the tiger to the Art House. Stripes was chosen because in the Chinese calendar, 1998 was the Year of the Tiger.

The Year of the Tiger Stripes comes in a soft, flexible acrylic box filled with red zig-zag confetti. The red ribbon around his neck carries a picture of a tiger in gold, the Chinese characters for "good luck," and the year (1998).

The Year of the Tiger Stripes comes with a "Certificate of Authenticity"—a red card printed in gold and black inks, with information on the Chinese Year of the Tiger. In the center, the Art House placed a special commemorative stamp issued by the

Canadian Postal Service honoring the Year of the Tiger. The card is dated January 28, 1998.

Though the Year of the Tiger Stripes originally sold for only $24.95 (Cdn), the fund-raiser was interrupted by Stripes' retirement. The Art House had reported at one time that only 512 of these special fund-raiser Beanies had been produced, thus limiting the amount of money raised to be able to donate to the designated charities.

In an attempt to limit secondary market selling of the Year of the Tiger Stripes, the Art House limited purchases to one Stripes per family per week, and even then, only in-store purchases were allowed.

Get the Scoop

Because the Year of the Tiger Stripes was a Canadian promotion, the Stripes Beanies wear the Canadian tush tag in addition to the usual Ty Beanie tush tag.

Broadway Beanies

Of course, nonprofit organizations aren't the only ones to notice the value of a Beanie Baby promotion. Professional sports promotions are big news (see Chapter 3). But Beanies are also benefiting Broadway!

Hoping to introduce the theater to a new audience—especially children—theater producers Livent, Inc., decided to sell special Beanies in theater gift shops where the musicals were being presented. Livent hoped to boost sales while creating interest in Broadway musicals.

At first, anyone could dash in and buy the special "Broadway Beanies," but demand became so high the shops began to limit the sales to ticket holders and to require an additional purchase in the gift shops.

The Beanies chosen for each of the musicals had some association with the plot or style of the musical itself. For example, the musical "Ragtime," set at the turn of the century, seemed to fit well with the old-fashioned-looking Curly the bear. For the special promotion, the maroon ribbon with each Curly was replaced with one of burgundy, ivory, or navy and stamped with the musical's name "Ragtime," in an old-fashioned lettering style.

When choosing a Beanie to represent Livent's production of "Joseph and the Amazing Technicolor Dreamcoat" (starring Donny Osmond), the company chose Garcia the bear with a rainbow-striped ribbon to represent Joseph. When Garcia was retired, the company turned to the technicolors of Peace, Inch (of many colors), and Fleece.

Fish gotta swim and birds gotta fly, and Beanies Goldie and Scoop do just that for Livent's "Show Boat," complete with light-blue ribbons with the show's title in gold ink. When Goldie retired from the stage, Scoop was left to fly alone.

Beanie Tails

Just as with the professional sports Beanie promotions, documentation is a very important part of the value of a commemorative Beanie. Ticket stubs and programs can add to the value of your promotional Beanie almost as much as the commemorative card (if one is available). When collecting one of these special Beanies, try to collect as many other associated bits of paraphernalia as you can!

Can you imagine going to see "Phantom of the Opera" and coming away with a Maple? Maple was actually one of the "Phantom" Beanies available in the theater gift shop when the production was touring in Canada. In the United States, Velvet, Congo, Bongo, and Peanut were the Beanie stars in the "Phantom" gift shop.

Regardless of which show you attend, you can combine an evening of terrific entertainment, wonderful music, *and* Beanies!

Beanie Mania Congo

What do you think of when you think of New York City—the Empire State Building? That's what many people think of, which is what led Becky Phillips and Becky Estenssoro to select Congo for their "King Congo," a limited edition promotion for the 1998 Toy Fair. Held February 9–16, 1998, in New York City, "the Beckys" wanted to promote their book *Beanie Mania* (now *Beanie Mania II*) in a memorable way. They turned to the Beanie Mania Congo, making it available to retailers who ordered 36 copies of their book.

Beanie Mania Congo comes with a red velveteen ribbon embroidered with gold thread (not heat-stamped), giving Congo a very classy look. His commemorative card, numbered from 1 to only 1998, is gold foil on one side with the Beanie Mania logo, and dark blue on the other (with the number).

Because this promotion was only available to retailers and in such a limited number, the Beanie Mania Congo is only rarely available on the secondary market, and when he does appear, you'll end up paying a premium for this rare gorilla.

Tie a Yellow Ribbon 'Round That Old Beanie

Let's face it…almost anyone can tie a ribbon around a Beanie's neck and create a commemorative card or second tag to go with it. The promotional and fund-raising Beanies mentioned in this chapter are among the most popular with collectors.

Don't buy any old promotional Beanie unless it's something you really like. If you can, try to buy it from the source if it's a fund-raiser Beanie, to ensure that the money will be funneled to the worthy cause for which it was intended—and not just into the pocket of a secondary market dealer. Or if you choose, try to donate at least 10 percent of the cost of the promotional Beanie to the charity that created it. It's more in keeping with the original intent, and it'll make you feel good, too!

When you're shopping for promotional Beanies, look at the documentation that comes with the promotion. Make sure that you get anything and everything you can, including ticket stubs, programs, commemorative cards, and certificates of authenticity. The documentation can authenticate your Beanie and add to its value.

If the promotion is considered "limited" (not an on-going promotion), a Beanie that comes with a serial number (like the Toys for Tots Valentino or the Beanie Mania Congo) will hold its value over the years better than those without a serial number. The serial number helps to document that there were only X number of Beanies available during the promotion.

On the Sly

Not all promotions are really worthwhile. For example, a "Nagano Valentino" was promoted during the 1998 Winter Olympics. Released with an additional ear tag with a serial number, the "Nagano Valentino" wasn't endorsed by either Ty or the International Olympics Committee. Once collectors realized this, the market for this Beanie virtually disappeared. He's rarely been heard of since.

From the Horse's Mouth

So, I'll bet you want to know what the Ty company itself thinks of all the "follow the leaders" in Beanie promotions. Ty published the following letter on its Web site (**http://www.ty.com**) in August 1998. The letter pretty much says it all.

NEWSFLASH!

BEWARE OF UNAUTHORIZED PROMOTIONS!

Recently, some companies and sports teams have attempted to re-create the phenomenon of our popular Beanie Babies promotions. As you know, NBA, WNBA, NFL, NHL, and MLB teams have given away Beanie Babies to their fans, and these promotions have been incredibly successful.

Please be aware that the only authorized Beanie Babies promotions are with those areas of sports listed above. If you want to be sure that a promotion is authorized by Ty, please review our Web site where we announce upcoming promotions.

Any sports promotion that features Beanie Babies, and is conducted by a team that is not affiliated with the NBA, WNBA, NFL, NHL, or MLB, or that is not listed on our Web site, is done without our permission and is unauthorized. For

Get the Scoop

Keep checking the Ty Web site to keep up with more upcoming Beanie promotions as they are offered.

example, the recent Orlando Predators Arena Football promotion was not authorized, approved, or sponsored by Ty. Ty will not authenticate the product or commemorative cards associated with this event, or with any other unapproved promotion.

Ty-sponsored promotions are obviously more "important" in the collecting market than those not sponsored by Ty. But sometimes, even though Ty doesn't sponsor the given promotion, the company allows the creators to purchase quantities of a certain style to help with their promotion (as with the Livent Broadway Beanies).

The Least You Need to Know

➤ The Princess bear has raised more than $2 million for the Diana, Princess of Wales Memorial Fund.

➤ Beanies have helped publicize many organizations and raise money for many of them at the same time.

➤ The most popular, sought-after fund-raiser Beanie is the Special Olympics Maple.

➤ Almost any group can use Beanies to raise funds—the trick lies in getting enough Beanie stock to back up the idea!

Chapter 5

Political Power

In This Chapter

➤ Read about both Beanie bears who bear the Stars and Stripes

➤ Find out which two different Beanies shared the same poem

➤ Discover the bilingual Beanie

➤ Learn about the first Beanie not available in North America

---

When I started collecting Beanies to cheer up my dad in the hospital, I bought him Curly, Chocolate, and Righty. My dad's in his 70s, so I figured that I'd probably get them back as soon as he was feeling better.

I figured wrong.

I finally faced facts: If I wanted to add these Beanies to my collection, I'd have to schlepp down to the local gift emporium and buy my own Curly, Chocolate, and Righty, because he wasn't giving them up!

I can't really object to this. After all, they were a gift, and you don't give gifts expecting to get them back—but these were stuffed animals, and this was my father! I just assumed he'd consider them clutter and be happy to let them come home with me.

To my surprise, once he was released from the hospital, the "clutter" took positions of honor in his den at home, on top of his TV. They're still there. Every time I go for a visit, I point to Righty and tell him what the current value is, and he always says, "Sell it!"—but I know he won't. At least, I don't think so.

My only regret? I took him Righty because I figured since he's a Republican, he wouldn't give house room to a Democrat donkey! Silly me. Not even a bred-in-the-bone Republican can resist the allure of a cuddly Beanie donkey, especially when they retire and their value goes up!

Life, Libearty, and the Pursuit of Beanies

Considered part of the "American Trio" (now the "American Quartet" with Glory's arrival on the scene), Libearty was actually released to commemorate the 1996 Summer Olympics in Atlanta. He's paired with Righty and Lefty because he has the Stars & Stripes sewn onto his chest and because he was released and retired in the same group as Righty and Lefty. Patriotically speaking, he is a red, white, and blue bear with white plush just like Maple and Valentino, but with both red and blue ribbons tied around his neck.

Being a member of the biggest "in" group in Beaniedom (that would be the Beanie bears), Libearty was always the most difficult to find in stores—even though he came out before the Beanie craze truly went national. Libearty also was the first on his block to wear the fourth-generation hangtag, many of which were connected to Libearty with a clear plastic connector rather than the more familiar red connector.

Get the Scoop

Lots of collectors have questions about how to pronounce Libearty's name. Many just refer to him as "Liberty," but the more accepted pronunciation is *lih-BEAR-tee,* with the accent on the "bear"— where it should be!

Get the Scoop

Libearty is the only Beanie to have a birthplace in addition to his birthday. Libearty was born in Atlanta, Georgia, USA, home of the 1996 Summer Olympics.

Ty used both clear and red plastic connectors for the Beanie hangtags through the first three generations of Beanies, though the red connectors are more common. The fourth- and fifth-generation swing tags (except for Libearty's) seem to have dibs on all-red connectors.

Unfortunately, it's apparently not as easy as it looks to get the right data on a hangtag. Poor Libearty's tags are notorious for problems, as are some of the other tags on the mid-1996 releases. Ty wanted to include the Internet address **www.ty.com** on the hangtags, but another company had already registered the domain "ty.com."

Ty eventually triumphed, and won the right to the domain name in court—but in the meantime, tags that had been printed with the invitation to "visit our Web site" together with the address, had to be modified. Some of the tags covered up the Internet address with stickers or a correction fluid, but other tags were simply missing the tip of the back part of the hangtag.

That's not all. Libearty's birthday was originally "Summer Olympics 1996," but the word "Olympic" didn't go down well over at the offices of the International Olympic Committee. As a result, the word "Olympic" was covered over on some of the earliest tags. Later tags just listed "Summer 1996," making Libearty the only Beanie with a season as a birthday instead of an actual birth date.

It turned out that Libearty was a troubled bear in more ways than one. Some Libearties have tush tags that spell the word "Beanie" in "The Beanie Babies Collection" as "Beanine." Although some collectors think the "Beanine" Libearty is more valuable, there are actually more of them around than his correctly-spelled counterpart. Along with the "Beanine" error, you may find that your Libearty's tush tag misspells the word "Surface" in "Surface Wash" as "Sufrace." The same misspelling can also be found on some Righty and Lefty tush tags.

Beanies to the Left

Ty sure has made good use of the pattern that was used to make Lefty! He shares his body style with Derby (all three versions), Mystic (all three versions) and Ziggy. Unlike Derby and Mystic, however, Lefty never came in a fine-maned version.

Lefty is a beautiful, shiny blue tone—the hue of freshly minted steel. His hooves, the insides of his ears, and the tip of his nose are black plush, and his mane and tail are black, too. His most distinguishing feature, however, is the U.S. flag sewn onto his left hip. Of course, nothing is perfect in Beaniedom—with flags come errors. Sometimes Lefty was shipped from the factory missing his flag, or with his flag sewn upside-down. (How unpatriotic!) If you can find one of the flag-error Lefties, you've got yourself one valuable donkey.

Like many of the mid-1996 releases, loads of Lefties had a typographical error on their tush tag. In the word "Surface" (part of "Surface Wash"), the "r" and the "f" were transposed so that the word is spelled "Sufrace." This typo doesn't really add any value to your Lefty, but it's amusing to consider what happens to errant typesetters at the company....

Lefty was released in honor of the 1996 Presidential election and was a popular Beanie even before President Clinton hit it big on the re-election trail. Sadly, after the election was over, Lefty's services were no longer required and Ty put him out to pasture in January 1997.

Right On!

Power to the pachyderm! Unlike donkeys, horses, unicorns, and zebras, an elephant's body style really can only be—well, elephantine. As a result, Righty looks a lot like his sister Peanut (in both color styles). But Righty is gray—regulation elephant gray to be exact—just like an elephant should be, with the same pink inner ears as Peanut. Though not quite as exotic-looking as Peanut (or even as classy as fellow-release Lefty), Righty is still cute and cuddly.

You would think that, being right-minded, Righty would display the Stars & Stripes proudly from his right hip, but to do so is politically incorrect. The stars in the flag represent the states of the union and to have them stuck at Righty's back end would be considered rude. Fortunately, Ty recognized this potential faux pas ahead of time and located the flag on Righty's left hip, but it didn't help the Republicans in their bid for the election that Righty honored.

Bob Dole may have lost the election that year, but the lucky people who voted for the Beanie pachyderm were big winners. Righty's worth—like that of the rest of the American Trio—has shot through the voting booth ceiling since his January 1997 retirement.

No matter how valuable he is, errors still happen. Righty suffers from the "Sufrace" error on his tush tag that plagues many of the mid-1996 releases, as well as other errors that come with trying to get those pesky flags on correctly.

Righty and his pals Lefty and Libearty have long been referred to as the "American Trio," but with Glory's arrival on the scene in mid-1998, the trio swelled to a quartet.

On the Sly

If you happen to find a Righty without a flag (or a Lefty for that matter), check the plush closely to make sure it's not crushed or that there aren't holes where the flag was sewn on. Although it's possible that a flag got missed by the machine that sews it on, it could also mean that someone removed the flag after Righty got shipped.

Glory! Glory! Hallelujah!

American collectors got to watch the American Trio retire at the same time Maple the bear made his opening bow exclusively in Canada. When Britannia was announced as a United Kingdom exclusive Beanie early in 1998, the U.S. crowd really began to feel left out of the fun. After all, the American collectors had been missing their own patriotic Beanies for a year by then. Finally, at the end of May, Ty gave collectors what they'd been clamoring for: a new U.S. flag bearer—Glory! The best news is that because Glory isn't tied to a particular event (unlike Libearty) he'll probably stick around at least for next year's July 4th celebration.

Get the Scoop

Glory made a big splash on the Beanie scene when Ty announced shortly before the Major League Baseball All-Star game that every fan attending the game would get both a Glory and a commemorative card. (You can read more about the sports promotions in Chapter 3.)

Unfortunately, Glory triggered mixed emotions among his eager fans. A lot of collectors looked at the pictures of his red and blue star-spangled white plush and weren't stirred to thoughts of patriotic songs and waving flags—what actually came to mind were visions of childhood diseases like chicken pox and measles. All those stars dotting his plush!

Fortunately, Glory in the plush was a lot more appealing than Glory in a photograph. It turns out he just wasn't very photogenic! Glory be!

As soon as he hit store shelves, Glory was an instant hit—like every other bear in the Beanie collection. Not only did he satisfy the desires of bear collectors *and* those wanting an American Beanie—those big and little red and blue stars gave each Glory a unique look and personality.

Collectors swarmed out to their local gift shops armed for bears, looking for Glorys that appealed to them personally—a star on each ear like earrings, or stars over each eye for a wide-eyed expression.

Don't worry if more than one Glory appeals to you—get them all! There's no rule saying "one per collection!"

Our Northern Neighbors, Eh?

Canadians can take pride in their very own patriotic bear, Maple. Like his southern cousin Libearty, Maple is a beautiful bright white bear with a brown oval nose and a red ribbon tied around his neck.

He wears a Canadian flag patch on his chest, with wide bands of red on either side of a white field containing an 11-point stylized red maple leaf. Red and white have been Canada's official colors since 1921, when they were officially appointed by King George V; the current Canadian flag was first raised at noon on February 15, 1965, on Parliament Hill in Ottawa.

Get the Scoop

The buzz on the street is that the word "Canada" was added to the flag on Maple's chest to match the flag proportions of Lefty, Righty, Libearty, and Glory. For those engineers out there: The flag is proportioned 2-to-1, length by height.

Though Maple was intended to honor Canada Day on July 1, he was actually released earlier in the year, about the time the American patriot bears were retired. Many collectors expected to see him retire as quickly as the American Trio did, but Maple just can't say goodbye—he's still current.

The funny thing about Maple is that he seems to have been renamed before he was released. Although all the hangtags list "Maple" as his name and use "Maple" in his poem, what was probably the first batch of Maples have tush tags that say "Pride," not "Maple." The Maple/Pride combo Beanie is very rare; most collectors believe that there are only about 3,000 of these dual-moniker Maples floating around in circulation. Maple himself is no slouch in the price department, selling for about $200 to 250 in the United States. The Maple/Pride version sells for almost three times that.

Get the Scoop

Beanies that have "classic" mistags are often referred to by their real name followed by their mistagged name, such as Maple/Pride, Sparky/Dotty, Echo/Waves, and so on.

Maple should *always* have a Canadian tush tag in addition to the regular Ty tush tag. The extra tag is required by Canadian law and gives consumer information (kind of like the tags you find on pillows and mattresses in the United States warning you not to remove them on pain of death!). In Maple's case, you don't want to remove his Canadian tush tag.

On the Sly

If Maple is missing his Canadian tush tag, he may be a counterfeit! Other counterfeit Maples may have the "Fabrique en Chine" (Made in China) in the middle of the bottom line of the tush tag so it crosses over to the English side. You can find more about counterfeit Beanies in Chapter 21.

Again to satisfy Canadian law, one side of the Canadian tag is printed in English and the other is printed in French.

While Maple on sale in Canada was a popular Beanie, Maple traveling south was another matter entirely. There was a lot of controversy when Canadian Beanies started crossing the border into the United States during the summer of 1998. Beanies manufactured in one country are intended for sale in that country only.

Ty, trying to help stem the tide of "gray market" Beanies being brought in for resale, asked the U.S. Customs Office for assistance. A limit of one Beanie per person coming through customs (whether from Canada or elsewhere) was instituted, and Customs officers began confiscating and (gasp!) even destroying excess, contraband Beanies. Unfortunately, this included the collections of some children who had inadvertently traveled into Canada with their own Beanies.

Beanie Tails

This import/export problem wasn't limited to Canada. In July, U.S. Trade Representative Charlene Barshefsky was caught Bean-handed when she tried to squeeze through U.S. Customs with a bunch of Beanies that she had bought in Beijing with President Clinton. Enforcing the one-Beanie-per-family rule, Barshefsky surrendered her stash. Staffers wouldn't say just how many she lost, but the Associated Press reported it as "several" and the Washington Post said "about 40."

During this time, Maple's price had skyrocketed. He was hard enough to find in Canadian stores, but problems in crossing the border made him downright impossible to find in the United States. In the end, Ty realized that the limitation might be a little too strict and relaxed it to 30 Beanies per person with no more than three of any one style. However, you should still be careful and check the limits before you go to Canada in search of Maples for all your friends and relatives.

Hail, Britannia

A year after Maple's release, Ty crossed the Big Pond. Though Beanies hadn't really caught on (yet!) in the United Kingdom, Ty honored that country by releasing Britannia, a close relative to the then-recently-retired brown new-faced Teddy.

Teddy Differences

The differences between twins Teddy and Britannia are small, but significant. First of all, the new-faced brown Teddy's neck ribbon is burgundy rather than red like Britannia.

The biggest difference between the two is that Teddy is plain, whereas Britannia carries an embroidered Union Jack (the flag of the United Kingdom) on her chest. Although other Beanies (Valentino, Peace, Princess, and Erin) display embroidered symbols on their chests, Britannia is the only embroidered flag bear-er.

Those Who Know suggest that there's evidence Ty may have originally designed Britannia with a patch flag similar to the ones found on U.S. Beanies Righty, Lefty, Libearty, and Glory, and Maple, the Canadian bear. Rare versions of a "patched" Britannia have been spotted (and priced accordingly). We can only surmise that Ty wasn't pleased with the look of the patch on Britannia and switched to the embroidered version instead.

On the Sly

Some collectors don't like the embroidered flag on Britannia's chest because they believe the embroidery is too tight, making the flag bow in or out and look too stiff.

Flag Facts

The Union Jack has been the flag of the United Kingdom since the "Act of Union" in 1801 and has been part of the flags of many other countries (such as Australia and Canada before 1965) that were at one time under English rule. The flag is actually a composite of three different flags, historically representing three of the countries of the United Kingdom.

Representing England in the Union Jack is the flag of the "Cross of St. George," with a red vertical cross (similar to the Red Cross logo) on a white background. The Cross of St. George decorated the tunics that covered soldiers' chain mail during the Crusades.

The background of the Union Jack represents Scotland, with the "Cross of St. Andrew." This flag has a white diagonal cross (X-shaped) on a dark blue field. You may notice that when the Cross of St. George is overlaid on the blue background of the Cross of St.

Andrew, the color white surrounds the red cross. It was taboo in heraldic times to place red directly on blue, so the white was used to separate the two colors. The first Union Flag consisted of only these two crosses and was first used in 1606.

Beanie Tails

Collectors have noticed that the blue on Britannia's flag seems to come in two distinct shades, one lighter and one darker. One may be more rare than the other, but there really shouldn't be a price difference. The color difference is probably caused by different dye lots in the thread that was used to embroider the flag. But do take a look at other parts of Britannia just to make sure you're not going to end up with a counterfeit!

In 1801, the "Cross of St. Patrick," representing Ireland, was added to the Union Flag to form the Union Jack we know today. The "Cross of St. Patrick" is a diagonal red cross on a white field. The trick for ancient flag designers was in combining the two diagonal crosses (one red and one white) so that neither color was "superior" to the other. They pulled it off by making white the superior (top) color on the "hoist" side of the flag (the side closest to the flag pole) and red the superior (top) color on the "fly" side (the side that waves in the breeze).

On the Sly

Check the tags on Britannia closely before you buy her. There are counterfeits galore, but fortunately, the most common ones have really bad and squished up printing in the gold star on the front of her hangtag.

British Beandamonium

If Ty's intention was to create a Beanie frenzy in the UK, it seems to have worked. Once a place where collectors from "The Colonies" could go to find long-retired Beanies, the quest for the Britannia bear seems to have given British retailers a ride on the Clue Bus—and brought UK collectors into the hobby as well. Even now, almost a year after her release, shipments of Britannia are few and far between and are often limited to 12 bears a month. Needless to say, with the demand for her in the United States alone, prices run high (between \$350 and \$450).

Another reason for the high price of importing this lovely patriotic bear was linked to the same U.S. Customs limitations that caused a squeeze on Maple during early and mid-1998. With luck, now that restrictions have been eased, we may be able to see more Britannias flying across the Pond. Don't expect her price to drop too much, though, until shipments become more plentiful.

The Least You Need to Know

➤ Libearty is the only Beanie to have both a birthplace and a season for a birthday.

➤ Glory is likely to be more long-lived than Libearty.

➤ Lefty and Righty were released for the 1996 Presidential election and share a poem.

➤ Maple was originally released with tush tags that said "Pride."

➤ Britannia has already had two different kinds of flags, a patch and an embroidered one.

Chapter 6

Special-Occasion Fun with Beanies

In This Chapter

➤ Get some new ideas on making Beanie gift baskets for any occasion

➤ Decorate for the holidays using Beanies

➤ Plan some fun kids' parties with Beanie decorations

While it's true that lots of folks are locking their Beanies up behind closed doors and waiting for their value to skyrocket, it's also true that Beanie Babies are highly ornamental.

If you're putting together a gift basket for a special occasion such as a get-well present or for a birthday, adding a little Beanie can really make it special. If you're decorating for the holidays and you'd like to make a Beanie statement, almost every possible holiday or special occasion you can think of has at least one Beanie that would fit in well with the theme.

For some holidays, such as Halloween, the plethora of costumes available in Beanie sizes means that almost every creature you own can come to the party dressed in an appropriately spooky outfit. Anyone who enjoys decorating for a holiday can find a gold mine of possibilities in the Beanie Baby collection, with its many holiday-theme–oriented creatures.

Read on to find out about some of our ideas!

Gift Baskets

Beanies are sweet, cuddly, and highly collectible—and they come in just about every known type of animal. This means they make wonderful additions to themed gift baskets. Whether you're looking for a hostess gift, a birthday basket, or something to send to a friend in the hospital, the addition of a Beanie or two can really brighten things up.

➤ *Picnic lover basket:* Fill a straw picnic basket with a bottle of wine, fine cheese, gourmet crackers, chocolate-dipped strawberries, a colorful picnic cloth, crusty French bread—and Ants the anteater.

Get the Scoop

Of course, if the recipient has a special collection—roosters, lambs, cows, dogs—your choice in gift baskets is easy.

➤ *Gardening basket:* Fill a window planter or container with some hard-to-find seeds (Mesclun, French filet beans, unusual sunflowers), a fine British gardening tool, a gardening book or magazine, a small, pretty flowering plant or cuttings—and Lucky the ladybug.

➤ *Down-east basket:* Fill an enameled lobster pot with a lobster bib, butter warmers (for dipping), a bag of oyster crackers, a gift certificate for a mail-order "clambake"—and Pinchers the lobster.

➤ *Cheese basket:* Fill a straw basket with a variety of gourmet cheeses, a container of imported olives, a small marble cheese board and knife, a few boxes of gourmet crackers, a fine bottle of red wine, a few polished red apples—and Trap the mouse.

➤ *Halloween basket:* Fill a straw pumpkin basket with some sacks of candy, a glow-in-the-dark skeleton, the latest Stephen King novel, an elegant sequined mask, a scary videotape, small holiday gourds, a jack-'o-lantern cutting kit—and Spooky the ghost or Radar the bat.

➤ *Chocolate basket:* For the chocoholic, make up a basket filled with gift chocolates, gourmet hot chocolate, specially wrapped chocolate bars, chocolate novelties—and Chocolate the moose.

➤ *Christmas cheer basket:* Fill a straw basket with a tin of gourmet hot chocolate, some special spice tea, a pretty Christmas ornament, an embroidered Christmas stocking, some holiday cloth napkins, Christmas cookies, tinsel—and Snowball the snowman or a 1997 Holiday Teddy.

➤ *Hanukkah cheer basket:* Fill a straw basket with a tin of gourmet hot chocolate, a dreidle, a bag of chocolate coins, some special spice tea, a miniature Menorah, a child's book about Hanukkah—and Snowball the snowman.

➤ *South of the border basket:* Fill a basket with a bag of blue corn tortilla chips, a jar of gourmet salsa, a book on Mayan culture, a stoneware tortilla warmer, recipes for Mexican food, a margarita glass and container of margarita mix—and Garcia the bear.

➤ *Endangered species basket:* Fill a straw basket with some Rainforest Crunch candy, an "adopt a whale" or "adopt a wolf" kit, a container of trail mix, a certificate for one square foot of rain forest, a coconut or pineapple—and Kiwi the toucan or Jabber the parrot.

➤ *Crabby basket:* Fill a basket with wooden mallets, a box of Old Bay seasoning, a colorful plastic tablecloth, a map of Baltimore's Harborplace or Chincoteague/Assateague, a gift certificate for steamed crabs—and Claude or Digger the crab.

➤ *New baby basket:* Fill a basket with a soft rattle, a pretty baby blanket, a book of baby names or parenting book, a small soft baby toy, a baby washcloth set, a gift certificate for a visit from a housecleaning service; a night light, a pair of booties—and Quackers the duck.

➤ *Smilin' Irish Eyes basket:* Fill a green basket with Irish tea and soda bread, a book on Irish cooking, a bag of Irish oatmeal, a shamrock keychain, a fine Waterford crystal wineglass, a compact disk of Gaelic music—and Erin the bear.

➤ *Anniversary basket:* Fill a basket with two crystal wine glasses, a bottle of fine wine or champagne, a container of scented massage oil, a video of *Dr. Zhivago*, a box of chocolates—and Valentino the bear.

Get the Scoop

Of course, you don't need to always choose a basket for your container. Try to come up with something that may fit the occasion—a birdhouse for a bird lover, a pet carrier for a cat lover, or a large clay pot for a gardener.

➤ *Young naturalist:* Fill a basket with a magnifying glass, a bug specimen jar, a videotape on wildlife, a pair of binoculars, an illustrated guide to nature—and Flutter the butterfly.

➤ *Goin' fishin' basket:* Depending on the type of fishing the person does, fill a fishing creel with lures, flies, a certificate for fly-fishing lessons, fly or lure boxes, a book on fishing, needlenose pliers—and Bubbles, Coral, or Goldie the fish.

➤ *Szechuan love basket:* Fill a basket with chopsticks, a box of fortune cookies, a jar of imported hoisin sauce, a book on the Chinese zodiac, some Chinese green tea, a bottle of rice wine, a sake set—and Fortune or Peking the panda.

➤ *Graduation basket:* Fill a basket with a book on housecleaning tips or cooking in a dorm, a watch, gift certificates to a local fast food restaurant, a book on investing for young adults, notepaper and stamped envelopes—and Hoot the owl.

Get the Scoop

If you're remembering a needy family during the holiday and filling a food basket for them, keep in mind that it's nice to include a toy for the family's children. A Beanie Baby makes a perfect basket stuffer—packing lots of love for a small price.

➤ *Anglophile basket:* Fill a basket with Devonshire clotted cream, British tea and a teapot, plum pudding, a video of *Upstairs Downstairs*, British marmalade, a London travel guide, Wallace and Gromit magnets—and Britannia or Princess bear.

➤ *Highland fling basket:* Fill a straw basket with Scottish shortbread, a bag of oatmeal, a plaid wool scarf, a compact disk of bagpipe music, a book about the Loch Ness monster, a tam o' shanter, a bottle of fine old Scotch whiskey—and Scottie the dog.

➤ *National Velvet basket:* Fill a basket with a book on horses, a set of spurs, saddle soap, ribbons for the horse's mane, a bottle of horse shampoo, carrots, a gift certificate for a riding lesson or a set of horseshoes, a hoof pick or brush—and Derby the horse.

➤ *Mystical basket:* Fill a basket with a crystal, a book on astrology, a pouch of healing gems, a small windchime, a New Age music tape or compact disk, some scented massage oil, herbal tea—and Magic the dragon or Mystic the unicorn.

➤ *Canada basket:* Fill a basket with a miniature Canadian flag, a bag of maple candy, a package of smoked Canadian salmon, tickets to a hockey game featuring a Canadian team, a jug of maple syrup, a block of cheddar cheese, the book *Anne of Green Gables*—and Maple the bear.

➤ *Bird lovers' basket:* Fill a basket with a pair of binoculars, several varieties of bird seed, a journal for recording bird sightings, an Audubon bird book, a birdhouse building kit, a gift certificate for a Purple Martin house—and Early the robin, Rocket the blue jay, or one of the other bird Beanies.

➤ *Cajun queen basket:* Fill a basket with a jar of Tabasco sauce, some Cajun spices, a can of gourmet seafood gumbo, a Mardi Gras mask and coins, a bag of beignet mix, a book by Anne Rice—and Ally the alligator.

➤ *Dog days basket:* Fill a large basket with a leather collar, a colorful dog bandanna, a dog brush or nail clippers, gourmet dog biscuits, a dog pin or tee shirt, a book about dogs, a video on dog training, a dog toothbrush—and Doby the Doberman, Bruno the terrier, or one of the other dog Beanies.

➤ *Skidoo basket:* Fill a basket with some ski wax, a knit ski cap, some toasty mittens or a scarf, a bag of gourmet microwave popcorn, a high-energy chocolate bar, a bag of gourmet hot chocolate, lift tickets for a favorite ski resort—and Bernie the St. Bernard.

Holiday Cheer

Gift baskets are just one way you can use Beanie Babies to help celebrate special events. They also make terrific party decorations for just about any holiday you can imagine. Take a look at some of our ideas.

New Year's Eve/Chinese New Year

If you want to ring in the new year (whether it's at a traditional New Year's party or a Chinese New Year's party), Beanies can help get the fun started: Just add Fortune or Peking the panda to your decorating scheme.

Love Is in the Air

If it's early February, Valentine's Day isn't far away. Take the time to make this day special for your partner and your family. Decorate the table in red and white, stir red food coloring into the butter, chill it, then cut it into heart shapes; make heart-shaped pancakes for breakfast; and set the table with a Valentine centerpiece featuring Valentino the bear.

Get the Scoop

If you're decorating your home with Beanies this year, get your kids involved in the act. Make some little holiday costumes and have your kids dress up their Beanies before arranging them around the home.

Faith and Begorrah!

You don't have to be Irish to celebrate St. Patrick's Day on March 17—but it helps! Decorate your home in green and serve corned beef and cabbage and mashed potatoes (go ahead—tint 'em green and see who notices!). Serve a fine Irish beer and be sure to include Erin the emerald-green bear as part of your table decorations.

Easter/Spring

Springtime is a time of renewal for people of all faiths—and for kids who celebrate Easter, nothing is more fun than discovering what the Easter bunny left behind. For a fun Easter basket decoration this year, include colored eggs, chocolate rabbits, a wind-up metal Easter toy, and one of the Beanie bunnies (Ears, Hippity, Hoppity, or Floppity). Other Easter decorations may feature one of the many animals we associate with spring:

➤ Chops or Fleece the lamb

➤ Early the robin

➤ Doodle or Strut the rooster

➤ Quackers the duck

➤ Roary the lion ("March comes in like a lion...")

➤ Rocket the blue jay

Happy Birthday USA

If it's July 4th, it must be time for outdoor picnics and fireworks. Red, white, and blue decorations are required, but you can also incorporate some of these patriotic Beanies into your scheme:

➤ Baldy the eagle

➤ Glory the bear

➤ Lefty the donkey

➤ Libearty the bear

➤ Righty the elephant

Get the Scoop

For a fun Halloween party game for your kids, try this version of "bean-bag toss": Toss Halloween-related Beanies into a large plastic pumpkin. The winner gets a Halloween-related Beanie!

Trick or Treat

It's Halloween, and one of the very best excuses for throwing a party. There are a wide variety of just-right Beanies you can use to spruce up your rumpus room for scary doin's, such as:

➤ Batty or Radar the bat

➤ Spooky the ghost

➤ Spinner or Web the spider

➤ Zip the all-black cat

Giving Thanks

There's really only one thing on everybody's mind when it comes to Thanksgiving dinner—and that's a turkey. In addition to the cornucopias, sheaves of wheat, and autumn gourds, why not add Gobbles the turkey to your holiday centerpiece?

Get the Scoop

You may want to set up your own Bethlehem stable scene, featuring Chops or Fleece the lamb, Bessie or Daisy the cow, Derby the horse, and Lefty the donkey.

A Little Holiday Cheer

Whether you celebrate Hanukkah, Christmas, Kwanzaa—or just getting off school because of a winter snowstorm—the winter months are ideal times for parties.

What could be more appropriate than decorating your home with some of these very special holiday Beanies:

➤ Chilly the polar bear

➤ Chocolate the moose

➤ Snowball the snowman

➤ 1997 Teddy the holiday bear

Parties

If you've got more than one child, the annual search for a birthday party theme can get desperate at times. That's where Beanies come in: Kids' parties are the perfect way to use Beanie Babies as decorative props, and kids love to help decorate with their favorite stuffed toys.

To get you started, here are some party themes and the Beanies that lend themselves to the topic. In addition to the Beanies, you can follow through on the theme with appropriate party bags, decorations, and games.

Under-the-Sea Theme

Use an ocean-blue tablecloth and paper goods; include fish-shaped pretzels and cheese snacks, seafood gummi candies, and a giant starfish cake; decorate the room with seashells from the shore, netting strung along the walls, and plastic starfish; and of course:

➤ Claude and Digger the crabs

➤ Crunch the shark

➤ Echo and Flash the dolphins

➤ Bubbles, Coral, and Goldie the fish

➤ Pinchers the lobster

➤ Manny the manatee

➤ Inky the octopus

➤ Seamore the seal

➤ Sting the stingray

➤ Splash and Waves the whales

Beanie Tails

Many kids get duplicate Beanies during birthdays or holidays. For a unique party twist, have each guest bring an "extra" or "unwanted" Beanie to trade. Either let the kids pick a different Beanie that they don't have and that they'd like, or put each one in a sack and have the child choose.

Jungle Theme

What little boy or girl wouldn't love to be the leader of his or her very own African safari? Decorate with mosquito netting, pop up all the tents you can find, and give each child a pith helmet before setting out on a scavenger hunt. Serve Rainforest crunch candy, "jungle juice," and a lion cake. Indoors, party decorations could include:

➤ Peanut and Righty the elephants

➤ Twigs the giraffe

➤ Congo the gorilla

➤ Happy the hippo

➤ Freckles the leopard

➤ Roary the lion

➤ Bongo and Nana the monkeys

➤ Velvet the panther

➤ Spike the rhinoceros

➤ Blizzard and Stripes the tigers

➤ Ziggy the zebra

Farm Theme

You'd be surprised how much kids love to go down on the farm (especially if they live in the city). Throw some old gingham on the tables, set up a chuckwagon in the back yard to serve beans and franks, and bake a red barn cake. Decorate the party with:

➤ Bumble the bee

➤ Snort and Tabasco the bulls

➤ Ears, Floppity, Hippity, and Hoppity the bunnies

➤ Bessie and Daisy the cows

➤ Lefty the donkey

➤ Jake and Quackers the ducks

➤ Derby the horse

➤ Chops and Fleece the lambs

➤ Squealer the pig

➤ Doodle and Strut the roosters

➤ Gracie the swan

➤ Gobbles the turkey

Teddy-Bear Picnic

Tea parties are still fashionable among the elementary school set, and what could be more fun than a teddy-bear picnic? Set up tables under the trees, serve lemonade, iced cookies, and delicate sandwiches on fine china, and make sure as many of these bears can attend as possible:

Get the Scoop

Take a photo of each child with her teddy at the picnic with an instant camera (or have a family member run out to a one-hour photo shop nearby to develop the film). Before the end of the party, slip each photo into the child's goody bag for a special memento of the party.

- ➤ 1997 Teddy
- ➤ Blackie
- ➤ Britannia
- ➤ Brownie
- ➤ Chilly
- ➤ Clubby
- ➤ Cubbie
- ➤ Curly
- ➤ Erin
- ➤ Fortune
- ➤ Garcia
- ➤ Glory
- ➤ Libearty
- ➤ Maple
- ➤ Mel
- ➤ Peace
- ➤ Peking
- ➤ Princess
- ➤ Teddy (colored, new and old face)
- ➤ Valentino

Dinosaur Theme

If your child can't seem to spell his own name but can give you the entire life history of *Tyrannosaurus Rex*, then you know you're dealing with dinosaur fever. In fact, if it's 50 feet tall, with feet like dinner plates and huge glistening teeth, kids automatically seem to love it. Any party with a "dino" theme is a guaranteed hit. Serve gelatin "dinosaur eggs," play pin-the-horn on the triceratops, bake a Stone Age cake—and if you're thinking about decorating with dinos, look no further than the following Beanie Babies:

- ➤ Bronty the brontosaurus
- ➤ Rex the tyrannosaurus
- ➤ Steg the stegosaurus

Beanie Tails

At the moment, there are only three Beanie dinosaurs, but in a party like this, there are other Beanies that would fit in well with the general theme: Ally the alligator, Ants the anteater, Grunt the razorback (he looks a bit like a triceratops, without the horn), Iggy the iguana (he seems dinosaur-like and appropriately terrifying), Rainbow the chameleon, Slither the snake, and Tank the armadillo.

Zodiac Theme

Slightly older kids (and grownups, too!) might enjoy a party with an astrological theme, using Beanies to represent some of the 12 signs of the zodiac. While not all signs use animals, those that do are all represented by Beanie Babies:

➤ Stinger the scorpion (Scorpio the scorpion: October 23–November 21)

➤ Snort or Tabasco the bull (Taurus the bull: April 20–May 20)

➤ Claude or Digger the crab (Cancer the crab: June 21–July 22)

➤ Roary the lion (Leo the lion: July 23–August 23)

➤ Bubbles, Coral, or Goldie the fish (Pisces the fish: February 19–March 20)

The Least You Need to Know

➤ Beanies can make terrific holiday decorations for every season.

➤ If you're looking for a very special themed gift basket, adding an appropriate Beanie Baby can really do the job right.

➤ Themed birthday parties can be a lot more fun if you incorporate Beanie Babies into the action.

Part 3
Family Album

Take a wide variety of sea creatures, cats, farm animals, birds, dogs, insects, lizards, bears, jungle critters, and woodland creatures—not to mention dinosaurs and the odd ghost—and you've got the basic Beanie Baby lineup. If you have trouble keeping 'em all straight, don't despair! We've rounded them all up in this section and grouped them by animal type so it will be easy to find the ones you want.

So, with book in hand, read on and find out the vital statistics on your favorites: birthdays, retirement dates, outstanding characteristics, and identifying marks...it's all here to help you separate the wheat from the chaff and the counterfeits from the true-blue Beanies.

Chapter 7

Down by the Sea

In This Chapter

➤ Get the history and details of each sea creature Beanie Baby

➤ Find out which sea creature Beanie Babies have been retired and which are active

➤ Identify photos of all Beanie Baby sea creatures

From gnashing of felt teeth and nibbling of cloth seaweed to cracking of felt claws, the Beanie Baby sea creatures are a fearsome lot! Still, things can get confusing under the sea, where everybody tends to look alike. Whether it's Pinchers vs. Punchers, Echo vs. Flash, Digger vs. Digger (same Beanie, different colors!)—well, you can't tell the swimmers without a scorecard.

So pull up a beach chair, shake the sand out of your shoes, and read on about all the ins and outs of the world of underwater Beanie Babies.

Bubbles the Fish

➤ Style: 4078

➤ Birthday: 7-2-95

➤ Released: 6-3-95

➤ Retired: 5-11-97

➤ Hangtag: 3-4

On the Sly

Things can get pretty fishy as Beanie values rise—so it should be no surprise that counterfeits of Bubbles exist. Before you buy, study her closely to make sure she's the real thing. (Counterfeit giveaway: uneven seams!)

Bubbles was part of the fish trio that included Coral and Goldie. Majestic in yellow and black stripes with yellow fins, she was retired in May 1997—but if you look around, you probably won't have any trouble reeling her in.

❑ It's mine!

Date purchased: _____

Price: _____

❑ Sold!

Date sold: _____

Price: _____

Claude the Crab

➤ Style: 4083
➤ Birthday: 9-3-96
➤ Released: 5-11-97

➤ Retired:
➤ Hangtag: 4-5

This jewel-colored, tie-dyed crab has a cocky attitude, flashy on the outside with a cream-colored underbelly. Many collectors have more than one because they can't decide which of these beautiful Beanies they like best. If you're lucky, you'll be able to dig one of these collectibles out of the sand.

❏ It's mine!

Date purchased: _____

Price: _____

❏ Sold!

Date sold: _____

Price: _____

Get the Scoop

Claude's one-of-a-kind, tie-dyed plush makes each Beanie unique, so plop a few into your crab pots the first chance you get.

Coral the Fish

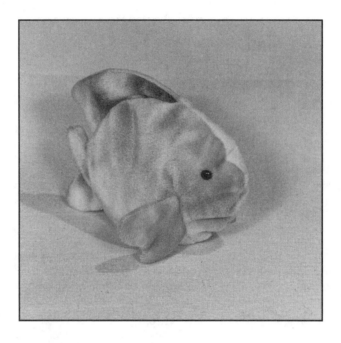

➤ Style: 4079
➤ Birthday: 3-2-95
➤ Released: 6-3-95

➤ Retired: 1-1-97
➤ Hangtag: 3-4

Get the Scoop

If you're convinced your Coral is looking a little squinty—one eye smaller than the other—you're not crazy! It's just that one eye is set more deeply into the plush.

Coral is one of a shoal of Beanie fish (she shares a similar body type to both Bubbles and Goldie). Because of the tie-dyed method of plush coloration, her plushy scales range from muted to very bright. No matter where your Coral falls along the finny continuum, she'll be unique.

❑ It's mine!

   Date purchased: _____

   Price: _____

❑ Sold!

   Date sold: _____

   Price: _____

Crunch the Shark

➤ Style: 4130
➤ Birthday: 1-13-96
➤ Released: 1-1-97

➤ Retired: 9-24-98
➤ Hangtag: 4-5

Long and skinny, Crunch's plush is steel blue (the same color as Echo the dolphin and Lefty the donkey) with a white underbelly. While the inside of his mouth is filled with red plush and lots of white teeth, don't worry! Crunch's teeth are felt.

❑ It's mine!

Date purchased: _____

Price: _____

❑ Sold!

Date sold: _____

Price: _____

Get the Scoop

Experts had been predicting Crunch was swimming toward retirement for quite some time (he was a bit of a slow seller).

Digger the Crab

- ➤ Style: 4027
- ➤ Birthday: (none) (orange)
- ➤ Birthday: 8-23-95 (red)
- ➤ Released: 6-25-94 (orange)
- ➤ Released: 6-3-95 (red)

- ➤ Retired: 6-3-95 (orange)
- ➤ Retired: 5-11-97 (red)
- ➤ Hangtag: 1-3 (orange)
- ➤ Hangtag: 3-4 (red)

Digger's original incarnation was bright all-orange, the same material as Chocolate's antlers and Caw's beak and feet. Sharing a body style with Claude, she was later redesigned with bright red plush. Don't get crabby if you have an orange Digger with the same style number—that's how they were produced.

Get the Scoop

While Digger comes in two colors, you'll find it easier to dig up the red version.

Orange

❑ It's mine!

 Date purchased: _____

 Price: _____

❑ Sold!

 Date sold:_____

 Price: _____

Red

❑ It's mine!

 Date purchased: _____

 Price: _____

❑ Sold!

 Date sold:_____

 Price: _____

Echo the Dolphin

➤ Style: 4180

➤ Birthday: 12-21-96

➤ Released: 5-11-97

➤ Retired: 5-1-98

➤ Hangtag: 4-5

Like her name, Echo the dolphin isn't unique. She's simply an echo of Flash the dolphin. The first release was a bit schizophrenic: Her hang- and tush tags said "Waves," and Waves' tags said "Echo." Her stomach and underside of her snout are white, and her back is the same steel blue as Crunch.

❑ It's mine!

Date purchased: _____

Price: _____

❑ Sold!

Date sold: _____

Price: _____

Get the Scoop

While she looks as graceful as any dolphin, Echo's is one of the more awkward Beanie styles; unless propped up, she tends to fall over on her steel blue back.

Flash the Dolphin

➤ Style: 4021
➤ Birthday: 5-13-93
➤ Released: 1-8-94

➤ Retired: 5-11-97
➤ Hangtag: 1-4

Get the Scoop

In the "they could be twins" department: The white underbelly and lack of nostrils are the main features that distinguish Flash from the strikingly similar Manny the manatee.

Flash and her counterpart Splash the whale were the first two of the Original Nine Beanies to be retired. Flash is light gray (like Righty and Manny) with a white underbelly.

❑ It's mine!

Date purchased: _____

Price: _____

❑ Sold!

Date sold: _____

Price: _____

Goldie the Goldfish

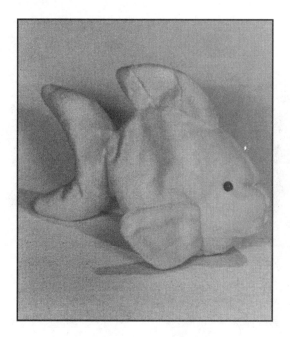

- ➤ Style: 4023
- ➤ Birthday: 11-14-94
- ➤ Released: 6-25-94

- ➤ Retired: 12-31-97
- ➤ Hangtag: 1-4

Goldie, the last of the piscatorial Beanie trio to be retired, sports the bright orange plush seen on Scoop's beak and feet. Her dorsal fin is more pointed than Bubbles' and Coral's, and her tail is split into a wide V-shape.

❏ It's mine!

Date purchased: _____

Price: _____

❏ Sold!

Date sold: _____

Price: _____

Get the Scoop

While Goldie was the last of the fish trio to be flushed away to retirement, she was the first of her fishy friends to be released.

69

Inky the Octopus

➤ Style: 4028

➤ Birthday: (none) (tan—no mouth)

➤ Birthday: (none) (tan—mouth)

➤ Birthday: 11-29-94 (pink)

➤ Released: 6-25-94 (tan—no mouth)

➤ Released: 9-12-94 (tan—mouth)

➤ Released: 6-3-95 (pink)

➤ Retired: 9-12-94 (tan—no mouth)

➤ Retired: 6-3-95 (tan—mouth)

➤ Retired: 5-1-98 (pink)

➤ Hangtag: 1-2 (tan—no mouth)

➤ Hangtag: 3 (tan—mouth)

➤ Hangtag: 3-5 (pink)

Inky is one of only seven Beanies to have gone through three different designs. The original Inky was a fine taupe with black-on-white eyes and no mouth. In his next incarnation, he had that same dull taupe. He also appeared with a thread mouth sewn under the eyes. Eventually, Ty got the message and replaced the duller taupe with a jazzier pink tone. The thread mouth stayed.

On the Sly

Check to make sure Inky's eyes aren't all scratched up and that the stitching for the mouth wasn't removed by hand. Counterfeiters have more ways to alter a Beanie than an octopus has arms!

Tan—no mouth	*Tan—mouth*	*Pink*
❏ It's mine!	❏ It's mine!	❏ It's mine!
Date purchased: ____	Date purchased: ____	Date purchased: ____
Price: ____	Price: ____	Price: ____
❏ Sold!	❏ Sold!	❏ Sold!
Date sold: ____	Date sold: ____	Date sold: ____
Price: ____	Price: ____	Price: ____

Jolly the Walrus

➤ Style: 4082
➤ Birthday: 12-2-96
➤ Released: 5-11-97

➤ Retired: 5-1-98
➤ Hangtag: 4-5

On the blazing Halley's Comet Scale of "cute," Jolly definitely scores higher than Tusk the walrus, whom he replaced. However, Jolly has the same design problem as co-releases Echo and Waves: He has no backbone! He doesn't sit up very well on his own, and if he's not propped up, you can expect him to roll over. He's covered in brown plush, but his most notable feature (besides his tusks) is his extremely fuzzy mustache.

❑ It's mine!

Date purchased: _____

Price: _____

❑ Sold!

Date sold: _____

Price: _____

Get the Scoop

If you're frustrated with your wobbly walrus, think about displaying him in a clear acrylic display box. He'll be guaranteed to sit up straight!

71

Legs the Frog

➤ Style: 4020
➤ Birthday: 4-25-93
➤ Released: 1-8-94

➤ Retired: 10-1-97
➤ Hangtag: 1-4

Get the Scoop

Earlier versions of Legs with swing tags are hard to come by, but the later tagged versions are as plentiful as june bugs on a lily pond—and still inexpensive.

An amphibian in the true Shaker style and one of the Original Nine Beanies, Legs is one of the plainest critters Ty makes. With the same medium-green plush that he shares with Speedy the turtle, he lacks any distinguishing features other than his eyes.

❑ It's mine!

   Date purchased: _____

   Price: _____

❑ Sold!

   Date sold: _____

   Price: _____

Manny the Manatee

➤ Style: 4081

➤ Birthday: 6-8-95

➤ Released: 1-7-96

➤ Retired: 5-11-97

➤ Hangtag: 3-4

No, you're not seeing double: Manny's shape and light gray plush are often confused with Flash the dolphin. Here's the difference: Manny has embroidered nostrils and a more rounded nose—and she lacks Flash's white stomach.

❏ It's mine!

   Date purchased: _____

   Price: _____

❏ Sold!

   Date sold: _____

   Price: _____

Get the Scoop

Manny's unpopularity on store shelves (she was an all-time sluggish seller) has helped boost her value since she retired.

Patti the Platypus

➤ Style: 4025

➤ Birthday: (none) (maroon)

➤ Birthday: 1-6-93 (fuchsia)

➤ Released: 1-8-94 (maroon)

➤ Released: 2-28-95 (fuchsia)

➤ Retired: 2-28-97 (maroon)

➤ Retired: 5-1-98 (fuchsia)

➤ Hangtag: 1-3 (maroon)

➤ Hangtag: 3-5 (fuchsia)

Call her "Patti the Flatty"—she's one of the flattest Beanies—and no matter how many times she's redesigned in different shades, she's consistently rolled off the conveyor belt with the same wide gold beak and "paddles." She comes in at least two different colors of plush: First came maroon, and then came fuchsia (also referred to as purple, orchid, or magenta).

Get the Scoop

Patti may come in as many as four colors, but some of the subtle variations may be the result of dye lot differences in the fabric.

Maroon

❏ It's mine!

    Date purchased: _____

    Price: _____

❏ Sold!

    Date sold: _____

    Price: _____

Fuchsia

❏ It's mine!

    Date purchased: _____

    Price: _____

❏ Sold!

    Date sold: _____

    Price: _____

Pinchers the Lobster/Punchers the Lobster

- ➤ Style: 4026
- ➤ Birthday: 6-19-93
- ➤ Released: 1-8-94 (Pinchers)
- ➤ Released: 1993 (Punchers)

- ➤ Retired: 5-1-98 (Pinchers)
- ➤ Retired: (pre-Beanies) (Punchers)
- ➤ Hangtag: 2-5 (Pinchers)
- ➤ Hangtag: 1 (Punchers)

The bright red Pinchers was one of the Original Nine Beanies released in January 1994. He has two black string whiskers of uneven length (either very long or very short). The difference between Pinchers and his earlier *pre-Beanie* version, Punchers, is in the spacing of the segments of the tail: The two inner segments on Pinchers are more narrow than the two outer segments.

❑ It's mine!

   Date purchased: _____

   Price: _____

❑ Sold!

   Date sold: _____

   Price: _____

Baby Talk

Pre-Beanie refers to the original beanbag animals produced by Ty before the official Beanie Baby craze began. (Pinchers' ancestor, Punchers, was a "pre-Beanie.")

Get the Scoop

The difference between Punchers and Pinchers is so slight that most people insist on carding Punchers to check out his hangtag as a way of proving his identity.

Seamore the Seal

➤ Style: 4029

➤ Birthday: 12-14-96

➤ Released: 6-25-94

➤ Retired: 10-1-97

➤ Hangtag: 1-4

Get the Scoop

Seamore is the most valuable Beanie from the October 1997 retirement group. Finding a mint condition Seamore is harder than balancing a beach ball on the end of your nose; but if you do, hang onto her!

Seamore is all white plush with a black plastic nose and whiskers and embroidered eyebrows. She was hard to find in stores before her October 1997 retirement, and afterwards her value briefly skyrocketed.

❑ It's mine!

  Date purchased: _____

  Price: _____

❑ Sold!

  Date sold: _____

  Price: _____

Seaweed the Otter

➤ Style: 4080
➤ Birthday: 3-19-96
➤ Released: 1-7-96
➤ Retired: 9-19-98
➤ Hangtag: 3-5

Unlike some of the floppier Beanie sea creatures, Seaweed's tail helps her maintain a sitting position—but she can also lie on her back just like real otters, who spend a great deal of time floating around this way. Seaweed has dark brown plush with a medium brown plush snout. Missing from action for the last couple months before her retirement, her value "ottter" go up fairly quickly.

❑ It's mine!

Date purchased: _____

Price: _____

❑ Sold!

Date sold: _____

Price: _____

Get the Scoop

Only a few Beanies boast felt as a decoration; Seaweed is one of them! A vegetarian, as are all good otters, she nibbles a tasty morsel of green felt seaweed in her paws.

Splash the Whale

➤ Style: 4022

➤ Birthday: 7-8-93

➤ Released: 1-8-94

➤ Retired: 5-11-97

➤ Hangtag: 1-4

Get the Scoop

Thar he blows! Some people think Splash is a tad more rare than Flash, his twin, but others don't believe it makes a whale of a difference. They are both good value if you can harpoon one.

Splash and his fraternal twin Flash were among the Original Nine Beanies, both of whom were retired in May 1997, and replaced with the moderately short-lived Waves and Echo. Splash has beautiful black plush on his back and fins, but his underbelly, like all proper Orca whales, is white.

❏ It's mine!

Date purchased: _____

Price: _____

❏ Sold!

Date sold: _____

Price: _____

Sting the Stingray

➤ Style: 4077

➤ Birthday: 8-27-95

➤ Released: 6-3-95

➤ Retired: 1-1-97

➤ Hangtag: 3-4

Sting and Bronty share the same deep blue, tie-dyed plush, but it seems far more appropriate to this beautiful sea creature. Who ever heard of a blue brontosaurus, anyway? Initial introduction photos of this guy sported a white belly, but he's been all blue up to his retirement New Year's Day 1997.

❑ It's mine!

Date purchased: _____

Price: _____

❑ Sold!

Date sold: _____

Price: _____

On the Sly

Beware! All those "beans" in Sting's tail can make it hard to bend, which can lead to some popped stitches where the tail connects to his body.

Tusk the Walrus

➤ Style: 4076

➤ Birthday: 9-18-95

➤ Released: 1-7-95

➤ Retired: 1-1-97

➤ Hangtag: 3-4

Much plainer than his toothy descendant Jolly the walrus, Tusk has brown plush over all but his snout, which is a lighter brown. His white felt tusks can face either forward or backward. Notice that Ty often uses the Beanies' poems to drive home an educational point to their younger customers.

Get the Scoop

Some of the later versions of Tusk had a hangtag with his name spelled "Tuck"—this error makes him slightly more valuable, despite being a poor speller.

❑ It's mine!

Date purchased: _____

Price: _____

❑ Sold!

Date sold: _____

Price: _____

80

Waddle the Penguin

➤ Style: 4075
➤ Birthday: 12-19-95
➤ Released: 6-3-95

➤ Retired: 5-1-98
➤ Hangtag: 3-5

He's a fat and sassy fellow, dressed in formal attire: black plush on his head, back, and the top of his wings. The underside of his wings and his belly are white plush. His beak and feet are bright orange and his "bow tie" is bright yellow plush. Waddle on over to your nearest store, where you may still find him on the shelves.

❑ It's mine!

   Date purchased: _____

   Price: _____

❑ Sold!

   Date sold: _____

   Price: _____

Get the Scoop

Although Waddle was reincarnated in midget form as one of the 1998 Teenie Beanies, full-sized Waddle was retired before his release in miniature.

Waves the Whale

➤ Style: 4084
➤ Birthday: 12-8-96
➤ Released: 5-11-97

➤ Retired: 5-1-98
➤ Hangtag: 4-5

Get the Scoop

The mistagged Waves and Echo are now worth slightly more than the correctly tagged versions, though neither is very expensive.

Waves was never as popular (or easy to display) as his predecessor Splash. It was a whale of a mixup as the first shipments of Waves arrived in the stores bearing Echo's hang- and tush tags (and vice versa).

❑ It's mine!

   Date purchased: _____

   Price: _____

❑ Sold!

   Date sold: _____

   Price: _____

The Least You Need to Know

➤ The world of sea creatures includes some of the cutest Beanies Ty makes.

➤ Beware of counterfeit Beanies—especially Bubbles.

➤ Don't adjust your set: Many of the Beanie sea creatures (especially the May 1997 releases) don't sit upright easily.

Chapter 8

Here Kitty, Kitty...

In This Chapter

➤ Get the history and details of all the Beanie Baby cats

➤ Find out which kitties have retired

➤ Check out all the cat Beanie Baby photos

Have trouble telling the Zips from the Chips, the Nips from the Snips? You're not alone! We're here to get this all straight for you, once and for all.

In this chapter, you'll find the lowdown on all the Beanie Baby cats. For convenience's sake (and because the "wildlife" chapter was already filled to overflowing) we've also included the wild cats in this group—so look here for Blizzard the tiger, Freckles the leopard, and Stripes the tiger.

Blizzard the Tiger

➤ Style: 4163
➤ Birthday: 12-12-96
➤ Released: 5-11-97

➤ Retired: 5-1-98
➤ Hangtag: 4-5

Get the Scoop

Rumors of retirement due to trademark claims (Dairy Queen already had a "Blizzard" frozen treat) followed her from the time of her release up until the day she was retired. In case you wondered: No, the rumors weren't true.

You might expect her to be pure white, but Blizzard has black stripes on that white body. You can tell the difference between her and Ziggy the zebra by measuring the stripes: Blizzard's are farther apart. With her pink nose, black whiskers, and blue eyes, she has been an extremely popular member of the leopard-tiger-panther group.

❑ It's mine!

　　Date purchased: _____

　　Price: _____

❑ Sold!

　　Date sold: _____

　　Price: _____

Chip the Cat

➤ Style: 4121
➤ Birthday: 1-26-96
➤ Released: 5-1-97

➤ Retired:
➤ Hangtag: 4-5

Chip looks like a Frankenstein version of Nip and Zip, with two-thirds of her face and one ear gold plush, and the other side and ear black. Her paws and the inside of her ears are white, and she's got a pink nose and white whiskers. Chip was a very popular addition to the Beanie cats, which include Flip, Nip, Snip, and Zip.

❏ It's mine!

Date purchased: _____

Price: _____

❏ Sold!

Date sold: _____

Price: _____

Get the Scoop

You won't find huge piles of Chips at your local store, but if you search you may still uncover some.

Flip the White Cat

➤ Style: 4012
➤ Birthday: 2-28-95
➤ Released: 1-7-96

➤ Retired: 10-1-97
➤ Hangtag: 3-4

On the Sly

Flip's baby blues are a standout, but like all white Beanies, Flip can be a pain to keep clean!

All bets were off (which cat would be retired first?) as Flip went sailing into retirement, the first of the Beanie cats to do so. All white with a pink nose and whiskers, her interior ears are pink plush as well.

❏ It's mine!

Date purchased: _____

Price: _____

❏ Sold!

Date sold: _____

Price: _____

Freckles the Leopard

➤ Style: 4066
➤ Birthday: 6-3-96
➤ Released: 6-15-96

➤ Retired:
➤ Hangtag: 4-5

Freckles is—well, freckled all over with leopard spots, but he's shaped like his cousins Stripes the tiger and Velvet the panther (both now retired). Pink-nosed and black-whiskered, his tail comes in two varieties: flat with visible stitching or round with hidden stitching.

❏ It's mine!

    Date purchased: _____

    Price: _____

❏ Sold!

    Date sold: _____

    Price: _____

Get the Scoop

Freckles' unusual plush design has had collectors clamoring for more; he's usually one of the first to get snapped up from store shelves.

Nip the Cat

- ➤ Style: 4003
- ➤ Birthday: (none) (white face)
- ➤ Birthday: (none) (all gold)
- ➤ Birthday: 3-6-94 (white paws)
- ➤ Released: 1-7-95 (white face)
- ➤ Released: 1-7-96 (all gold)
- ➤ Released: 3-10-96 (white paws)

- ➤ Retired: 1-7-96 (white face)
- ➤ Retired: 3-10-96 (all gold)
- ➤ Retired: 12-31-97 (white paws)
- ➤ Hangtag: 2-3 (white face)
- ➤ Hangtag: 3 (all gold)
- ➤ Hangtag: 3-4 (white paws)

Get the Scoop

The second variation of Nip is the hardest to get.

Another three-variation Beanie, Nip was first released with a very round face, pink inner ears, and a white plush triangle that extended over his belly. In his second incarnation, he appeared with a smaller, more triangular-shaped face in all gold (except for the pink in his ears). Both these first two versions had pink plastic noses and pink string whiskers. In his third appearance, he kept his all-gold plush but now sports white paws and white inner ears. The pink string whiskers turned white.

Tan—no mouth

❏ It's mine!

Date
purchased: ____

Price: ____

❏ Sold!

Date sold: ____

Price: ____

Tan—mouth

❏ It's mine!

Date
purchased: ____

Price: ____

❏ Sold!

Date sold: ____

Price: ____

Pink

❏ It's mine!

Date
purchased: ____

Price: ____

❏ Sold!

Date sold: ____

Price: ____

Pounce the Cat

➤ Style: 4122
➤ Birthday: 8-28-97
➤ Released: 12-31-97

➤ Retired:
➤ Hangtag: 5

When Pounce was first released, her tie-dyed brown plush was a fabric innovation. Many people thought there was something wrong with their Pounce, since the fabric wasn't an even color. (The tie-dye variations are very subtle.) Her paws, inner ears, and chin are off-white, and she has a pink nose and mouth and brown string whiskers.

❏ It's mine!

Date purchased: _____

Price: _____

❏ Sold!

Date sold: _____

Price: _____

Get the Scoop

No, Pounce is not going to be recalled because her name is the same as a popular cat treat—that's just a rumor!

Prance the Cat

➤ Style: 4123
➤ Birthday: 11-20-97
➤ Released: 12-31-97

➤ Retired:
➤ Hangtag: 5

Get the Scoop

Can't keep Pounce and Prance straight? Try remembering that alphabetically, brown comes before gray, so Pounce comes before Prance.

The black-on-gray striped plush on Prance is a first for the Beanie line; her paws and inner ears are white, and she has a white spot on her forehead. Blue eyes and a pink nose, mouth, and whiskers complete the package.

❏ It's mine!

Date purchased: _____

Price: _____

❏ Sold!

Date sold: _____

Price: _____

Roary the Lion

➤ Style: 4069

➤ Birthday: 2-20-96

➤ Released: 5-11-97

➤ Retired:

➤ Hangtag: 4-5

Roary borrowed the fake fur from Nuts the squirrel's tail in order to have a full mane and a ball of fur on the tip of his tail. Covered in brown plush, his inner ears and chin are off-white. He has black whiskers, but shares his small fuzzy plastic nose with Velvet the panther.

❏ It's mine!

   Date purchased: _____

   Price: _____

❏ Sold!

   Date sold: _____

   Price: _____

Get the Scoop

If you've got young friends, you know that Roary is a particular favorite of youngsters (perhaps because of Disney's *The Lion King*).

Snip the Siamese Cat

➤ Style: 4120

➤ Birthday: 10-22-96

➤ Released: 1-1-97

➤ Retired:

➤ Hangtag: 4-5

Get the Scoop

While there are more dog Beanies than there are cats at the moment, you feline aficionados can count on more cat breeds being born in the next two years to even the score.

Just as you'd expect from a Siamese, Snip has big blue eyes, cream-colored plush fur, and brown points on each paw, the tip of her tail, her inner ears, and her face just above her nose. The nose is black plastic, with dark brown whiskers.

❑ It's mine!

Date purchased: _____

Price: _____

❑ Sold!

Date sold: _____

Price: _____

Stripes the Tiger

- ➤ Style: 4065
- ➤ Birthday: (none) (dark)
- ➤ Birthday: 6-11-95 (light)
- ➤ Released: 1-7-96 (dark)
- ➤ Released: 6-3-96 (light)

- ➤ Retired: 6-3-96 (dark)
- ➤ Retired: 5-1-98 (light)
- ➤ Hangtag: 3 (dark)
- ➤ Hangtag: 4-5 (light)

Dark stripes/light stripes, old stripes/new stripes, thin stripes/fat stripes...if it's stripes you want, you can get 'em all in various Beanie Babies, all variations on the tiger theme. The older Stripes has black stripes on dark-gold material, while the newer, more common version has fewer black stripes on a yellow-tan plush. Both have fuzzy pink plastic noses and black whiskers.

Get the Scoop

If you're into collecting, try to bag the rare version of the darker Stripes with fuzzier material on the belly. It's worth significantly more money.

Dark

❑ It's mine!

　　Date purchased: _____

　　Price: _____

❑ Sold!

　　Date sold: _____

　　Price: _____

Light

❑ It's mine!

　　Date purchased: _____

　　Price: _____

❑ Sold!

　　Date sold: _____

　　Price: _____

Velvet the Panther

➤ Style: 4064
➤ Birthday: 12-16-95
➤ Released: 6-3-95

➤ Retired: 10-1-97
➤ Hangtag: 3-4

This beautiful black plush panther's most distinguishing feature is her fuzzy pink plastic nose found on many of the Beanie cats, both wild and domestic. (Those of you who like realism in your wild cats will be pleased with these details: You can even see the nostrils.)

Get the Scoop

Velvet comes in both round- and flat-tailed versions, but they're all worth the same.

❑ It's mine!

Date purchased: _____

Price: _____

❑ Sold!

Date sold: _____

Price: _____

Zip the Cat

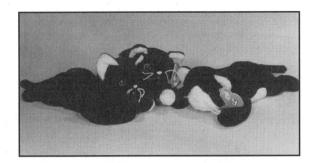

➤ Style:	4004	➤ Retired:	1-7-96 (white face)
➤ Birthday:	(none) (white face)	➤ Retired:	3-10-96 (all black)
➤ Birthday:	(none) (all black)	➤ Retired:	12-31-97 (white paws)
➤ Birthday:	3-28-94 (white paws)	➤ Hangtag:	2-3 (white face)
➤ Released:	1-7-95 (white face)	➤ Hangtag:	3 (all black)
➤ Released:	1-7-96 (all black)	➤ Hangtag:	3-4 (white paws)
➤ Released:	3-10-96 (white paws)		

Zip the cat, like his pal Nip, has worked his way through three variations of his nine lives. In his first life, he was born with a face as round as a pumpkin, with a triangle of white plush from the middle of his forehead extending under his chin and over his belly. The second and most rare (rarer than the all-gold Nip) variation is all black. Both versions come with pink inner ears, pink plastic noses, and pink string whiskers. The final variation has white inner ears, whiskers, and paws, and is the hardest to find among all the May 1998 retirees. All three Zips have green eyes.

Get the Scoop

The second-edition Zip (all black) is even rarer than the all-gold Nip. If you've got this one stashed in your collection, break out the catnip and celebrate!

White face

❏ It's mine!

Date purchased: _____

Price: _____

❏ Sold!

Date sold: _____

Price: _____

All black

❏ It's mine!

Date purchased: _____

Price: _____

❏ Sold!

Date sold: _____

Price: _____

White paws

❏ It's mine!

Date purchased: _____

Price: _____

❏ Sold!

Date sold: _____

Price: _____

97

The Least You Need to Know

➤ Each Beanie cat has her own personality—but all are loaded with charm.

➤ While all the cats are very popular, they are still outnumbered by dog Beanies—but more cats are on the way.

➤ Second-edition Zip (all black) is the rarest of the Beanie cats.

Chapter 9

Old McDonald Had a Farm

In This Chapter

➤ Learn how to tell the Beanie bunnies apart

➤ Find out which Beanie hit the sauce and got renamed

➤ Read all about a cow with a gender identity problem

If you live on a farm—or just dream of living the rural life—you'll find plenty of cuddly Ty Beanies to fulfill your country aspirations. In this chapter, we outline all you need to know about each one.

While you'll find all the traditional farm creatures here, you'll also find all of the rabbits, too. While technically "wild" critters, they are often raised on farms and seemed to fit in well with their fellow barn Beanies.

Bessie the Cow

➤ Style: 4009   ➤ Retired: 10-1-97

➤ Birthday: 6-27-95   ➤ Hangtag: 2-4

➤ Released: 6-3-95

Bessie is a brown and white "sit-up" style cow who was a companion to Daisy, the black and white "lay-down" cow, until Bessie got put out to pasture last October 1. Daisy followed just two weeks shy of a year later, having retired on September 15, 1998.

Get the Scoop

She's udderly divine, but why does this lady cow have horns?

❑ It's mine!

Date purchased: _____

Price: _____

❑ Sold!

Date sold: _____

Price: _____

Chops the Lamb

➤ Style: 4019
➤ Birthday: 5-3-96
➤ Released: 1-7-96

➤ Retired: 1-1-97
➤ Hangtag: 3-4

If you're counting sheep, Chops was the first of two Beanie ovines (Fleece was the other) to hit the market. Chops has cream-colored plush with a black face and black interior ears, and a pink nose.

❏ It's mine!

Date purchased: _____

Price: _____

❏ Sold!

Date sold: _____

Price: _____

Get the Scoop

It was rumored that Chops was retired (way too early, many say!) due to a name conflict with the late Shari Lewis' puppet, Lamb Chop.

Daisy the Cow

➤ Style: 4006
➤ Birthday: 5-10-94
➤ Released: 6-25-94

➤ Retired: 9-15-98
➤ Hangtag: 1-5

Get the Scoop

Daisy sported a special hangtag for the Chicago Cubs in memory of legendary broadcaster Harry Caray (see Chapter 3) as part of a promotion.

Daisy is a lay-down cow, unlike her similarly retired bovine sister, Bessie. Mostly black with a broad white stripe down her face and white inner ears, Daisy also sports a white spot on the left side of her back and has light tan horns.

❑ It's mine!

Date purchased: _____

Price: _____

❑ Sold!

Date sold: _____

Price: _____

Derby the Horse

➤ Style: 4008

➤ Birthday: (none) (fine-mane)

➤ Birthday: 9-16-95 (coarse-mane)

➤ Birthday: 9-16-95 (star)

➤ Release: 6-3-95 (fine-mane)

➤ Release: (unknown) (coarse-mane)

➤ Release: 12-15-97 (star)

➤ Retired: (unknown) (fine-mane)

➤ Retired: 12-15-97 (coarse-mane)

➤ Retired: (star)

➤ Hangtag: 3 (fine-mane)

➤ Hangtag: 3-4 (coarse-mane)

➤ Hangtag: 5 (star)

Derby is one of the few Beanies who have undergone two design changes. In his initial entry into the Ty stable, he came equipped with a mane and tail of fine brown yarn to contrast his lighter-brown plush. The fine yarn gave way to thicker, coarser brown yarn, and then at the start of 1998, Derby earned a white star on his forehead.

Fine mane	*Coarse mane*	*Star*
❑ It's mine!	❑ It's mine!	❑ It's mine!
Date purchased: ____	Date purchased: ____	Date purchased: ____
Price: ____	Price: ____	Price: ____
❑ Sold!	❑ Sold!	❑ Sold!
Date sold: ____	Date sold: ____	Date sold: ____
Price: ____	Price: ____	Price: ____

Get the Scoop

The fine-maned Derby version is very rare, so if you want this one you'll have to pony up quite a bit of spare change.

Doodle the Rooster (now Strut)

➤ Style:	4171		➤ Retired:	7-12-97 (Doodle)
➤ Birthday:	3-8-96		➤ Retired:	(Strut)
➤ Released:	5-11-97		➤ Hangtag:	4

Doodle wasn't long for the Beanie world when apparently he was retired due to a name conflict. (There was already a "Doodles" chicken—the mascot of restaurant chain Chick-Fil-A.) This Beanie rooster is no chicken: He's colorfully made of pink, magenta, yellow, and green tie-dye with long yellow legs and beak. His wings and tail are bright red plush to match his felt comb and waddle. He was not redesigned after the renaming.

Get the Scoop

There weren't a whole lot of Doodles to start with, and he was only distributed on a limited basis. Once news of his new name dribbled out, his worth skyrocketed from $10 to more than $100!

❏ It's mine!

Date purchased: _____

Price: _____

❏ Sold!

Date sold: _____

Price: _____

Ears the Brown Rabbit

➤ Style: 4018
➤ Birthday: 4-18-95
➤ Released: 1-7-96

➤ Retired: 5-1-98
➤ Hangtag: 3-5

Ears was the first and most realistic of the Beanie rabbits, since he's designed to stretch out just like living, breathing lagomorphs. Brown with a cute white tail, the insides of his long ears and his mouth are also white, and he has pink string whiskers and nose. He retired along with his three pastel compatriots in May 1998, but should still be easy to find.

❏ It's mine!

Date purchased: _____

Price: _____

❏ Sold!

Date sold: _____

Price: _____

Get the Scoop

If you're looking for a unique way to decorate your home for the Easter holidays, what could be more festive than little brown Ears peeking out of a spring flower arrangement?

Fleece the Lamb

➤ Style: 4125
➤ Birthday: 3-21-96
➤ Released: 1-1-97

➤ Retired:
➤ Hangtag: 4-5

On the Sly

Be careful of how you display Fleece; her fur can quickly mutate from white as snow to dull as dishwater if you're not careful.

Fleece is as white as snow (at least, she is when she's new!), but her plush is unique among most Beanies in that it's nappy rather than smooth. The sweet-faced replacement for Chops, the black-faced lamb, Fleece has a cream-colored face and small pink nose.

❑ It's mine!

Date purchased: _____

Price: _____

❑ Sold!

Date sold: _____

Price: _____

Floppity the Lilac Bunny

➤ Style:	4118		➤ Retired:	5-1-98
➤ Birthday:	5-28-96		➤ Hangtag:	4-5
➤ Released:	1-1-97			

Lovely light-lilac, Floppity is one of a trio of pastel bunnies as pretty as a row of Easter eggs on a spring morning. (Hippity and Hoppity are the other two.) Floppity has a pink nose, whiskers, and pink plush under the ears. A totally color-coordinated bunny, she has a lavender bow that matches her plush.

❑ It's mine!

Date purchased: _____

Price: _____

❑ Sold!

Date sold: _____

Price: _____

Get the Scoop

Have trouble remembering which bunny is which color? Put the colors in alphabetical order—lilac, mint, and rose—and you have the order of their names, too.

Gobbles the Turkey

➤ Style: 4023
➤ Birthday: 11-27-96
➤ Released: 10-1-97

➤ Retired:
➤ Hangtag: 4-5

Gobbles is decorated in harvest colors of red, yellow, brown, and white. Her head is red with a yellow beak. Yellow is also found under her wings and on her feet. She has a red felt waddle and two embroidered nostrils. Her body and the base of her tail are brown plush with a middle arc of red and outer arc of white. She is a large, impressive Beanie—quite beautiful when her tail is fanned out.

Get the Scoop

Having a Thanksgiving dinner and stumped for party favors for the kids' table? Look no further. Gregarious Gobbles will be a sure-fire holiday hit!

❑ It's mine!

Date purchased: _____

Price: _____

❑ Sold!

Date sold: _____

Price: _____

Hippity the Mint Bunny

➤ Style: 4119
➤ Birthday: 6-1-96
➤ Released: 1-1-97

➤ Retired: 5-1-98
➤ Hangtag: 4-5

The middle of the bunny trio of Floppity, Hippity, and Hoppity, Hippity is a medium mint-green with a matching ribbon around his neck. He has a pink nose and whiskers, and the undersides of his long ears are pink as well.

❏ It's mine!

    Date purchased: _____

    Price: _____

❏ Sold!

    Date sold: _____

    Price: _____

Get the Scoop

Hippity is usually considered the most difficult of the three pastel bunnies to dig up. If you find him, hop right out and snap him up!

Hoppity the Rose Bunny

➤ Style: 4117
➤ Birthday: 4-3-96
➤ Released: 1-1-97

➤ Retired: 5-1-98
➤ Hangtag: 4-5

This little bunny is all pink, from the tip of her nose down to her toes. Like her buddies Floppity and Hippity, the undersides of her ears are pink, but with her coloring you don't notice. Like the other bunnies, Hoppity's ribbon around her neck matches her plush.

❏ It's mine!

Date purchased: _____

Price: _____

❏ Sold!

Date sold: _____

Price: _____

Lefty the Donkey

➤ Style: 4086

➤ Birthday: 7-4-96

➤ Released: 6-15-96

➤ Retired: 1-1-97

➤ Hangtag: 4

Lefty and Righty the elephant are the only Beanies that share both a birthday and a poem. Ty trotted out the same body style as Derby the horse for this steel-blue donkey, but his mane and tail are black instead of brown.
He also has black hooves, nose, and inner ears.

❑ It's mine!

   Date purchased: _____

   Price: _____

❑ Sold!

   Date sold: _____

   Price: _____

Get the Scoop

As the Democratic candidate for the 1996 Presidential election, Lefty was retired before the inauguration.

Snort the Bull

➤ Style: 4002
➤ Birthday: 5-15-95
➤ Released: 1-1-97

➤ Retired: 9-15-98
➤ Hangtag: 4-5

Get the Scoop

Some Snorts were shipped with Tabasco's tag, and some Canadian Snorts have "Snort" as the name on the tag, but Tabasco's name in the poem.

When Tabasco the bull was benched, Snort came to play center court. The two are almost identical; the only difference is that Snort has cream-colored hooves.

❏ It's mine!

   Date purchased: _____

   Price: _____

❏ Sold!

   Date sold: _____

   Price: _____

Squealer the Pig

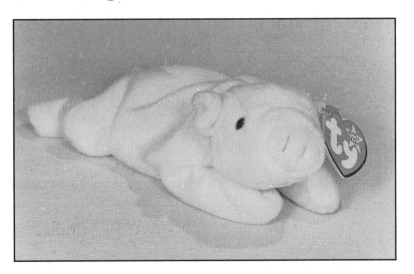

➤ Style: 4005
➤ Birthday: 4-23-93
➤ Released: 1-8-94

➤ Retired: 5-1-98
➤ Hangtag: 1-5

Squealer's little folded ears and pink knotted tail are endearing, though I have to admit a personal attachment to this Original Nine Beanie as he was one of the first I got.

❏ It's mine!

   Date purchased: _____

   Price: _____

❏ Sold!

   Date sold: _____

   Price: _____

Get the Scoop

Squealer, like his fellow retiree Zip, seemed to disappear from store shelves for several months prior to his retirement. As a result, he's generally a little more expensive than the rest of his retirement class.

Tabasco the Bull

➤ Style: 4002

➤ Birthday: 5-15-95

➤ Release: 6-3-95

➤ Retirement: 1-1-97

➤ Hangtag: 3-4

It's the bull, NOT the sauce! But due to the name conflict, he had an untimely retirement—Snort was introduced with the same poem but the different name. You'll have to work hard to steer around the differences between these two: Tabasco's hooves are red, while Snort's are cream-colored like his nose, horns, and inner ears.

Get the Scoop

Thanks to his quick retirement, Tabasco's value shot through the barn roof—but now has finally stabilized.

❏ It's mine!

Date purchased: _____

Price: _____

❏ Sold!

Date sold: _____

Price: _____

The Least You Need to Know

➤ The barnyard Beanies are some of the cutest Beanies around.

➤ If you put the pastel bunnies' colors in alphabetical order (lilac, mint, and rose) you get the order of their names (Flippity, Hippity, Hoppity).

➤ There's been a lot of naming complications down on the farm: Chops (vs. Lamb Chop the puppet), Doodle (vs. the Chick-Fil-A mascot), and Tabasco (vs. the sauce).

Chapter 10

Birds of a Feather

In This Chapter

➤ Learn which bird Beanies make good holiday decorations

➤ Discover which Beanies make good gifts for patriotic collectibles, hunting themes, and bird lovers

➤ Tell the difference between some common counterfeit birds and the real thing!

If you've been flocking to the stores to stock up on bird Beanies, this chapter will tell you all you need to know! There is lots to learn about in the bird department: common counterfeits, some gorgeous plumage, and some connections to baseball promotions that are sure to continue. Read on for the details!

Baldy the Eagle

➤ Style: 4074

➤ Birthday: 2-17-96

➤ Released: 5-11-97

➤ Retired: 5-1-98

➤ Hangtag: 4-5

Get the Scoop

Because of his association with our national emblem, Baldy is a favorite among collectors of patriotic items as well as bird collectors and Beanie Baby fans.

Baldy's black plush body makes a striking contrast to his white head and bright yellow beak and feet. Only released for a year, he flew into retirement recently enough that he's fairly easy to find if you want to start in on your collection of retired Beanies.

❏ It's mine!

  Date purchased: _____

  Price: _____

❏ Sold!

  Date sold: _____

  Price: _____

Batty the Bat

➤ Style: 4035

➤ Birthday: 10-29-96

➤ Released: 10-1-97

➤ Retired:

➤ Hangtag: 4-5

Batty's plush is a difficult color to describe—it's a pinky-colored light brown, not a deep chocolate-colored brown like you might expect after watching all those old Boris Karloff movies. His felt ears and feet are the same color.

❏ It's mine!

Date purchased: _____

Price: _____

❏ Sold!

Date sold: _____

Price: _____

Get the Scoop

Unlike any other Beanie in the collection, Batty has Velcro on the edges of his wing tips so he can be stuck on you.

Caw the Crow

➤ Style: 4071

➤ Birthday: (none)

➤ Released: 6-3-95

➤ Retired: 6-15-96

➤ Hangtag: 3

Get the Scoop

Caw wasn't on the market very long, which means people will pay more money to cage him in their collections.

Caw is a short, squat black plush with long tail and wings. His beak and feet are a bright orange plush. Though simple in name and design, he's very appealing in person, especially to bird lovers.

❑ It's mine!

  Date purchased: _____

  Price: _____

❑ Sold!

  Date sold: _____

  Price: _____

120

Early the Robin

➤ Style:	4190	➤ Retired:	
➤ Birthday:	3-20-97	➤ Hangtag:	5
➤ Released:	5-30-98		

Early's plush is a deep brown tie-dye (the same as Pounce). Naturally, he sports a bright red plush chest like every good robin. He's one of the shortest Beanies and appeared with a whole flock of birds in the May 30, 1998 release.

❑ It's mine!

Date purchased: _____

Price: _____

❑ Sold!

Date sold: _____

Price: _____

Get the Scoop

If you're looking for a cheerful way to celebrate the spring, consider hosting a springtime brunch, and decorate your buffet table with Early.

Gracie the Swan

➤ Style: 4126
➤ Birthday: 6-17-96
➤ Released: 1-1-97

➤ Retired: 5-1-98
➤ Hangtag: 4-5

Get the Scoop

The Chicago Cubs used Gracie in a promotion to honor their first baseman, Mark Grace.

Gracie is another of those hard-to-keep-clean white Beanies, with bright orange feet and beak and black plastic eyes. Many felt she was too plain, but as a newly retired Beanie, she has gained popularity.

❑ It's mine!

Date purchased: _____

Price: _____

❑ Sold!

Date sold: _____

Price: _____

Hoot the Owl

➤ Style: 4073

➤ Birthday: 8-9-95

➤ Released: 1-7-96

➤ Retired: 10-1-97

➤ Hangtag: 3-4

Like many other bird Beanies, Hoot is another shortie. His rounded head, body, and the tops of his wings are dark-brown plush. His face, chest, and the undersides of his wings are a lighter brown (the same color as Derby), and he has a small orange felt beak. Some tags have an error where "quite" is spelled "qutie."

❏ It's mine!

Date purchased: _____

Price: _____

❏ Sold!

Date sold: _____

Price: _____

Get the Scoop

For a long time, buyers did not exactly flock to the stores to stock up on this poor little bird, whom many consider to be a less–than–exciting example of the Beanie Baby art. As a retiree, he may gain slowly in value.

Jabber the Parrot

➤ Style: 4197
➤ Birthday: 10-10-97
➤ Released: 5-30-98

➤ Retired:
➤ Hangtag: 5

Jabber is one of the most colorful Beanies of all, similar in style to his predecessors Caw and Kiwi. A bright red Beanie, the top of his head is bright blue, while the top of his beak, the undersides of his wings, and his feet are yellow. The wings closest to the body are green, changing to blue plush halfway down, and his eyes are yellow surrounded by black-and-white striped plush.

Get the Scoop

Jabber was one of a group of 14 new babies introduced May 30, 1998.

❑ It's mine!

Date purchased: _____

Price: _____

❑ Sold!

Date sold: _____

Price: _____

Jake the Mallard Duck

➤ Style: 4199

➤ Birthday: 4-16-97

➤ Released: 5-30-98

➤ Retired:

➤ Hangtag: 5

Jake is a beautiful rendition of the real thing: His head is a deep teal green (deeper than teal Teddy), and he has a white neck band, light gray sides and back, and dark gray on his wing tops. The teal material is repeated on the top of his tail. His chest matches the tie-dyed brown material worn by Pounce and Early, and his beak is gold felt, stitched in black around the edge with embroidered nostrils. His feet are the same material as his beak.

❏ It's mine!

   Date purchased: _____

   Price: _____

❏ Sold!

   Date sold: _____

   Price: _____

Get the Scoop

Jake is popular not just with Beanie fans, but with those who enjoy decorating their dens in a hunting motif.

125

Kiwi the Toucan

➤ Style: 4070

➤ Birthday: 9-16-95

➤ Released: 6-3-95

➤ Retired: 1-1-97

➤ Hangtag: 3-4

Bright Kiwi looks a lot like Caw in the body department: The plush on the top of his head, back, wings, and tail is black, but his chest and the bottom of his wings are bright red. The underside of his head and neck is bright yellow, and the blue used on his long beak is the same as the royal blue used in the rare version of Peanut.

On the Sly

Accept no substitutes! The counterfeit Kiwi's beak is a lighter blue and much shorter than the legitimate version.

❏ It's mine!

Date purchased: _____

Price: _____

❏ Sold!

Date sold: _____

Price: _____

Kuku the Cockatoo

- ➤ Style: 4192
- ➤ Birthday: 1-5-97
- ➤ Released: 5-30-98

- ➤ Retired:
- ➤ Hangtag: 5

Besides his bright white plush body and wings and gray beak and feet, it's hard to miss Kuku's shocking crown of bright pink fluff on the top of his head.

❑ It's mine!

Date purchased: _____

Price: _____

❑ Sold!

Date sold: _____

Price: _____

Get the Scoop

Looking a bit like a punk rock star without the nose ring, Kuku is one of six Beanie birds released at the end of May 1998.

Pinky the Flamingo

➤ Style: 4072
➤ Birthday: 2-13-95
➤ Released: 6-3-95

➤ Retired:
➤ Hangtag: 3-5

Pinky truly fits her name: Her body plush is bright pink, a color not found on any other Beanie. Her long, dangling light pink legs allow her to be draped over almost anything, and her bright orange beak is the same color as Goldie. Pinky's Teenie Beanie counterpart is the most rare and valuable Teenie from the 1997 set.

On the Sly

The "red Pinky" rumored as a new Ty release turned out to be nothing more than another counterfeit.

❑ It's mine!

Date purchased: _____

Price: _____

❑ Sold!

Date sold: _____

Price: _____

Puffer the Puffin

➤ Style: 4181

➤ Birthday: 11-3-97

➤ Released: 12-31-97

➤ Retired: 9-18-98

➤ Hangtag: 5

Puffer's black back and white chest look terrific next to her red feet and beak banded with yellow and red. The sides of her face are white plush with a small triangle of black material surrounding her eyes.

❏ It's mine!

　　Date purchased: _____

　　Price: _____

❏ Sold!

　　Date sold: _____

　　Price: _____

Get the Scoop

After the May 1998 retirement, Puffer was left with only two other birds in the current category until the May 1998 new releases that brought in six new birds. Retired only nine months after his release, look for his value to rise a bit more than the average Beanie.

Quackers the Duck

- ➤ Style: 4024
- ➤ Birthday: (none) (wingless)
- ➤ Birthday: 4-19-94 (winged)
- ➤ Released: 6-25-94 (wingless)
- ➤ Released: 1-7-95 (winged)

- ➤ Retired: 1-7-95 (wingless)
- ➤ Retired: 5-1-98 (winged)
- ➤ Hangtag: 1-2 (wingless)
- ➤ Hangtag: 2-5 (winged)

The awkward-looking original version of Quackers is quite rare. Without his wings and with generally less "beans" than the later winged version, Quackers had a hard time keeping his balance. Both versions are covered in bright yellow plush, with stuffed orange beaks, orange feet, and embroidered eyebrows.

Get the Scoop

Either version of Quackers (winged or plucked) may have old swing tags that made his name singular (Quacker).

Wingless

❏ It's mine!

Date purchased: _____

Price: _____

❏ Sold!

Date sold: _____

Price: _____

Winged

❏ It's mine!

Date purchased: _____

Price: _____

❏ Sold!

Date sold: _____

Price: _____

Radar the Bat

➤ Style: 4091
➤ Birthday: 10-30-95
➤ Released: 9-1-95

➤ Retired: 5-11-97
➤ Hangtag: 3-4

The only break from Radar's all-black plush and felt feet and "fingertips" is the white plush inside his ears and two little beady red eyes. Though finding Radar isn't difficult, finding one in mint condition that hasn't been played with into oblivion is a little more challenging!

❑ It's mine!

   Date purchased: _____

   Price: _____

❑ Sold!

   Date sold: _____

   Price: _____

Get the Scoop

If you're looking for a good Halloween decoration, search no farther! This cute little black bat will look smashing as part of your holiday decorations.

131

Scoop the Pelican

➤ Style: 4107
➤ Birthday: 7-1-96
➤ Released: 6-15-96

➤ Retired:
➤ Hangtag: 4-5

Dressed in the same steel-blue plush as Echo and Crunch, Scoop's distinguishing feature is a huge stuffed bill of bright orange plush. Too bad for Scoop it's not stuffed with fish! Scoop's feet are made from the same bright orange plush.

Get the Scoop

Scoop gained popularity when he was included in the 1998 Teenie Beanie set.

❑ It's mine!

Date purchased: _____

Price: _____

❑ Sold!

Date sold: _____

Price: _____

Stretch the Ostrich

➤ Style: 4182   ➤ Retired:

➤ Birthday: 9-21-97   ➤ Hangtag: 5

➤ Released: 12-31-97

Stretch was the hardest to find of the new year's releases for quite a while. Resembling her cousin Pinky the flamingo, Stretch shares Pinky's long dangling legs, but in tan rather than pink. Her long slender neck is the same color. Her body is brown, but her wing tips are white. Most notable is the fluffy white necklace of fur she wears day and night.

❑ It's mine!

Date purchased: _____

Price: _____

❑ Sold!

Date sold: _____

Price: _____

Get the Scoop

A commemorative Stretch was given away as a memento at the St. Louis Cardinals game on May 22, 1998.

Wise the Owl

➤ Style: 4194
➤ Birthday: 5-31-97
➤ Released: 5-30-98

➤ Retired:
➤ Hangtag: 5

What a hoot! Don't expect this Beanie to be flapping around for long. The second of what Ty seems to intend as "annual Beanies" sells out quickly in anticipation of a year-end retirement. Similarly styled to Hoot, Wise is taller even without the black mortarboard and bright orange tassel proclaiming his graduation.

Get the Scoop

Wait to see if you can find Wise in a store before paying secondary prices for him.

❏ It's mine!

  Date purchased: _____

  Price: _____

❏ Sold!

  Date sold: _____

  Price: _____

> ### The Least You Need to Know
>
> ➤ Many of the birds are among the shortest of all Beanies.
>
> ➤ Batty is the only Beanie with Velcro feet.
>
> ➤ Hoot's tag may carry a misspelled "qutie."
>
> ➤ Jake and Jabber are two of the most colorful Beanies.

Chapter 11

Bow-Wowing
the Critics

In This Chapter

➤ Learn why Sparky was transformed into Dotty

➤ Discover why Fetch the Golden Retriever is so plain

➤ Collar all the details on which Beanie pups are the most popular, and why

It's a dog's life, and nobody knows that better than the Ty company, which seems to delight in releasing packs of hounds in a variety of irresistible shapes, sizes, and designs. In this chapter you'll read about some of the extraordinarily well-done details of the Beanie dogs, such as the sewn-in wrinkles on Pugsly and Wrinkles, the tiny red bows on Gigi the poodle, and those soulful sad eyes of Tracker the basset.

Whether you're a dog lover who would like to buy a few Beanies, or a Beanie fanatic who's interested in some excellent designs, you'll find out all you need to know in this chapter.

Bernie the St. Bernard

➤ Style: 4109
➤ Birthday: 10-3-96
➤ Released: 1-1-97

➤ Retired: 9-22-98
➤ Hangtag: 4-5

If you love St. Bernards but hate the slobber, this one's for you! Bernie is a lay-down St. Bernard with tan, black, and cream plush. He sports a cream streak along the top of his head and around his muzzle, with black patches of plush around his eyes (but no whiskey under his chin).

❏ It's mine!

Date purchased: _____

Price: _____

❏ Sold!

Date sold: _____

Price: _____

Get the Scoop

This St. Bernard was fairly common, so you shouldn't have much trouble rescuing one at your neighborhood Beanie dealer, even though he's retired.

Bones the Dog

➤ Style: 4001   ➤ Retired: 5-1-98
➤ Birthday: 1-18-94   ➤ Hangtag: 1-5
➤ Released: 6-25-94

Bones has that hang-dog, hound-dog look, with a tan body and long brown ears and tail. His wide black nose and eyebrows give him a "surprised" look, and he's one of the earliest Beanies you can still find on the shelves.

❑ It's mine!

   Date purchased: _____

   Price: _____

❑ Sold!

   Date sold: _____

   Price: _____

Get the Scoop

Bones was one of the Teenie Beanie Babies released in May 1998 in the second, overwhelmingly popular McDonald's promotion.

Bruno the Terrier

➤ Style: 4183
➤ Birthday: 9-9-97
➤ Released: 12-31-97

➤ Retired: 9-18-98
➤ Hangtag: 5

Get the Scoop

Bruno's retirement in September, 1998, came as a surprise to collectors. As a "short-timer" in the Beanie kennel, his value will probably increase more than some of the Beanies retired in the same time frame.

Most likely modeled after a bull terrier, Bruno was a January 1998 release with dark brown back and ears, and white belly, paws, nose, and tail tip. Pictures of him don't do him justice: In person, he's irresistible.

❑ It's mine!

Date purchased: _____

Price: _____

❑ Sold!

Date sold: _____

Price: _____

Doby the Doberman

➤ Style: 4110   ➤ Retired:
➤ Birthday: 10-9-96   ➤ Hangtag: 4-5
➤ Released: 1-1-97

Like the look of a Doberman but worry about all those teeth? Park this little fellow by your door and relax! Little black Doby has brown paws, underbelly, under ears, and nose, with two brown eyebrows giving him a perpetual look of surprise. His ears are long, just the way real Dobermans are born.

❏ It's mine!

   Date purchased: _____

   Price: _____

❏ Sold!

   Date sold: _____

   Price: _____

Get the Scoop

Doby had the distinction of being number one in the second series of McDonald's Teenie Beanie Babies.

Dotty the Dalmatian

➤ Style: 4100

➤ Birthday: 10-17-96

➤ Released: 5-11-97

➤ Retired:

➤ Hangtag: 4-5

Get the Scoop

Alert Beanie collectors were tipped off to Dotty's impending birth when "Dotty" tush tags started cropping up on the last of the Sparkys.

Dotty replaced Sparky quicker than a dog can bury a pork chop, as a result of yet another name conflict. If you're looking for the difference between Dotty and Sparky, check out the ears and tail: Dotty's are black, while Sparky's are white-spotted.

❏ It's mine!

   Date purchased: _____

   Price: _____

❏ Sold!

   Date sold: _____

   Price: _____

Fetch the Golden Retriever

➤ Style: 4189

➤ Birthday: 2-4-97

➤ Released: 5-30-98

➤ Retired:

➤ Hangtag: 5

Needless to say, this little pup is made of golden plush. The plain-faced Fetch dismayed owners of the breed, but for those of you who want to split doghairs: Golden Retriever puppies don't develop their "feathers" until later in life, so this little guy is anatomically correct.

❏ It's mine!

   Date purchased: _____

   Price: _____

❏ Sold!

   Date sold: _____

   Price: _____

Get the Scoop

As the mascot of one of the most popular of all dog breeds, many collectors suspect that Fetch will soon become hard to find.

Gigi the Poodle

➤ Style: 4191
➤ Birthday: 4-7-98
➤ Released: 5-30-98

➤ Retired:
➤ Hangtag: 5

Get the Scoop

Poodles are said to be among the very most intelligent of all dog breeds. Gigi's lively little face should be a very popular seller among poodle lovers and Beanie collectors alike.

Gigi is the first Beanie to be made of both smooth and napped plush as a nod to the typical tufted hairdo you'll find on real poodles. Similar in body shape to retired Scottie, Gigi is beautifully made, with all the elegant details you'd expect in a Parisian pooch: black fur, black nose, and tiny twin red ribbons decorating her ears.

❑ It's mine!

Date purchased: _____

Price: _____

❑ Sold!

Date sold: _____

Price: _____

Nanook the Husky

➤ Style:	4104
➤ Birthday:	11-21-96
➤ Released:	5-11-97

➤ Retired:	
➤ Hangtag:	4-5

If you've got a yen for a Beanie with a big, round head, pudgy body, and sweet blue eyes, you'll want to rub noses with Nanook the husky dog. It's been a real sled race among collectors, who began searching for this pooch once he became hard to find in 1997. His back, head, and the backs of his ears are dark gray plush; while his face, inner ears, belly, and paws are white.

❏ It's mine!

    Date purchased: _____

    Price: _____

❏ Sold!

    Date sold: _____

    Price: _____

Get the Scoop

If you've spent long months fruitlessly mushing down the trails looking for Nanook, you'll be pleased to know collectors report that he is becoming easier to find.

Pugsly the Pug Dog

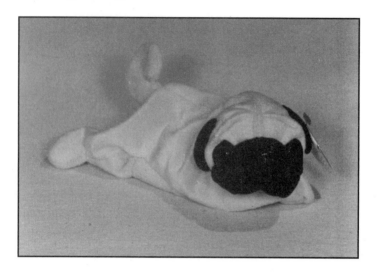

➤ Style: 4106
➤ Birthday: 5-2-96
➤ Released: 5-11-97

➤ Retired:
➤ Hangtag: 4-5

Little Pugsly is created from beige plush with black inner ears and snout to resemble the real thing. Like all self-respecting pugs, Pugsly has a wrinkly forehead, thanks to rows of wrinkles stitched into his forehead that give him a worried frown. If you're pugnacious, you'll be able to find this current release fairly easily in stores.

❑ It's mine!

Date purchased: _____

Price: _____

❑ Sold!

Date sold: _____

Price: _____

Get the Scoop

Pugsly was one of four dogs introduced on Mother's Day 1997.

146

Rover the Dog

➤ Style: 4101   ➤ Retired: 5-1-98
➤ Birthday: 5-30-96   ➤ Hangtag: 4-5
➤ Released: 6-15-96

With his bright, lobster-colored plush and long, round face, Rover closely resembles Clifford the Big Red Dog, hero of a series of children's books. Rover has long ears and an oval black plastic nose like those used on many of the new-faced bears. He's one of the more difficult-to-find Beanies from the May 1998 retirements, in part because he was snatched up so eagerly by preschoolers already familiar with Clifford.

❑ It's mine!

Date purchased: _____

Price: _____

❑ Sold!

Date sold: _____

Price: _____

Get the Scoop

If you've got preschoolers on your gift list, think about putting a leash around Rover, a real favorite among this age group because of his similarity to Clifford.

Scottie the Scottish Terrier

➤ Style: 4102
➤ Birthday: 6-15-96
➤ Released: 6-15-96

➤ Retired: 5-1-98
➤ Hangtag: 4-5
➤ Price: ?

Get the Scoop

Don't be surprised if your Scottie has a birthday of June 6 instead of June 15! Both dates exist on the tags, but neither is considered more valuable than the other.

You don't need to be the Laird of Loch Lomond to hanker after this little Scottie, one of the few Beanies sharing nappy plush. Jet black with a body style similar to Gigi the poodle, some collectors growl that Scottie's face is too dark to stand out properly.

❏ It's mine!

Date purchased: _____

Price: _____

❏ Sold!

Date sold: _____

Price: _____

Sparky the Dalmatian

➤ Style: 4100
➤ Birthday: 2-27-96
➤ Released: 6-15-96

➤ Retired: 5-11-97
➤ Hangtag: 4

Some days, it must seem like a dog's life at the Ty company, where name complications seem to pop up faster than toadstools after a spring rain. Case in point: Sparky, who produced yet another "renaming" when the National Fire Protection Association folks pointed out they had first dibs on the "Sparky the Fire Dog". As a result, his name and image were subsequently re-released as Dotty. The difference between the two? Sparky's white-spotted ears and tail (Dotty's are black).

❑ It's mine!

  Date purchased: _____

  Price: _____

❑ Sold!

  Date sold: _____

  Price: _____

Get the Scoop

Alert collectors noted that the last Sparkys to come rolling off the assembly line were equipped with "Dotty" tush tags.

Spot the Dog

- ➤ Style: 4000
- ➤ Birthday: (none) (no spot)
- ➤ Birthday: 1-3-93 (spot)
- ➤ Released: 1-8-94 (no spot)
- ➤ Released: 4-13-94 (spot)

- ➤ Retired: 4-13-94 (no spot)
- ➤ Retired: 10-1-97 (spot)
- ➤ Hangtag: 1 (no spot)
- ➤ Hangtag: 1-4 (spot)

No matter how hard you try, you won't be able to spot the spot on the original Spot. This little Beanie was first issued with a partly black face, black ears, and tail—but strangely enough, no spot on the back. Hence, his nicknames: "Spotless Spot" or "Spot without a Spot." The spotless version didn't last long and was replaced with the more common spotted variety, with a half-circle on the left half of his back.

On the Sly

There have been reports of false spotless Spots—beware! The real spot-free pooch is extremely rare and pricey. If you don't see spots when you're shopping for Spot, it pays to put on your specs to make sure you've got the real thing.

No spot

❏ It's mine!

 Date purchased: _____

 Price: _____

❏ Sold!

 Date sold: _____

 Price: _____

Spot

❏ It's mine!

 Date purchased: _____

 Price: _____

❏ Sold!

 Date sold: _____

 Price: _____

Spunky the Cocker Spaniel

➤ Style: 4184

➤ Birthday: 1-14-97

➤ Released: 12-31-97

➤ Retired:

➤ Hangtag: 5

Spunky quickly became one of the most popular Beanies from the December 31, 1997 releases. Handsome in tan plush, he's got that typical big domed head so characteristic of cockers. If you're lucky, you'll be able to sniff out a Spunky to add to your collection!

❑ It's mine!

   Date purchased: _____

   Price: _____

❑ Sold!

   Date sold: _____

   Price: _____

Get the Scoop

Like the true Cocker Spaniels who inspired him, Spunky's ears are covered with long, soft curls—the only Beanie Baby with such curly plush.

Tracker the Basset Hound

➤ Style: 4198
➤ Birthday: 6-5-97
➤ Released: 5-30-98

➤ Retired:
➤ Hangtag: 5

Get the Scoop

No doubt those doleful eyes (unique to Tracker) and long plush ears will make him one of the more popular dogs in the Beanie kennel.

If you've got a nose for a good buy, sniff your way to the nearest shop with the most recently released Beanie pup—the sad-eyed Tracker. It may take some time before this brown-and-white hound shows up as a regular on store shelves.

❑ It's mine!

   Date purchased: _____

   Price: _____

❑ Sold!

   Date sold: _____

   Price: _____

Tuffy the Terrier

➤ Style: 4108
➤ Birthday: 10-12-96
➤ Released: 5-11-97

➤ Retired:
➤ Hangtag: 4-5

Tuffy is a nappy (not a yappy) terrier. Similar in body style to Gigi and Scottie, Tuffy is the only two-tone nappy Beanie. Ty uses the same tan plush on Tuffy and Curly the bear, but the brown nappy plush on Tuffy's back is unique to him.

❏ It's mine!

   Date purchased: _____

   Price: _____

❏ Sold!

   Date sold: _____

   Price: _____

Get the Scoop

What's the doggone quickest way to find out whether you have an older or a newer Tuffy? Check out his name on the tag. Early releases spelled his name in capital letters.

Weenie the Dachshund

➤ Style: 4013

➤ Birthday: 7-20-95

➤ Released: 1-7-96

➤ Retired: 5-1-98

➤ Hangtag: 3-5

Quite a hot dog before his retirement (Weenie was easy to find in just about every retail store!), Weenie is now one of the harder-to-find members of the May 1998 retirement pack. His plush may be plain bone-brown, but his long body and wide-spread ears make him a popular pooch.

❏ It's mine!

    Date purchased: _____

    Price: _____

❏ Sold!

    Date sold: _____

    Price: _____

Get the Scoop

Weenie's plush comes in two kinds of brown: shiny and less shiny. Make no bones about it, though—either coat is worth about the same.

Wrinkles the Bulldog

➤ Style: 4103
➤ Birthday: 5-1-96
➤ Released: 6-15-96

➤ Retired: 9-22-98
➤ Hangtag: 4-5

This gold and white plush pup lives up to his name, with more wrinkles than a day-old leisure suit. His sewn-in wrinkles on back and face guarantee that authentic worried look of the bulldog, and resemble Pugsly, the other wrinkled Beanie.

❏ It's mine!

Date purchased: _____

Price: _____

❏ Sold!

Date sold: _____

Price: _____

Get the Scoop

The recently retired Wrinkles has two larger cousins in the plush line (named Winston and Churchill) as well as a Pillow Pal cousin. Collect all four for a great display!

The Least You Need to Know

➤ Since there are more than 100 breeds of dogs and many more dog lovers for each, the Ty company should have the inspiration for an endless supply of new canine Beanies.

➤ Sparky was replaced by Dotty.

➤ Rover is NOT modeled after Clifford the Big Red Dog from the children's books.

➤ The original Spot had no spots at all and is extremely rare and pricey now.

Chapter 12

Creepy-Crawlers

In This Chapter

➤ Learn the different permutations of Lucky the ladybug and all her spots

➤ Uncover the manufacturing mix-up between Iggy and Rainbow

➤ Find lots of decorating ideas with these Beanie Babies

If it's creepy and crawly, lizardy or spidery, you'll likely find it in this chapter. Yet even these stuffed critters, despite their names, are more cuties than creepies. We've taken quite a few liberties with the Beanies we've included here—after all, alligators are not really anywhere near the same genus as a bumblebee or a butterfly. But if you look at one of these animals and shiver, you'll likely find its Beanie counterpart within this chapter!

Ally the Alligator

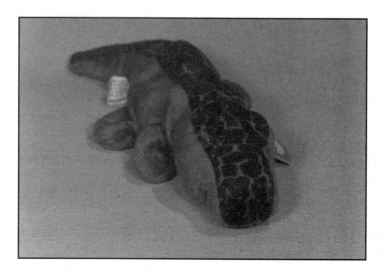

➤ Style: 4032
➤ Birthday: 3-14-94
➤ Released: 6-25-94

➤ Retired: 10-1-97
➤ Hangtag: 1-4

Get the Scoop

How can you tell whether an alligator is a boy or a girl? By the poem! (At least you can if it's a Ty Beanie Baby...) Even though Ally often gets referred to as a "she" because of his name, the poem definitely indicates he's all boy.

If you're a University of Florida grad, you've probably already wrestled this little alligator from the gift shop out to the parking lot. The rest of you are probably lining up for Ally not because he's a mascot, but just because he's so cute! About a foot long with avocado-green sides and stomach, he's got a strip of brown spots on avocado-green along his back.

❏ It's mine!

  Date purchased: _____

  Price: _____

❏ Sold!

  Date sold: _____

  Price: _____

Bumble the Bee

➤ Style: 4045
➤ Birthday: (none)
➤ Released: 6-3-95

➤ Retired: 6-15-96
➤ Hangtag: 3-4

Feeling down in the dumps? Buying this little fellow can take the sting out of a bad day! Bumble is small, even as Beanies go—he can fit right into the palm of your hand. Looking typically bee-like with a yellow-and-black striped back, he also has a black head, wings, and underbelly.

❏ It's mine!

   Date purchased: _____

   Price: _____

❏ Sold!

   Date sold: _____

   Price: _____

Get the Scoop

Bumble is the one exception to the "older tags are more valuable" rule—his fourth-generation version is more rare than the one before it.

Flutter the Butterfly

➤ Style: 4043
➤ Birthday: (none)
➤ Released: 6-3-95

➤ Retired: 6-15-96
➤ Hangtag: 3

On the Sly

Look closely and you'll see that Flutter has knotted eyes rather than the hard plastic ones found on most other Beanies. One variation of a counterfeit Flutter has appeared with hard plastic eyes, so if you see these—fly away and don't buy!

If you really want to butter up a collecting friend, try giving Flutter as a gift! Usually found in bright rainbow tie-dye, Flutter can also appear in more subtle tones. Only the lower rounded part of her wings are heavily stuffed with "beans"; both her body and the upper part of her wings contain little stuffing. Her black plush body is matched by long black antennae waving at the top of her head.

❏ It's mine!

Date purchased: _____

Price: _____

❏ Sold!

Date sold: _____

Price: _____

Hissy the Snake

➤ Style: 4185
➤ Birthday: 4-4-97
➤ Released: 12-31-98

➤ Retired:
➤ Hangtag: 5

If you're the type who likes to fiddle with something in your hands, then Hissy is the Beanie for you. One of Ty's most innovative Beanie designs, Hissy's natural stretchy coil just begs to be played with. The top of Hissy's plush is blue tie-dyed like Bronty and Sting, but his underside is bright yellow like Quackers the duck. A red ribbon tongue completes his reptilian charm.

❑ It's mine!

Date purchased: _____

Price: _____

❑ Sold!

Date sold: _____

Price: _____

Get the Scoop

Because of the unique coiled design of this Beanie, you can get some really nifty display effects by wrapping him around another object. Don't just line 'em all up—be creative! Coil, drape, hang, or weave this beautiful Beanie to add zest to your collection.

Iggy the Iguana

On the Sly

If you're the type who gets confused as to who's on first, then don't try to decipher the saga of Iggy the iguana and Rainbow the chameleon! For months collectors thought it was their tags that were reversed, but as it turns out, it really was their plush coats. Just remember that no matter what his coat color, whether it be bright tie-dye like Peace, Garcia, or Coral, or blue tie-dye like Bronty and Sting, you're looking at Iggy the iguana. If you're looking at a Beanie reptile with a flap of plush behind his head (and no felt spikes along his back), you've got Iggy's pal Rainbow in your hands, even if he's blue. The second variation of Iggy (a bright tie-dyed version) has a soft pink tongue, but when the plush was corrected, the tongue moved, too, leaving poor Iggy tongue-tied.

➤ Style: 4038
➤ Birthday: 8-12-97
➤ Released: 12-31-97 (bright tie-dye without a tongue)
➤ Released: about mid-May, 1998 (bright tie-dye with a tongue)
➤ Released: about mid-August, 1998 (blue tie-dye without a tongue)
➤ Retired: about mid-May, 1998 (bright tie-dye / without a tongue)
➤ Retired: about mid-August, 1998 (bright tie-dye with a tongue)
➤ Retired: (blue tie-dye without a tongue)
➤ Hangtag: 5

It's doubtful that Bette Davis had Iggy in mind when she agreed to star in Tennessee Williams' "Night of the Iguana"—but although he's never been onstage, this version is pretty darn cute!

❑ It's mine!

Date purchased: _____

Price: _____

❑ Sold!

Date sold: _____

Price: _____

Inch the Worm

➤ Style: 4044

➤ Birthday: 9-3-95

➤ Released: 6-3-95 (felt)

➤ Released: 10-15-96 (yarn)

➤ Retired: 10-15-96 (felt)

➤ Retired: 5-1-98 (yarn)

➤ Hangtag: 3-4 (felt)

➤ Hangtag: 4-5 (yarn)

He's long, he's wiggly, and he's stiff enough to stand up on end—he's Inch, the multicolored Beanie who's wormed his way into many collectors' hearts! Unlike many other Beanies, he's not a tie-dye—his colors are divided neatly into sections, sort of like a patchwork quilt laid end-to-end. His head starts off in yellow, followed by sections of bright orange, lime green, royal blue, and bright orchid.

Felt

❏ It's mine!

   Date purchased: _____

   Price: _____

❏ Sold!

   Date sold: _____

   Price: _____

Yarn

❏ It's mine!

   Date purchased: _____

   Price: _____

❏ Sold!

   Date sold: _____

   Price: _____

Get the Scoop

If you've packed your Inch up into a Ziploc bag to put away as an investment, inch on over and check out his antennae. Originally released with felt antennae, these gave way to yarn in late 1996; the felt feelers are worth more than the yarn variety. Which have you got?

Lizzy the Lizard

- ➤ Style: 4033
- ➤ Birthday: (none) (tie-dyed)
- ➤ Birthday: 5-11-95 (blue)
- ➤ Released: 6-3-95 (tie-dyed)
- ➤ Released: 1-7-96 (blue)

- ➤ Retired: 1-7-96 (tie-dyed)
- ➤ Retired: 12-31-97 (blue)
- ➤ Hangtag: 3 (tie-dyed)
- ➤ Hangtag: 3-4 (blue)

Unbeknownst to many collectors, the original-release Lizzy was resplendent in an earth-toned tie-dye plush rather than the black-on-blue spotted plush she now wears. As with all tie-dyed Beanies, each of these Lizzies is unique and her value may depend on her coloring as well as her condition. The black-on-blue version has orange-on-yellow plush on her belly.

On the Sly

Lizzy's felt tongue seems to end up taking most of the abuse, so if you're a collector who wants to preserve the condition of your Beanies, you might take particular care of this lizard part.

Tie-Dyed

❑ It's mine!

   Date purchased: _____

   Price: _____

❑ Sold!

   Date sold: _____

   Price: _____

Blue

❑ It's mine!

   Date purchased: _____

   Price: _____

❑ Sold!

   Date sold: _____

   Price: _____

Lucky the Ladybug

➤ Style: 4040

➤ Birthday: (none) (7 spot)

➤ Birthday: 5-1-95 (21 spot)

➤ Birthday: 5-1-95 (11 spot)

➤ Released: 6-25-94 (7 spot)

➤ Released: circa 2-25-96 (21 spot)

➤ Released: circa 6-15-96 (11 spot)

➤ Retired: circa 2-27-96 (7 spot)

➤ Retired: circa 6-15-96 (21 spot)

➤ Retired: 5-1-98 (11 spot)

➤ Hangtag: 1-3 (7 spot)

➤ Hangtag: 4 (21 spot)

➤ Hangtag: 4-5 (11 spot)

A leopard may not be able to change his spots, but that hasn't stopped Lucky the ladybug: Proving that a lady can always change her mind, she's swapped her spots at least five times. Her original design included 7 spots of felt glued onto her red plush back—but when those spots started falling off, it was back to the drawing board for Ty. Voilá! Her plush changed to preprinted spots—21 of them. However, the 21-spot version turned out to be short-lived; while a more common recent variation has about 11 printed spots, she may appear with as few as 8 and as many as 14. In addition to her spots, she also has a black head, black string antennae, black belly, and six felt legs.

Get the Scoop

When she first appeared, Lucky the 21-spotted ladybug wasn't exactly flying off the shelves—but today those few who bought her are glad they did!

7 Spot

❏ It's mine!

    Date purchased: _____

    Price: _____

❏ Sold!

    Date sold: _____

    Price: _____

21 Spot

❏ It's mine!

    Date purchased: _____

    Price: _____

❏ Sold!

    Date sold: _____

    Price: _____

11 Spot

❏ It's mine!

    Date purchased: _____

    Price: _____

❏ Sold!

    Date sold: _____

    Price: _____

Rainbow the Chameleon

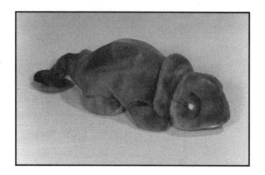

➤ Style: 4037

➤ Birthday: 10-14-97

➤ Released: 12-31-97 (blue tie-dyed without a tongue)

➤ Released: about mid-August, 1998 (bright tie-dye with a tongue)

➤ Retired: about mid-August, 1998 (blue tie-dyed without a tongue)

➤ Retired: (bright tie-dye with a tongue)

➤ Hangtag: 5

It's true that chameleons change their color at the drop of a hat, so you shouldn't be surprised if the creature you've been calling Rainbow because of his bright tie-dyed plush really turned out to be Iggy the iguana sporting the wrong coat! Most people thought their tags were mixed up, but those collectors really in the know about all things reptilian figured out that it was the chameleons that wore that little hood behind their heads and iguanas had spikes. They called it right, and the old blue tie-dyed Rainbow hit the streets while the new and improved bright tie-dyed Rainbow came in from the cold. And if that wasn't enough to keep your tongue wagging, the pink tongue that the second version of Iggy had has migrated to the new and improved Rainbow!

It makes you wonder if it should be on the blue Iggy, though.

Get the Scoop

Check out that little pink velveteen tongue flapping in the front of the brightly tie-dyed Rainbow since around mid-August. Beginning with mid-year shipments, that same tongue had been found on Iggy the iguana, not Rainbow! All bets are off as to whether it stays on the bright tie-dyed chameleon or wags its way back to the now-blue Iggy.

❑ It's mine!

　Date purchased: _____

　Price: _____

❑ Sold!

　Date sold: _____

　Price: _____

Slither the Snake

➤ Style: 4031

➤ Birthday: (none)

➤ Released: 6-25-94

➤ Retired: 6-15-95

➤ Hangtag: 1-3

This two-foot-long reptile's back is covered in the spotted brown-on-green plush found on both Ally and Speedy. He's a real yellow-belly—bright yellow, the same plush as Quackers. He's also quite rare and very pricey—so if you're cold-blooded enough to stand the sticker shock, slither on over and check him out!

❑ It's mine!

   Date purchased: _____

   Price: _____

❑ Sold!

   Date sold: _____

   Price: _____

On the Sly

Slither's long red felt tongue is split down the middle and isn't as sturdy as the rest of him, so take care you don't pull it out by the roots when you're playing with him!

Smoochy the Frog

➤ Style: 4039
➤ Birthday: 10-1-97
➤ Released: 12-31-97

➤ Retired:
➤ Hangtag: 5

Perhaps this design was Ty's way of contrasting Smoochy with the plain styling of Legs the frog, but this amphibian got all the looks in the family. He's bright and far more intricate, with lime-green plush covering his back and neon yellow on all four feet and the front of his eyes. If you have to kiss a lot of frogs before you find your prince, here's hoping they all are as irresistible as Smoochy!

Get the Scoop

Smoochy's lips are red and created out of several different materials, none of which has earned a higher value than another at this point. So choose the one you like and wait and see!

❏ It's mine!

   Date purchased: _____

   Price: _____

❏ Sold!

   Date sold: _____

   Price: _____

Spinner the Spider

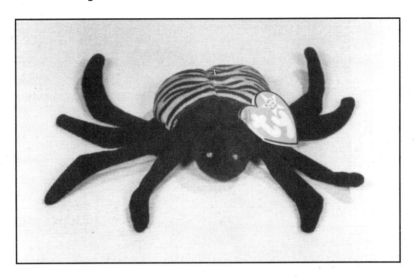

➤ Style: 4026

➤ Birthday: 10-28-96

➤ Released: 10-1-97

➤ Retired: 9-19-98

➤ Hangtag: 4-5

Most collectors agree that Spinner is pretty creepy—creepy enough that some were released with tush tags emblazoned with the name "Creepy." Nobody's sure if the Creepy tags are a harbinger of Beanies-to-be or a last-minute renaming of Spinner. Spinner's back is black-on-dark gold stripes, and he's also inherited Radar's red eyes. Retired after only one year as a current, Spinner spent only one Halloween scaring collectors away. They'll be running to entangle him now.

❏ It's mine!

   Date purchased: _____

   Price: _____

❏ Sold!

   Date sold: _____

   Price: _____

Get the Scoop

Planning a Halloween party and just can't find the right decorating touch? Don't look any further than the evil-looking Spinner, who's been known to give little kids nightmares. However, you may have to search quite a few webs before you land this little retired fellow: He's rare and getting rarer every minute.

Stinger the Scorpion

➤ Style: 4193   ➤ Retired:

➤ Birthday: 9-29-97   ➤ Hangtag: 5

➤ Released: 5-30-98

If astrology's your game, then all you Scorpios out there will be clamoring for this little stuffed scorpion, the sign of the eighth house of the zodiac. While a tad creepy-looking, his plush color is unique among Beanies: It's a deep taupe color. He's a Beanie who's not very photogenic; he's much cuter in person.

On the Sly

Like his multi-legged friend Inky, Stinger sometimes gets a leg added or subtracted in his manufacture, so count them closely.

❑ It's mine!

Date purchased: _____

Price: _____

❑ Sold!

Date sold: _____

Price: _____

Web the Spider

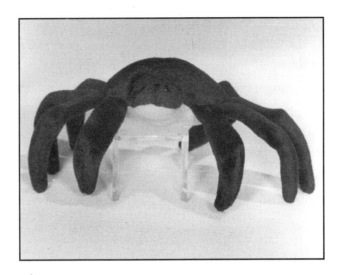

➤ Style: 4041   ➤ Retired: 1-7-96

➤ Birthday: (none)   ➤ Hangtag: 1-3

➤ Released: 6-25-94

From the top, Web looks plain as can be, but flip this fellow over and you'll get a surprise: No, not an hourglass, but a belly of bright red plush. Unlike the later spider (Spinner), Web's eyes are black, not red, although red would be a perfect complement to his stomach.

❏ It's mine!

   Date purchased: _____

   Price: _____

❏ Sold!

   Date sold: _____

   Price: _____

Get the Scoop

If you've managed to trap this Beanie Baby, you'll want to spin a web around him quick, because he's hard to find and getting harder by the minute. Expect his value to rise, especially around Halloween!

> ### The Least You Need to Know
>
> ➤ Iggy and Rainbow were first released with each other's plush. Iggy shipped as bright tie-dye while Rainbow shipped with blue tie-dye. The rightly plushed versions are now shipping.
>
> ➤ Some Spinners were manufactured with the tag "Creepy."
>
> ➤ Lucky the ladybug can be found with many different numbers of spots, including 21, 7, and 11.

Chapter 13

Unbearably Cute

In This Chapter

➤ Learn about the yearly Teddies

➤ Find out which bears are truly international

➤ Discover which are worth more: old- or new-faced bears

Even if you've bearly begun collecting Beanies, you'll probably be attracted to these colorful ursines—a whole wide range of adorable bears in a variety of colors. In fact, collectors of all sorts of stuffed bears enjoy collecting the bear group of Beanies, which are available in a huge range of colors (black, brown, cranberry, jade, magenta, teal, violet, white, and tie-dyed). Most of the bears are retired: fifteen of them in all, including Chilly, Garcia, Libearty, Peking, all the colored Teddies, and all the old-faced Teddies.

While many people may think of Beanie bears as the traditional "teddy" type, we've also included other bear varieties, such as the black bear and the polar bear—so if it's a bear of any type you're hankering for, you're sure to find it here!

Blackie the Bear

➤ Style: 4011
➤ Birthday: 7-15-94
➤ Released: 6-25-94

➤ Retired: 9-15-98
➤ Hangtag: 1-5

Get the Scoop

The Chicago Bears used Blackie (he's a natural!) as a promotion for their Kids' Fan Club.

If you like to keep your bears just lying around, then Blackie is the one for you; he's one of four "lay-down" style bears available in the Ty collection. And surprise, surprise! He's all black (except for his snout, which is brown). If you want to collect the rest of the entire set of lay-down bears, here's what you should be looking for: Chilly, Cubbie, and Peking. All of the lay-down bears have been retired now, with Blackie being the last of the Quad Squad. Blackie and Cubbie should be pretty easy to find. Don't count on the same being true for Chilly and Peking!

❑ It's mine!

   Date purchased: _____

   Price: _____

❑ Sold!

   Date sold: _____

   Price: _____

Britannia the Bear

➤ Style: 4601
➤ Birthday: 12-15-97
➤ Released: 12-31-97

➤ Retired:
➤ Hangtag: 5

It's a long hike from London to the United States, so if you manage to snag a Britannia—the bear that is exclusively distributed in the United Kingdom—you're either a world traveler or you've plopped down quite a few pounds sterling to cage this critter! Although some of these little ladies have found their way to the States, they are generally quite expensive—even though they haven't yet been retired. Britannia is a brown "new-faced" bear with a Union Jack embroidered on her chest and a deep red ribbon.

❑ It's mine!

   Date purchased: _____

   Price: _____

❑ Sold!

   Date sold: _____

   Price: _____

On the Sly

Check Britannia's tags closely for errors to make sure you're getting the real thing and not a counterfeit. These errors include a "scrunchy"-looking font on the yellow star on the front of her tag, misplacement of the ™ symbol, and a smaller print than normal on the tush tag.

Brownie the Bear

➤ Style: 4010

➤ Birthday: (none)

➤ Released: 1993

➤ Retired: (pre-Beanies)

➤ Hangtag: 1

Brownie the bear is a predecessor of Cubbie (one of the Original Nine Beanies)—in fact, you'll bearly notice the difference unless you take a close peek at the swing tag. In order to be Brownie and not Cubbie, he must have that tag with his name on it; otherwise, he's just considered to be a Cubbie and not worth as much money. Brownie is a "lay-down" style bear with brown plush and a tan snout.

Get the Scoop

Brownie is usually considered a "pre-Beanie," and so if you're armed and hunting for bears, you may not find him in every checklist.

❏ It's mine!

Date purchased: _____

Price: _____

❏ Sold!

Date sold: _____

Price: _____

Chilly the Polar Bear

➤ Style: 4012

➤ Birthday: (none)

➤ Released: 6-25-94

➤ Retired: 1-7-96

➤ Hangtag: 1-3

Chilly is probably the most popular of the four "lay-down" style bears—and like all highly desirable Beanies, one of the hardest to find. His all-white plush is difficult to keep clean. If you're a collector and you manage to trap one, put him in hibernation behind a plastic or glass case to keep him in mint condition. Dust and dirt are Chilly's enemy.

❑ It's mine!

Date purchased: _____

Price: _____

❑ Sold!

Date sold: _____

Price: _____

Get the Scoop

Two of the bear Beanies have collectible mistakes, so if you're in the mood for unique Beanie Babies, check out these two: Maple with the "Pride" tush tag (which makes him about three times more valuable than a "regular" Maple); and Libearty with a misspelled "beanine" tush tag (which is a common error).

Curly the Bear

➤ Style: 4052

➤ Birthday: 4-12-96

➤ Released: 6-15-96

➤ Retired:

➤ Hangtag: 4-5

Get the Scoop

Curly was used by Livent Productions as their Broadway Beanie for the show "Ragtime." He was sold with maroon, ivory, or navy ribbon, with "Ragtime" heat-stamped on the ribbon.

If you're on a bear hunt, Curly is one of only five Beanies with nappy plush. Tan and curly, he comes equipped with a maroon ribbon around his neck.

❑ It's mine!

    Date purchased: _____

    Price: _____

❑ Sold!

    Date sold: _____

    Price: _____

Erin the Bear

➤ Style: 4186
➤ Birthday: 3-17-97
➤ Released: 1-31-98

➤ Retired:
➤ Hangtag: 5

As bright kelly green as the rolling hills of Ireland itself, Erin the Irish bear comes equipped with an embroidered white shamrock on her chest—and no ribbon around her neck. If you're wanting your collection to be wearin' the green, better start looking for Erin today!

❑ It's mine!

　　Date purchased: _____

　　Price: _____

❑ Sold!

　　Date sold: _____

　　Price: _____

On the Sly

Part of the ever-popular new-faced bear group, Erin is harder to find than a four-leaf shamrock in a peat bog, so don't be surprised if she's difficult to find in stores for a long time to come.

Fortune the Panda

➤ Style: 4196

➤ Birthday: 12-6-97

➤ Released: 5-30-98

➤ Retired:

➤ Hangtag: 5

On the Sly

Although Fortune has only just lumbered off the production line, counterfeit Fortunes have already turned up on the secondary market. So if you're seeking your Fortune, check him out closely!

Fortune marks a whole new era in Beanie Baby bears, a completely different design from previous bears. Though a sit-up style, Fortune doesn't have the pouty nose of the other new-faced bears, nor the stitch under the chin that forms the nose. This black-and-white descendant of Peking the lay-down Panda also has a bright red ribbon around his neck.

❑ It's mine!

    Date purchased: _____

    Price: _____

❑ Sold!

    Date sold: _____

    Price: _____

Garcia the Bear

➤ Style: 4051
➤ Birthday: 8-1-95
➤ Released: 1-7-96

➤ Retired: 5-11-97
➤ Hangtag: 3-4

Garcia was created in honor of the late Jerry Garcia, from the rock band the Grateful Dead, with a combination of Jerry's birth month and day combined with the year of his death as Garcia's birthday. All you Beanie bear groupies can search out your own Garcia, the first of the new-faced bears to be released without a ribbon on his neck.

❑ It's mine!

   Date purchased: _____

   Price: _____

❑ Sold!

   Date sold: _____

   Price: _____

Get the Scoop

Garcia is unique, thanks to his tie-dye plush, so search out several and start your own rainbow collection!

Glory the Bear

➤ Style: 4188

➤ Birthday: 7-4-97

➤ Released: 5-30-98

➤ Retired:

➤ Hangtag: 5

Glory is the fourth Beanie to bear the Stars and Stripes. The others (Righty, Lefty, and Libearty) are all retired. Resplendent in white plush decorated with all-over red and blue stars and a fluttering Old Glory on his chest, expect him to be hard to find for quite a while due to his fairly recent release. Counterfeit Glorys can be found with a different poem.

Get the Scoop

The placement and size of the stars makes each individual Glory unique.

❑ It's mine!

Date purchased: _____

Price: _____

❑ Sold!

Date sold: _____

Price: _____

Libearty the Bear

➤ Style: 4057

➤ Birthday: Summer '96

➤ Released: 6-15-96

➤ Retired: 1-1-97

➤ Hangtag: 4

The typographical error spelling Beanie as "Beanine" on Libearty's tush tag was one of the Beanie tag errors collectors consider a "classic." The version with the error is actually more common than the correct tag!

❏ It's mine!

   Date purchased: _____

   Price: _____

❏ Sold!

   Date sold: _____

   Price: _____

Get the Scoop

Libearty is the only Beanie whose birthday is a season (summer 1996) rather than a specific date. This is especially unusual since Libearty was one of the first releases with the fourth-generation hangtags, all of which come with birthdays.

Maple the Bear

➤ Style: 4600
➤ Birthday: 7-1-96
➤ Released: 1-1-97

➤ Retired:
➤ Hangtag: 4-5

Canadians may complain that their culture is overrun with goods, technology, and culture imported from the United States—but now the tide is turning with the introduction of this all-white, new-faced bear. Maple is highly sought after by Americans because he is sold exclusively in Canada, whose flag he wears proudly on his chest. Maple also wears a bright red ribbon around his neck. Be careful of that white plush!

Get the Scoop

Extremely rare (doubt it? check the price tag!) are versions with the name "Pride" on the tush tag rather than the correct name, "Maple."

❑ It's mine!

   Date purchased: _____

   Price: _____

❑ Sold!

   Date sold: _____

   Price: _____

Peace the Bear

➤ Style: 4053

➤ Birthday: 2-1-96

➤ Released: 5-11-97

➤ Retired:

➤ Hangtag: 4-5

Peace was given a chance once Garcia left the
Beanie Baby stage and headed into retirement. The
only difference between the two (other than the
tags, of course) is the rainbow-colored peace
symbol embroidered on Peace's chest. Even now,
Peace can be very elusive in stores.

❏ It's mine!

   Date purchased: _____

   Price: _____

❏ Sold!

   Date sold: _____

   Price: _____

Get the Scoop

More recent shipments of Peace
have a pastel tie-dye rather than the
rainbow tie-dye that is so familiar;
collectors still debate whether this is
a temporary or permanent color
change.

Peking the Panda

➤ Style: 4013
➤ Birthday: (none)
➤ Released: 6-25-94

➤ Retired: 1-7-96
➤ Hangtag: 1-3

On the Sly

There are three ways to spot a counterfeit Peking. First, they are generally a narrow shadow of the real thing (they have fewer pellets, making them very thin). Second, counterfeits have a much larger and more rounded black plastic nose. And third, the umlaut above the "u" in "Nürnberg" is missing if he has a third-generation swing tag.

There's no mistaking this black-and-white plush lay-down bear—he's all panda (the only thing missing are those bamboo shoots). Peking has black felt ovals through which his plastic eyes peer. Unfortunately, many of the Pekings on the market today are counterfeit.

❑ It's mine!

Date purchased: _____

Price: _____

❑ Sold!

Date sold: _____

Price: _____

Princess the Bear

➤ Style: 4300
➤ Birthday: (none)
➤ Released: 10-29-97

➤ Retired:
➤ Hangtag: special

Born to the purple, the Princess bear is a Beanie of firsts, released to honor Diana, the Princess of Wales, after her tragic death in 1997. Princess is the only Beanie created after June 1996 who comes without a birthday. Her hangtag is printed in a special italic font, and Ty donates profits from her sale to Diana's Memorial Fund (more than $2 million so far). The beautiful deep-purple Princess has a white rose with green stem embroidered on her chest and wears a deep purple ribbon around her neck.

❑ It's mine!

   Date purchased: _____

   Price: _____

❑ Sold!

   Date sold: _____

   Price: _____

Get the Scoop

The Princess bear comes stuffed with one of two types of pellets; the PVC pellets are more valuable than the PE pellets.

Teddy the Bear (New-Faced)

- ➤ Style: 4050 (brown)
- ➤ Style: 4052 (cranberry)
- ➤ Style: 4057 (jade)
- ➤ Style: 4056 (magenta)
- ➤ Style: 4051 (teal)
- ➤ Style: 4055 (violet)
- ➤ Birthday: (none) (all colors except brown)
- ➤ Birthday: 11-28-95 (brown)
- ➤ Released: 1-7-95 (all colors)
- ➤ Retired: 1-7-96 (all colors except brown)
- ➤ Retired: 10-1-97 (brown)
- ➤ Hangtag: 2-3 (all colors except brown)
- ➤ Hangtag: 2-4 (brown)

The "new-faced" bears are the ones you're probably more familiar with, as it's the same style used on the current "sit-up" style of bears like Princess, Glory, and Erin. These bears all have a stitch under their chin that runs over the top of their snout and back down to help form their pouty-nosed look. Sometimes these stitches can break (or not be tied completely), giving the bears the look of an "old-faced" bear. However, it's easy to tell the difference: The new-faced bears' eyes are on the inside of the plush triangle that helps form their face, while the old-faced bears' eyes are on the outside.

McDonald's Teenie Beanie Babies, the first batch.

Kiwi with kiwifruit.

Peanuts with peanuts.

Jabber, Kuku, Caw, Early, Rocket, Kiwi, and Baldy.

Bernie, Pugsly, Wrinkles, Nanook, Fetch, Doby, Spunky, Scottie, Dotty, Bruno, Tuffy, Gigi, and Tracker.

Bones, spotless Spot, Rover, Spot, Weenie, and Sparky.

Flip, Chip, Snip, Zip, Pounce, Prance, Nip, and Trap.

Bongo and Congo go bananas.

Twigs.

The wolf in sheep's clothing.

Hippity and Valentino confuse ears.

Derby, Snort, Squealer, Bessie, Chops, Doodle, Prance, and Quackers down on the farm.

Floppity, Hippity, and Hoppity.

All dressed up and no place to go: Magenta (new face), Violet (old face), Cranberry (new face), Teal (old face), Valentino, Inch, Magenta (old face), Bongo, and Rex.

I ♥ Beanies: Britannia the Engineer, Snip the Clown, Fortune ready for bed, Brown Moose (old face), Glory the spaceman, Blackie the ladybug, Princess in her jogging suit, Violet Bee (new face), Teal Clown (old face), and Valentino out of the shower.

McDonald's Teenie Beanie Babies, the second time around.

Blank Bernie.

No flag Lefty.

Milwaukee Batty.

Ty catalogs.

Tie-dye Claude, Flutter, Sting, Iggy-Rainbow, Coral, tie-dye Lizzy, Steg, Rex, Peace, Bronty, Garcia, and Doodle.

Pumpkin Curly.

Patriotic Righty, Lefty, Britannia, Libearty, Glory, and Maple.

NYPD Blues, Cubbie (playing Smokey the Bear), and Squealer the Pig.

Noah's Ark: Scottie, Patti, Pugsly, Humphrey, Chilly, Prance, Strut, Chops, Bongo, Ally, Quackers, Hissy, Legs, Happy, Peanut, Daisy, Derby, Squealer, Bones, and Fleece.

The wedding: Valentino, Cranberry (new face), Teal (new face), Daisy, and Snort.

Peace with no peace sign.

Chicago Cubs promos.

Chocolate, Chip, cookies, and milk.

Promos: Reds Rover, Special Olympics Maple, Beanie Mania Congo, Pacers Strut, and Cavs Bongo.

Garcia, Peace, and Woodstock tickets.

Jacksonville Pinky, Toys for Tots Valentino, and Special Olympics Maple.

Mid-1995 releases: (darkish) magenta Patti, Nana/Bongo, tan Inky with mouth, Valentino, all-gold Nip, white-face Nip, white-face Zip, all-black Zip, Quackers with wings, Jade (new face), Violet (new face), Cranberry (new face), Brown (new face), Teal (new face), Magenta (new face), and Spooky.

The original nine: Chocolate, Squealer, Cubbie, Patti, Flash, Splash, Pinchers, Legs, and Spot.

1997 Teddy Santa.

Peking and Fortune.

The colored Teddys.

Valentino with candy.

Blackie and Cubbie find Bumble's honey.

Reading Teddy.

Princess and Erin.

*The Garden of Eden: Valentino, Hissy,
and Teal (old face).*

*Mid-1994 releases: Slither, Daisy, Speedy, Blackie, Chilly, Web, Ally, Lucky,
Humphrey, tan Inky (no mouth), Mystic, Quackers (wingless), orange Digger,
gray Happy, Bones, Goldie, Teal (old face), Magenta (old face), Violet (old
face), Brown (old face), and Jade (old face).*

Of all the colored bears, the only one not retired back in early 1996 was the NF Brown Teddy, who hung around until October 1997. Because we've been seeing so much of him, his retirement value is much less than those of the other colored NF bears.

If you find it's easier to unstick your nose from a honey jar than tell the difference between OFs and NFs, check this out: Each of the new-faced bears comes with a ribbon around its neck, something the old-faced bears don't have. Just to keep you from getting complacent, the mad seamstresses at Ty gave Cranberry a dark green ribbon and Jade a cranberry ribbon. (They make great Christmas season decorations with those color combinations!) Magenta's ribbon is pink, Teal's ribbon is navy blue, and Violet (the rarest NF bear) has a green ribbon.

Get the Scoop

When you read about Beanie bears, you may feel as if you're drowning in alphabet soup: You'll often see these bears referred to as NF (new face) or OF (old face). Many folks collect only one style or the other rather than both, especially because of their rarity and cost. The new-faced bears tend to be more popular.

Brown

❑ It's mine!

　　Date purchased: _____

　　Price: _____

❑ Sold!

　　Date sold: _____

　　Price: _____

Cranberry

❑ It's mine!

　　Date purchased: _____

　　Price: _____

❑ Sold!

　　Date sold: _____

　　Price: _____

Jade

❑ It's mine!

　　Date purchased: _____

　　Price: _____

❑ Sold!

　　Date sold: _____

　　Price: _____

Magenta

❑ It's mine!

　　Date purchased: _____

　　Price: _____

❑ Sold!

　　Date sold: _____

　　Price: _____

Teal

❑ It's mine!

　　Date purchased: _____

　　Price: _____

❑ Sold!

　　Date sold: _____

　　Price: _____

Violet

❑ It's mine!

　　Date purchased: _____

　　Price: _____

❑ Sold!

　　Date sold: _____

　　Price: _____

Teddy the Bear (Old-Faced)

➤ Style: 4050 (brown)

➤ Style: 4052 (cranberry)

➤ Style: 4057 (jade)

➤ Style: 4056 (magenta)

➤ Style: 4051 (teal)

➤ Style: 4055 (violet)

➤ Birthday: (none) (all colors)

➤ Released: 6-25-94 (all colors)

➤ Retired: 1-7-95 (all colors)

➤ Hangtag: 1-2 (all colors)

You'll have to poke your way through quite a few caves before you uncover the old-faced brown bear, the rarest of any of the bears—old or new. Finding him in any condition is difficult at best, and if you find him you'll be faced with sticker shock: His price is generally several hundred to a thousand dollars more than the other old- or new-faced colored bears.

As you'd expect from their name, the OF bears are more Victorian in style, with pointier noses than those upstart pouty NF bears. Old-faced bears peer out of eyes set beyond the top triangle of plush that runs from their ears down to their noses.

The old-faced bears are plain, no-nonsense sort of bears, and don't go in for lots of fancy doodads like the decorative ribbons you'll see on the new-faced bears. If you notice a ribbon on an OF bear, be careful that it's just an add-on and not someone trying to pass off a counterfeit.

Get the Scoop

Though not quite as popular as the new-faced bears, the fact that the new-faced Teddys are older—with fewer survivors—helps keep their value closely in line with their younger cousins.

190

Brown

❑ It's mine!

Date purchased: _____

Price: _____

❑ Sold!

Date sold: _____

Price: _____

Cranberry

❑ It's mine!

Date purchased: _____

Price: _____

❑ Sold!

Date sold: _____

Price: _____

Jade

❑ It's mine!

Date purchased: _____

Price: _____

❑ Sold!

Date sold: _____

Price: _____

Magenta

❑ It's mine!

Date purchased: _____

Price: _____

❑ Sold!

Date sold: _____

Price: _____

Teal

❑ It's mine!

Date purchased: _____

Price: _____

❑ Sold!

Date sold: _____

Price: _____

Violet

❑ It's mine!

Date purchased: _____

Price: _____

❑ Sold!

Date sold: _____

Price: _____

Teddy, 1997

- ➤ Style: 4200
- ➤ Birthday: 12-25-96
- ➤ Released: 10-1-97

- ➤ Retired: 12-31-97
- ➤ Hangtag: 4

Get the Scoop

When originally introduced on the Ty Web site, the 1997 Teddy appeared in his publicity shots sporting red and green ribbons rather than a scarf. Actually, very few of these bears with ribbons are actually known to exist.

The first in what appears to be Ty's decision to offer annual Beanies, the 1997 Teddy was not introduced until almost the end of the year. As a result, he was still arriving at stores when in fact he was retired, much to everyone's surprise. His value has bearly changed, but is expected to increase during the holiday season. His plush is lighter than the new-faced brown Teddy.

❏ It's mine!

Date purchased: _____

Price: _____

❏ Sold!

Date sold: _____

Price: _____

Valentino the Bear

➤ Style: 4058
➤ Birthday: 2-14-94
➤ Released: 1-7-95

➤ Retired:
➤ Hangtag: 2-5

Valentino is often the butt of retirement rumors, but the thing about retirement rumors is that sooner or later, they'll be right (and it will probably be sooner). Another of those hard-to-keep-clean white Beanies obviously related to Libearty and Maple, Valentino wears a red embroidered heart on his chest and a matching red ribbon around his neck.

❏ It's mine!

   Date purchased: _____

   Price: _____

❏ Sold!

   Date sold: _____

   Price: _____

Get the Scoop

If you're searching for that just-right Valentine's gift—or just a little something to let your sweetheart know how much you care—what could be better than a sweet Valentino bear?

The Least You Need to Know

➤ For those of you who like to collect the entire set, there are 23 different styles of Beanie Baby bears to track down!

➤ You'll need to like travel if you collect Beanie bears: Maple is sold only in Canada and Britannia is available only in the United Kingdom.

➤ Ty appears to be offering a yearly Beanie: Teddy 1997 was the first.

➤ "Old-faced" bears are generally worth more than "new-faced" bears.

Chapter 14

It's a Jungle Out There

In This Chapter

➤ Discover which shade of hippo most collectors hope for

➤ Learn how to tell counterfeit Grunts from the real thing

➤ Read up on the color evolution of Peanut the royal blue elephant

Some folks like to jet off to Kenya on safari to bag their prey. As far as I'm concerned, it's a heck of a lot cheaper (and easier on the wild animals) to go hunting for Beanie Baby jungle creatures instead. In fact, these critters are exotic enough for anyone's taste, and rare enough to pique the pride of any poacher.

Ants the Anteater

➤ Style: 4195
➤ Birthday: 11-7-97
➤ Released: 5-30-98

➤ Retired:
➤ Hangtag: 5

Ants is one of the May 30, 1998, releases and is generally considered to appeal to the kind of Beanie Baby fans who go for this type of creature in a big way. Odds are, if you like Tank, the retired armadillo, you'll love Ants. He's made of a light gray plush, and has a black plush stripe on his neck with white plush stripes on either side.

Get the Scoop

Ants has a real nose for his work; the size of his nose is surpassed only by his tail.

❏ It's mine!

Date purchased: _____

Price: _____

❏ Sold!

Date sold: _____

Price: _____

Bongo/Nana the Monkey

➤ Style: 4067
➤ Birthday: 8-17-95
➤ Released: 2-6-96 (brown-tailed)
➤ Released: 6-3-95 (tan-tailed)

➤ Retired: 6-29-96 (brown-tailed)
➤ Retired: (tan-tailed)
➤ Hangtag: 3-4 (brown-tailed)
➤ Hangtag: 3-5 (tan-tailed)

Bongo's first release went for the "total look," where his tan tail matched his face and paws. He was later released with a brown tail matching his body. Apparently the designers at Ty just couldn't make up their minds: Eventually, the tan-tailed version reappeared and now is valued more highly. Bongo is also found with the name Nana, a highly prized Beanie.

Brown-tailed

❑ It's mine!

   Date purchased: _____

   Price: _____

❑ Sold!

   Date sold: _____

   Price: _____

Tan-tailed

❑ It's mine!

   Date purchased: _____

   Price: _____

❑ Sold!

   Date sold: _____

   Price: _____

Get the Scoop

Not wanting to beat around the bush, marketing execs gave away 5,000 Bongos (together with a commemorative card) on April 5, 1998, at a Los Angeles Clippers–Cleveland Cavaliers basketball game.

Congo the Gorilla

➤ Style: 4160
➤ Birthday: 11-9-96
➤ Released: 6-15-96

➤ Retired:
➤ Hangtag: 4-5

Get the Scoop

If you thought you'd noticed lots of giant Congos on store shelves, you could be right. Congo look-alikes (called "George") were created in various sizes for Ty's plush line.

Gentle Congo's black plush is offset by a brown face, ears, and paws. Unlike his buddy Bongo, Ty's designers haven't tampered with perfection: Congo hasn't undergone any design changes to date.

❑ It's mine!

Date purchased: _____

Price: _____

❑ Sold!

Date sold: _____

Price: _____

Grunt the Razorback

➤ Style: 4092

➤ Birthday: 7-19-95

➤ Released: 1-7-96

➤ Retired: 5-11-97

➤ Hangtag: 3-4

Often mistaken for Snort and Tabasco, Grunt will never be thought dull—his bright-red plush stands out at 50 paces, together with a fine set of white felt tusks (easily dirtied, alas), and a red felt spiky ridge along his back.

❑ It's mine!

   Date purchased: _____

   Price: _____

❑ Sold!

   Date sold: _____

   Price: _____

On the Sly

If you're rooting around for Grunt, beware! Counterfeit Grunts are thick on the ground. You know you've got a counterfeit if your Grunt has a more wrinkled appearance than the real thing.

Happy the Hippo

➤ Style: 4061
➤ Birthday: (none) (gray)
➤ Birthday: 2-25-94 (lavender)
➤ Released: 6-25-94 (gray)
➤ Released: 6-3-95 (lavender)

➤ Retired: 6-3-95 (gray)
➤ Retired: 5-1-98 (lavender)
➤ Hangtag: 1-3 (gray)
➤ Hangtag: 3-5 (lavender)

With a name sounding more like a flirtatious debutante than a fierce jungle creature, Happy was first released in light gray plush. Deciding that gray plush was on the drab side—not really happy enough for Happy—he was reformulated in a brighter lavender color that's sure to make anyone smile. We hope he's Happy in his retirement!

Get the Scoop

If you can find a gray Happy hippo, hang onto him. He's worth more than the lovely lavender shade.

Gray

❑ It's mine!

Date purchased: _____

Price: _____

❑ Sold!

Date sold: _____

Price: _____

Lavender

❑ It's mine!

Date purchased: _____

Price: _____

❑ Sold!

Date sold: _____

Price: _____

Humphrey the Camel

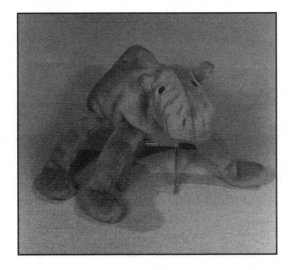

➤ Style: 4060
➤ Birthday: (none)
➤ Released: 6-25-94

➤ Retired: 6-15-95
➤ Hangtag: 1-3

Perhaps the most beloved of the Beanies, Humphrey has floppy legs and a goofy plump face that make him almost irresistible. Elegant in a lighter, rich tan plush, he was put out to pasture for a well-earned retirement long ago.

❏ It's mine!

   Date purchased: _____

   Price: _____

❏ Sold!

   Date sold: _____

   Price: _____

Get the Scoop

Today, Humphrey is difficult to find. If you're lucky enough to get one, don't be surprised if he's missing his swing tag.

Peanut the Elephant

- ➤ Style: 4062
- ➤ Birthday: (none) (royal blue)
- ➤ Birthday: 1-25-95 (light blue)
- ➤ Released: 6-3-95 (royal blue)
- ➤ Released: 10-2-95 (light blue)
- ➤ Retired: 10-2-95 (royal blue)
- ➤ Retired: 5-1-98 (light blue)
- ➤ Hangtag: 3 (royal blue)
- ➤ Hangtag: 3-5 (light blue)

You'll never sing the blues if you've managed to snag one of these Peanuts dressed in royal blue! Possibly the most coveted of all Beanies, the blue fabric on Peanut is thought by many to have been a goof on the production line. The royal blue is the same color used on Kiwi's beak and in a section on Inch. Shortly after her release, Peanut was redesigned in a baby blue fabric. Both versions have pink plush on the inside of their ears.

Get the Scoop

All dressed up with no place to go, the newly-dyed light blue Peanut was part of an Oakland Athletics' giveaway on August 1, 1998.

Royal Blue

❏ It's mine!

    Date purchased: _____

    Price: _____

❏ Sold!

    Date sold: _____

    Price: _____

Light Blue

❏ It's mine!

    Date purchased: _____

    Price: _____

❏ Sold!

    Date sold: _____

    Price: _____

Pouch the Kangaroo

➤ Style: 4161
➤ Birthday: 11-6-96
➤ Released: 1-1-97

➤ Retired:
➤ Hangtag: 4-5

Pouch is covered in brown plush except for her inner ears, chin, and stomach, which are off-white plush. She does have a pouch in there for stowing away her joey—but don't look too closely! Joey's actually a bodyless kangaroo with just a head! Joey is made of the same brown plush and has brown felt ears.

❏ It's mine!

   Date purchased: _____

   Price: _____

❏ Sold!

   Date sold: _____

   Price: _____

On the Sly

If you've tried to yank Pouch's baby out to get up close and personal, forget it! He's stitched into the pouch to help keep him safe.

Righty the Elephant

➤ Style: 4085

➤ Birthday: 7-4-96

➤ Released: 6-15-96

➤ Retired: 1-1-97

➤ Hangtag: 4

Get the Scoop

Made of light gray plush with pink inner ears, Righty sports an American flag on his left hip. To have put it on his right side, where it should be politically, would make him politically incorrect (the stars would be too close to his hind end, considered an insult to the flag).

Part of the American Trio (Righty, Lefty the donkey, and Libearty) released in the summer of 1996, Righty shares his birthday and his poem with Lefty. These are the only two Beanies brought out at the same time who share a poem, so these guys really are special.

❑ It's mine!

Date purchased: _____

Price: _____

❑ Sold!

Date sold: _____

Price: _____

Spike the Rhinoceros

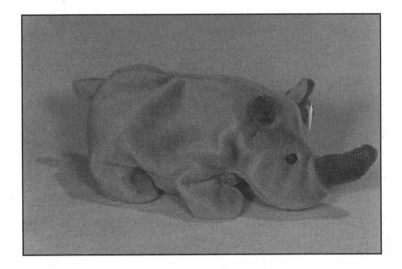

➤ Style: 4060
➤ Birthday: 8-13-96
➤ Released: 6-15-96

➤ Retired:
➤ Hangtag: 4-5

Short and stout, Spike has medium gray plush accented with a brown horn and inner ears. Until recently, Spike has been considered a "hard to find" Beanie, but has become more plentiful as shipments started coming to retailers regularly.

❑ It's mine!

   Date purchased: _____

   Price: _____

❑ Sold!

   Date sold: _____

   Price: _____

Get the Scoop

Will he be retired in the next Beanie wave? Will he remain current? Only Spike's creators know for sure!

Tank the Armadillo

- ➤ Style: 4031
- ➤ Birthday: (none) (7 lines, no shell)
- ➤ Birthday: 2-22-95 (9 lines, no shell)
- ➤ Birthday: 2-22-95 (shell)
- ➤ Released: 1-7-95 (7 lines, no shell)
- ➤ Released: circa 6-3-95 (9 lines, no shell)
- ➤ Released: (unknown) (shell)
- ➤ Retired: circa 1-7-96 (7 lines, no shell)
- ➤ Retired: (unknown) (9 lines, no shell)

- ➤ Retired: 10-1-97 (shell)
- ➤ Hangtag: 3 (7 lines, no shell)
- ➤ Hangtag: 4 (9 lines, no shell)
- ➤ Hangtag: 4 (shell)

Get the Scoop

When you're counting Tank's lines, count the number of lines of stitching, not the number of lines between the stitching.

Just the way you can count lines on a tree to figure out the age, you can count the number of lines on Tank to tell apart different varieties. The first two variations were longer than the final version, and both had embroidered nostrils. Finally, Ty seemed to understand that an armadillo should be armed with a shell and used a row of stitching along the bottom edge to form one. The last variation has a more rounded look to him and he has lost his nostrils. The 9-line, no-shell variation is probably the rarest.

7 lines, no shell

❑ It's mine!

    Date purchased: _____

    Price: _____

❑ Sold!

    Date sold: _____

    Price: _____

9 lines, no shell

❑ It's mine!

    Date purchased: _____

    Price: _____

❑ Sold!

    Date sold: _____

    Price: _____

Shell

❑ It's mine!

    Date purchased: _____

    Price: _____

❑ Sold!

    Date sold: _____

    Price: _____

Twigs the Giraffe

➤ Style:	4068		➤ Retired:	5-1-98
➤ Birthday:	5-19-95		➤ Hangtag:	3-5
➤ Released:	1-7-96			

If you thought you'd already spotted Twigs' orange-on-yellow spotted plush, you have—it also appears on the later version of Lizzy's stomach. Twigs' hooves are brown plush and he has a thin insert of brown plush as his mane.

Get the Scoop

Twigs' laid-back, sit-down body style was revisited in the May 1998 release of Whisper the deer.

❑ It's mine!

Date purchased: _____

Price: _____

❑ Sold!

Date sold: _____

Price: _____

Ziggy the Zebra

➤ Style: 4063   ➤ Retired: 5-1-98

➤ Birthday: 12-24-95   ➤ Hangtag: 5

➤ Released: 6-3-95

Introduced in 1995 and retired three years later, Ziggy's plush coat was transformed from the less stylish narrow stripe to the far more fashionable wide-stripe look.

❏ It's mine!

Date purchased: _____

Price: _____

❏ Sold!

Date sold: _____

Price: _____

Get the Scoop

Ziggy has never appeared with a fine-yarn mane as have other Beanies.

The Least You Need to Know

➤ Bongo and Nana are the same monkey, but with different name tags.

➤ Gray hippos are worth more than lavender hippos.

➤ Humphrey is one of the most beloved Beanies, and one of the hardest to find.

Chapter 15

Wild and Wooly

In This Chapter

➤ Find two kinds of beavers: one-toothed and two-toothed

➤ Learn more about koalas: Are they bears or aren't they?

➤ Discover what woodland creature is the only current Beanie who was one of the Original Nine

While their counterparts in the jungle are more than fierce, woodland creatures have more guile than growl. All the critters you'd be likely to find in an American woods are corralled into this chapter, such as the fox, the deer, and the raccoon. The jungle hotheads are all contained in Chapter 14.

Bucky the Beaver

➤ Style: 4016
➤ Birthday: 6-8-95
➤ Released: 1-7-96

➤ Retired: 12-31-97
➤ Hangtag: 3-4

Get the Scoop

One tooth or two? Bucky inadvertently comes in both varieties: His teeth are made of one piece of felt, cut in the middle to make two teeth. However, sometimes the felt didn't get cut, leaving him with one huge tooth.

You'll be as busy as the proverbial you-know-what as you try to search out this little fellow. Bucky the beaver was created with body shape similar to Ringo, Sly, and Stinky. One of more than 30 Beanies colored mostly brown, he has darker brown ears and tail with an oval nose, whiskers, and felt teeth.

❑ It's mine!

  Date purchased: _____

  Price: _____

❑ Sold!

  Date sold: _____

  Price: _____

Chocolate the Moose

➤ Style: 4015

➤ Birthday: 4-27-93

➤ Released: 1-8-94

➤ Retired:

➤ Hangtag: 1-5

Chocolate is the only Beanie you can still find sitting on store shelves of the Original Nine. Looking good enough to eat in his chocolate brown plush (no surprise there), he's also got bright orange antlers. If you put him side-by-side with the ever-popular Humphrey the Camel, you'd see a fairly identical face.

❑ It's mine!

   Date purchased: _____

   Price: _____

❑ Sold!

   Date sold: _____

   Price: _____

Get the Scoop

Cartons of Chocolates (5,000 individual Chocolates) were given away as a sports promotion during the Denver Nuggets—Portland Trailblazers basketball game April 17, 1998.

Mel the Koala

➤ Style: 4162
➤ Birthday: 1-15-96
➤ Released: 1-1-97

➤ Retired:
➤ Hangtag: 4-5

Get the Scoop

We would have filed Mel under "bears," except for the fact that koalas are really marsupials and not bears at all. Still, many people classify Mel as one of the Beanie bears.

Mel's plush is primarily medium-gray, though the insides of his ears and his stomach are white and his black plastic nose is rounder than the plastic noses you'll run across on other Beanies.

❑ It's mine!

   Date purchased: _____

   Price: _____

❑ Sold!

   Date sold: _____

   Price: _____

Nuts the Squirrel

➤ Style: 4114
➤ Birthday: 1-21-96
➤ Released: 1-1-97

➤ Retired:
➤ Hangtag: 4-5

If you don't immediately fall in love with this little critter, then nuts to you! This Beanie Baby is popular because of the transmutation from plush to faux fur on his S-shaped tail. His brown plush matches his furry tail except for off-white plush on his stomach, chin, and the inner part of his ears.

❑ It's mine!

   Date purchased: _____

   Price: _____

❑ Sold!

   Date sold: _____

   Price: _____

Get the Scoop

Notice that your Nuts can sit up and beg without really trying? It's because he seems to be filled with more stuffing rather than "beans" in order to help keep him in his upright position.

Ringo the Raccoon

➤ Style: 4014
➤ Birthday: 7-14-95
➤ Released: 1-7-96

➤ Retired: 9-16-98
➤ Hangtag: 3-5

Get the Scoop

You'll be running rings around your collector competition if you managed to snag a Ringo made with true-to-life gray-brown color before he retired in mid-September as part of the multiday retirement announcements.

Primarily covered in brown plush, Ringo's tail is sewn vertically with black plush rings. His ears are black and white, and his snout is covered in white plush, with small areas of black plush around each eye to give him the masked look of real raccoons. His nose and whiskers are black.

❑ It's mine!

Date purchased: _____

Price: _____

❑ Sold!

Date sold: _____

Price: _____

Sly the Fox

➤ Style: 4115
➤ Birthday: 9-12-96
➤ Released: 6-15-96 (brown belly)
➤ Released: 8-6-96 (white belly)

➤ Retired: 8-6-96 (brown belly)
➤ Retired: 9-22-98 (white belly)
➤ Hangtag: 4 (brown belly)
➤ Hangtag: 4-5 (white belly)

The original brown-bellied version of Sly is possibly the most undervalued of all the Beanies even though he was only available for about two months. Perhaps in an attempt to make their Beanie fox more anatomically correct, the belly was changed to the white plush matching his chin and the inside of his ears.

Brown belly

❏ It's mine!

   Date purchased: _____

   Price: _____

❏ Sold!

   Date sold: _____

   Price: _____

White belly

❏ It's mine!

   Date purchased: _____

   Price: _____

❏ Sold!

   Date sold: _____

   Price: _____

Get the Scoop

Amazingly, the brown-bellied version of Sly still is reasonably priced (in the $125–$150 range), but I don't expect it to stay that way—especially now that Sly is retired.

Speedy the Turtle

➤ Style: 4030
➤ Birthday: 8-14-94
➤ Released: 6-25-94

➤ Retired: 10-1-97
➤ Hangtag: 1-4

Get the Scoop

Except perhaps for youngsters with a penchant for all things reptilian, most collectors consider Speedy cute but not a Beanie with great emotional appeal.

Speedy's body is lime green, the same color as Legs the frog. His shell is brown-on-green spotted like Slither's and Ally's backs. Even though he's been retired for a year, he's still easy to find at shows.

❑ It's mine!

   Date purchased: _____

   Price: _____

❑ Sold!

   Date sold: _____

   Price: _____

Stinky the Skunk

➤ Style: 4017
➤ Birthday: 2-13-95
➤ Released: 6-3-95

➤ Retired: 9-28-98
➤ Hangtag: 3-5

Fortunately for collectors, Stinky doesn't live up to his odiferous name. Needless to say, he has black plush with a white stripe running from his nose to the tip of his tail.

❏ It's mine!

   Date purchased: _____

   Price: _____

❏ Sold!

   Date sold: _____

   Price: _____

Get the Scoop

He was around for quite a while (check out the fact that he's run through *all the* tush tags!) and therefore, he was fairly easy to find before, and probably will be even after, his recent retirement.

Trap the Mouse

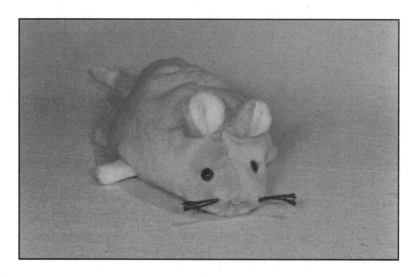

➤ Style: 4042

➤ Birthday: (none)

➤ Released: 6-25-94

➤ Retired: 6-15-95

➤ Hangtag: 1-3

Get the Scoop

Taking bets on what animals will be released next, many collectors are hoping to trap a replacement for the dearly departed Trap.

This light gray rodent with his pink plush feet, tail, and inner ears is one of the most popular of the older retired Beanies. Armed with sweet pink plastic nose and black (not pink!) whiskers, he fits easily into the palm of even the tiniest collector.

❑ It's mine!

   Date purchased: _____

   Price: _____

❑ Sold!

   Date sold: _____

   Price: _____

Whisper the Deer

➤ Style: 4194

➤ Birthday: 4-5-97

➤ Released: 5-30-98

➤ Retired:

➤ Hangtag: 5

One of the last of the May 1998 releases, Whisper has a body style that is reminiscent of the late great Twigs the giraffe. Her brown plush is speckled with white spots along her back (indicating that she is still a young Beanie); her stomach and inner ears are white, but her hooves are brown.

❑ It's mine!

Date purchased: _____

Price: _____

❑ Sold!

Date sold: _____

Price: _____

Get the Scoop

Still hoofing it into the stores, she'll be hard to find for a while as every collector will want to add this "Bambi" look-alike to their herd.

> **The Least You Need to Know**

➤ You may run from the real thing, but Stinky is easy to find in stores.

➤ Bucky the beaver comes in a one- and two-toothed variety.

➤ Nuts the squirrel is filled with more stuffing than usual to help him sit upright.

Chapter 16

Still Life

> ### In This Chapter
>
> ➤ Get some holiday and party decorating ideas with these Beanies
>
> ➤ Learn all about Magic's shades of thread and what they mean
>
> ➤ Get the scoop on Mystic's varieties: brown and shiny horns, fine and coarse manes

If your taste runs to the mystical and evanescent, this little group of non-living creatures—a small but captivating part of the Beanie Baby family—should be just your cup of Beanie tea. Even the scarier versions—ghosts and dragons—won't give the smallest child nightmares, so feel free to add all of these to your collection. In fact, some of the most beautiful creations of all the Beanies can be found here, with the hauntingly lovely, iridescent glimmer of a dragon's wing or a unicorn's horn. You'll also find the three versions of dinosaurs in this group—since dinosaurs are extinct, we felt they'd fit right in with the other "still life" group.

These Beanies also lend themselves very well to holiday decorations (Spooky can liven up a Halloween display, and Snowball is a great winter holiday-maker). They also make great birthday party favors—what little archaeologist wouldn't love a grab bag filled with Beanie dinosaurs!

Bronty the Brontosaurus

➤ Style: 4085

➤ Birthday: (none)

➤ Released: 6-3-95

➤ Retired: 6-15-96

➤ Hangtag: 3

Bronty's plush is a deep blue tie-dye (the same as Sting's) with shades of light blue and green running through it. No two Brontys are exactly alike, since the material isn't a consistent color. He was released with dino pals Rex (a red tie-dye) and Steg, an earth-toned tie-dye.

Get the Scoop

Bronty is the rarest of the three dinosaurs, so try to add him to your collection before he becomes extinct!

❑ It's mine!

    Date purchased: _____

    Price: _____

❑ Sold!

    Date sold: _____

    Price: _____

Magic the Dragon

➤ Style: 4088e
➤ Birthday: 6-8-95
➤ Released: 6-3-95

➤ Retired: 12-31-97
➤ Hangtag: 3-4

One of the two tallest Beanies, the all-white Magic is truly beautiful—and one of the most popular of all critters in the Ty collection. Magic's wings are crafted from an iridescent material and stuffed with filler (not beans) to help retain their shape. (Even dragons must bow to economic pressure; these wings were supposedly expensive for Ty to produce and were believed to be a factor in Magic's retirement.)

❑ It's mine!

   Date purchased: _____

   Price: _____

❑ Sold!

   Date sold: _____

   Price: _____

Get the Scoop

The stitching on Magic's wings and nostrils is a real evolutionary story. Originally, the thread was a very light pink, giving way to a standard pink stitching with lighter pink nostrils. This evolved into a dark (or "hot pink") stitching with light pink nostrils. Most collectors believe that the hot pink stitching is the rarest, although some insist that the lightest pink is more valuable since it's found in the oldest examples of the dragon.

Mystic the Unicorn

- ➤ Style: 4007
- ➤ Birthday: (none) (fine mane)
- ➤ Birthday: 5-21-94 (brown horn)
- ➤ Birthday: 5-21-94 (iridescent horn)
- ➤ Released: 6-25-94 (fine mane)
- ➤ Released: (unknown) (brown horn)
- ➤ Released: 10-23-97 (iridescent horn)

- ➤ Retired: (unknown) (fine mane)
- ➤ Retired: 10-23-97 (brown horn)
- ➤ Retired: (iridescent horn)
- ➤ Hangtag: 1-3 (fine mane)
- ➤ Hangtag: 3-4 (brown horn)
- ➤ Hangtag: 4-5 (iridescent horn)

Get the Scoop

The fine-mane version of Mystic is easier to find than the fine-mane version of Derby, which is a real rarity.

Here's another of those tough-to-keep-clean white Beanies. The original version of Mystic—like Derby the horse—had a mane and tail of fine yarn. Eventually, the fine yarn was replaced with coarser yarn, but both versions still had a stuffed gold felt horn. In the fall of 1997, however, Mystic's horn was transmuted into the same shiny material as Magic's wings, with a spiral of hot pink thread as an additional flourish. All three variations have blue eyes.

Fine mane

❏ It's mine!
   Date purchased: _____
   Price: _____
❏ Sold!
   Date sold: _____
   Price: _____

Brown horn

❏ It's mine!
   Date purchased: _____
   Price: _____
❏ Sold!
   Date sold: _____
   Price: _____

Iridescent horn

❏ It's mine!
   Date purchased: _____
   Price: _____
❏ Sold!
   Date sold: _____
   Price: _____

Rex the Tyrannosaurus

➤ Style:	4086	➤ Retired:	6-15-96
➤ Birthday:	(none)	➤ Hangtag:	3
➤ Released:	6-3-95		

Released and retired before birthdays and poems were added to Beanie tags, Rex is the most popular of the dinosaur trio—Bronty, Rex, and Steg—and that's saying something, since all three of this group are real crowd-pleasers. Looking more colorful than a day-old bruise, Rex's tie-dyed plush varies from reds, pinks, and oranges all the way through purple, burgundy, and blue.

❑ It's mine!

Date purchased: _____

Price: _____

❑ Sold!

Date sold: _____

Price: _____

Get the Scoop

This little fellow's value is expected to soar, so try to find one in mint condition today for your collection.

Snowball the Snowman

➤ Style: 4201   ➤ Retired: 12-31-97

➤ Birthday: 12-22-96   ➤ Hangtag: 4

➤ Released: 10-1-97

Released and retired quicker than a snowball melts in spring, Snowball was the second "non-animal" Beanie ever produced. (The first was Spooky the ghost.) Snowball sports a jaunty black felt hat with a red band, a red scarf with white fringe, orange felt for his carrot nose, and black plastic bits of "coal" for his eyes. He's a favorite choice for holiday winter party decorations, which is one reason why he was popular.

Get the Scoop

Snowball's early retirement came as a surprise to collectors. Expect his value to snowball during the holiday season!

❑ It's mine!

  Date purchased: _____

  Price: _____

❑ Sold!

  Date sold: _____

  Price: _____

228

Spooky the Ghost

➤ Style: 4090   ➤ Retired: 12-31-97

➤ Birthday: 10-31-95   ➤ Hangtag: 3-4

➤ Released: 9-1-95

Until Snowball came along and shoved him out of the limelight, Spooky had the distinction of being Ty's only non-living Beanie Baby. However, both of these creatures were retired in 1997, leaving only animals in the Ty company stable. Spooky was unique in another way: He's the only Beanie whose designer (Jenna Boldebeck) was listed in the third-generation hangtag. These same third-generation tags also mistakenly call him "Spook" (but it's not certain whether someone hit the wrong key on the computer, or whether this was an intentional renaming). As usual, Ty's not talking.

❑ It's mine!

    Date purchased: _____

    Price: _____

❑ Sold!

    Date sold: _____

    Price: _____

On the Sly

Don't get spooked if you notice that your Spooky's mouth looks different than somebody else's. Spooky's mouth correctly comes in several different configurations.

Steg the Stegosaurus

➤ Style: 4087   ➤ Retired: 6-15-96

➤ Birthday: (none)   ➤ Hangtag: 3

➤ Released: 6-3-95

The last of the dino trio to be released, Steg is covered in tie-dye plush in mostly earth tones of yellow, tan, and green. The muted colors tend to make him less popular than his chums Bronty and Rex, but he's still got that unmistakable Beanie charm.

Get the Scoop

While he might not win any beauty contests, Steg was never released in Europe and is considered to be rarer than his cousin Rex.

❑ It's mine!

Date purchased: _____

Price: _____

❑ Sold!

Date sold: _____

Price: _____

The Least You Need to Know

➤ All three of the Beanie Baby dinosaurs are retired and expected to become valuable as time goes on.

➤ Check out the nostril and stitching color to figure out which Magic you own.

➤ Spooky and Snowball are the only two non-animal Beanies to be released.

Chapter 17

A Teenie Tribute

In This Chapter

➤ Learn how Ty and McDonald's collaborated on the most popular McDonald's promotion ever held.

➤ Get the scoop on the worth of a complete set of Teenie Beanies

➤ Find out when the next McDonald's promotion may occur

When a company like Ty gets together with a company like McDonald's—both known for their marketing wizardry—you can expect something amazing to happen, and that's just what occurred on April 11, 1997, when the Teenie Beanie promotion began.

The First Set of Teenie Beanie Babies

The deal: McDonald's would give away one of 10 different styles of miniature versions of Ty's Beanie Babies (called "Teenie Beanies") with each purchase of a Happy Meal at participating restaurants. The Teenie Beanies were licensed by Ty, but produced by an independent McDonald's supplier. When news leaked out that the Teenie Beanies had arrived, McDonald's employees were stunned by the pandemonium that followed. Once the dust had settled, hundreds of thousands of new Beanie Baby collectors were born—and McDonald's was forced to run national TV ads apologizing to customers for running out of the furry little creatures. In less than two weeks, more than 100,000 Teenie Beanies were distributed in the promotion, which was termed the most successful McDonald's promotion ever devised.

After each McDonald's received the first set of 10 Teenie Beanies, many restaurants found they had used up their entire supply, which should have lasted for a week, within a day or two.

1997 Teenie Beanie set #1

234

Chocolate the Moose

- ➤ Number in set: 4
- ➤ Released: April 1997
- ➤ Retired: April 1997

❏ It's mine!
Date purchased: _____
Price: _____

❏ Sold!
Date sold: _____
Price: _____

Get the Scoop

The next official date for the McDonald's Teenie Beanie promotion is scheduled for April 23, 1999, according to *Advertising Age* magazine.

Chops the Lamb

- ➤ Number in set: 3
- ➤ Released: April 1997
- ➤ Retired: April 1997

❏ It's mine!
Date purchased: _____
Price: _____

❏ Sold!
Date sold: _____
Price: _____

Baby Talk

The letters **TBB** stand for Teenie Beanie Baby.

Goldie the Fish

- ➤ Number in set: 3
- ➤ Released: April 1997
- ➤ Retired: April 1997

❏ It's mine!
Date purchased: _____
Price: _____

❏ Sold!
Date sold: _____
Price: _____

Baby Talk

The abbreviation **HTF** is used among collectors to mean "hard to find."

Lizz the Lizard

- ➤ Number in set: 10
- ➤ Released: April 1997
- ➤ Retired: April 1997

❏ It's mine!
Date purchased: _____
Price: _____

❏ Sold!
Date sold: _____
Price: _____

Get the Scoop

Teenie Patti is almost as rare as Pinky. If you've got a mint-in-the-bag Patti, she's worth between $30 and $35.

Get the Scoop

Pinky is the rarest TBB from the first set (worth about $40 if she's mint and still in her package).

Get the Scoop

Quacks the duck (and Lizz the lizard) are the only Teenie Beanies from the first set to not use the same name as their larger "Moms" or "Dads."

Get the Scoop

While the Teenies originally were offered free with a McDonald's Happy Meal, today a complete set in the original packages sells for about $75 or more.

Patti the Platypus

➤ Number in set: 1
➤ Released: April 1997
➤ Retired: April 1997

❏ It's mine!   ❏ Sold!
  Date purchased: _____   Date sold: _____
  Price: _____   Price: _____

Pinky the Flamingo

➤ Number in set: 2
➤ Released: April 1997
➤ Retired: April 1997

❏ It's mine!   ❏ Sold!
  Date purchased: _____   Date sold: _____
  Price: _____   Price: _____

Quacks the Duck

➤ Number in set: 9
➤ Released: April 1997
➤ Retired: April 1997

❏ It's mine!   ❏ Sold!
  Date purchased: _____   Date sold: _____
  Price: _____   Price: _____

Seamore the Seal

➤ Number in set: 7
➤ Released: April 1997
➤ Retired: April 1997

❏ It's mine!   ❏ Sold!
  Date purchased: _____   Date sold: _____
  Price: _____   Price: _____

Snort the Bull

➤ Number in set: 8

➤ Released: April 1997

➤ Retired: April 1997

❏ It's mine!   ❏ Sold!

    Date purchased: _____   Date sold: _____

    Price: _____   Price: _____

Get the Scoop

The home offices of both Ty, Inc., and McDonald's are located in Oak Brook, Illinois.

Speedy the Turtle

➤ Number in set: 6

➤ Released: April 1997

➤ Retired: April 1997

❏ It's mine!   ❏ Sold!

    Date purchased: _____   Date sold: _____

    Price: _____   Price: _____

Get the Scoop

Rumors suggest that McDonald's had 10 million of each Teenie Baby produced, for a total of 100 million Teenies.

The Second Set of Teenie Beanie Babies

The first promotion was so popular, a second McDonald's Teenie Beanie giveaway was scheduled May 22, 1998, as part of a Memorial Day weekend promotion. This time, 12 teenie-tiny Teenie Beanies (again licensed by Ty, but produced by an independent McDonald's supplier) were included in the promotional offerings. It was up to the individual stores to decide how many would be offered at one time. Some stores offered one, some offered two—and some offered all 12 at once.

Customers could see which toys were available at any one time by reading posters in the windows of the store, or checking out the signs in the drive-through lane. Rumor has it that there were 240 million produced.

Interestingly, if you're into collecting, remember that it might not be a good idea to toss that Happy Meal bag away while you're grappling for the Teenie Beanie inside. Even the Happy Meal bag the TBBs came in is being traded on the secondary market. Some Teenie Beanie bag trivia:

➤ Some areas got Happy Meal boxes, not bags.

➤ There are two different styles of Teenie Beanie Baby bags for the second set.

➤ Happy meal bags may sell for between $1 and $5.

➤ In the second promotional set, some of the Teenie plastic bags are printed in three languages (English, French, and Spanish)—later shipments added German.

1998 Teenie Beanie set #2

Bones the Dog

➤ Number in set: 9

➤ Released: May 1998

➤ Retired: May 1998

Get the Scoop

In the second McDonald's promotion, three different Beanies were offered at one time, but while the promotion was intended to last for a month, once again the incredible Beanie frenzy depleted supplies within a few days.

❑ It's mine!

   Date purchased: _____

   Price: _____

❑ Sold!

   Date sold: _____

   Price: _____

Bongo the Monkey

➤ Number in set: 2

➤ Released: May 1998

➤ Retired: May 1998

❑ It's mine!

   Date purchased: _____

   Price: _____

❑ Sold!

   Date sold: _____

   Price: _____

Doby the Doberman

➤ Number in set: 1

➤ Released: May 1998

➤ Retired: May 1998

❑ It's mine!

    Date purchased: _____

    Price: _____

❑ Sold!

    Date sold: _____

    Price: _____

Happy the Hippo

➤ Number in set: 6

➤ Released: May 1998

➤ Retired: May 1998

❑ It's mine!

    Date purchased: _____

    Price: _____

❑ Sold!

    Date sold: _____

    Price: _____

Inch the Inchworm

➤ Number in set: 4

➤ Released: May 1998

➤ Retired: May 1998

❑ It's mine!

    Date purchased: _____

    Price: _____

❑ Sold!

    Date sold: _____

    Price: _____

Mel the Koala

➤ Number in set: 7

➤ Released: May 1998

➤ Retired: May 1998

❑ It's mine!

    Date purchased: _____

    Price: _____

❑ Sold!

    Date sold: _____

    Price: _____

Get the Scoop

While the Teenie Beanies were included free as part of the McDonald's Happy Meal, consumers also could buy a toy for about $1.50 (depending on the store) if they also purchased one meal item.

Get the Scoop

A Beanie that is the most recent is called a **new release**. Beanies referred to as **current** are those easily found at local stores.

Baby Talk

The abbreviation **MIB** stands for "Mint In Bag," meaning that the Beanie is in mint condition and comes in its original bag.

Get the Scoop

McDonald's produced a mass of Teenie Beanie accessories in 1998 for their employees, such as a group of enameled lapel pins.

Peanut the Elephant

➤ Number in set: 12

➤ Released: May 1998

➤ Retired: May 1998

❏ It's mine!   ❏ Sold!

   Date purchased: _____   Date sold: _____

   Price: _____   Price: _____

Pinchers the Lobster

➤ Number in set: 5

➤ Released: May 1998

➤ Retired: May 1998

❏ It's mine!   ❏ Sold!

   Date purchased: _____   Date sold: _____

   Price: _____   Price: _____

Get the Scoop

The original McDonald's Teenie Beanie promotion was slated to have lasted for five weeks, but it was so popular—causing hour-long lines at the drive-through windows across the country—that all the 100,000 Teenie Beanies had been given out within a week or so.

Scoop the Pelican

➤ Number in set: 8

➤ Released: May 1998

➤ Retired: May 1998

❏ It's mine!   ❏ Sold!

   Date purchased: _____   Date sold: _____

   Price: _____   Price: _____

Get the Scoop

Twigs is rumored to be the most rare in the second set due to a manufacturing error that rendered about half the production run unusable.

Twigs the Giraffe

➤ Number in set: 3

➤ Released: May 1998

➤ Retired: May 1998

❏ It's mine!   ❏ Sold!

   Date purchased: _____   Date sold: _____

   Price: _____   Price: _____

Waddle the Penguin

➤ Number in set: 11

➤ Released: May 1998

➤ Retired: May 1998

❑ It's mine!   ❑ Sold!

Date purchased: _____   Date sold: _____

Price: _____   Price: _____

Zip the Cat

➤ Number in set: 10

➤ Released: May 1998

➤ Retired: May 1998

❑ It's mine!   ❑ Sold!

Date purchased: _____   Date sold: _____

Price: _____   Price: _____

Get the Scoop

The complete set from the first promotion is worth between $150 and $200; the second set is worth between $50 and $75. If you've already ripped open the package to play with your Teenie Beanie, too bad for you. Out of the bags, the first set is worth about $50 and the second, about $20.

The Least You Need to Know

➤ There were two McDonald's Teenie Beanie promotions and a third one is expected in 1999.

➤ Teenie Beanie promotions are the most successful ever run by McDonald's.

➤ Both promotions were called off weeks early because all of the promotional Beanies had been given away.

Part 4
A Little Something Special

Tush tags and hangtags and price tags, oh my! If you're interested in collecting Beanies, there's a lot more you need to know than a few names and birth dates. You'll find the details on what to look for in a tush tag and hangtag, and whether that mistake on your Beanie's hangtag or elsewhere will allow you and your Beanie to retire to Miami Beach.

You'll also get the scoop on outfitting your Beanie with clothing, furniture, and other accessories; and we'll tell you how you can become a member of Ty's Beanie Babies Official Club.

Tag! You're It!

Every Beanie has a heart (tag, that is!). At least, they were all born with one, a hangtag connected to the Beanie's ear, leg, paw, side...well, somewhere on the Beanie's left side. It's that little red heart-shaped flap of paper that announces to the world this toy is a *real* Beanie Baby—not one of those cheap imitations!

You know you've cornered a genuine Beanie Baby if the tag:

➤ Is heart-shaped

➤ Is red on the front

➤ Is outlined in gold foil (not ink)

Baby Talk

The phrases **hangtag**, **swing tag**, and **heart tag** all refer to the same thing and can be used interchangeably.

Get the Scoop

While most hangtag connectors are red plastic, clear plastic has also been used, mostly on older Beanies.

➤ Has the name "ty" in white on the front

➤ Carries "The Beanie Babies Collection" phrase

➤ Has a style number (sometimes the last four digits of the bar code)

➤ Announces it was "Handmade" in China, Korea, or Indonesia

➤ Directs you to "Surface Wash," although the word "surface" may be spelled incorrectly

The Heart of the Beanie

Today, the Beanie Baby hangtags have gone through five generations—so getting the lowdown on tag details can help you pinpoint the approximate time period in which a Beanie was manufactured. However, this isn't rocket science, folks—nobody was really paying much attention for the first year or two of Beanie existence, so some of the time frames are estimates.

In each generation, Beanie Babies go through more mutations than an influenza virus. Some tags originated only in the United Kingdom. Sometimes Ty would shuffle an office around and note it on the tag without changing the basic style of the tag, thus preserving its "generation."

Trying to keep all the Beanie Baby tag generations straight can give you a migraine, so sit tight and read up on the general guidelines that will help you identify your Beanie's family tree. ("Generation" refers to the style of the hangtag and gives you a general idea of when that individual Beanie Baby was manufactured.)

The First-Generation Hangtag ("Pre-Beanies" to Mid-1994)

If you've got a Beanie Baby with a single tag that doesn't open up, rejoice! That's a first-generation hangtag, the only generation that's not a hinged tag that opens up like a book. Here are more details on the first-generation hangtag:

➤ The single-sided heart is more compact and wider than it is tall.

➤ The word "ty" on the front is known as the "skinny ty"—for obvious reasons.

➤ Gold foil outlines the edges of the heart, but there's also gold foil around the "ty" on the front of the heart.

➤ The hole through which the plastic connector passes is on the side of the hangtag, not at the upper-left corner.

➤ On the flip side, you'll see the words "The Beanie Babies."

The rest of the tag may vary slightly depending on whether that particular Beanie was made in China or Korea, or if it was intended for distribution in the United Kingdom. There's also a caution about removing the tag before giving the Beanie to a child. If you were one of those early conscientious parents who ripped that tag right off, you're probably kicking yourself now for obeying the rules! Some of the earliest Beanies are very valuable, but not without their tags.

The first-generation hangtag.

First-generation hangtag

The Second-Generation Hangtag (Mid-1994 to Mid-1995)

The Ty folks really got industrious with the second-generation hangtag, which now folds in the middle like a book, making four sides to the tag: front, inner front, inner back, and back. The front of the tag looks a lot like the first-generation tag, but the hole for the connector is now almost at the upper edge. Here are the other details about the second-generation hangtag:

➤ The white "skinny ty" is outlined with gold foil on a red background.

➤ The inner front carries the words "The Beanie Babies Collection," the copyright and corporate information, the warning, the country of origin, and the laundering information.

➤ Beanies available in Europe will list the corporate address for either the United Kingdom or Germany.

➤ The inner back side has the Beanie's name and style number, "to" and "from" gift tag lines, followed by the phrase "with love."

➤ The inner back of the European tags includes the information found on the inner front of the American tags, but the Beanie's name and style number are found under "The Beanie Babies Collection."

➤ The back of the tag includes the bar code and the words "Retain Tag For Reference" (the last four numbers of the bar code are the same as the style number!).

The second-generation hangtag.

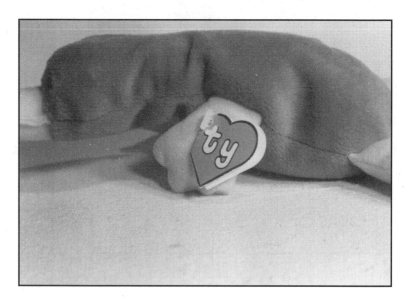

The Third-Generation Hangtag (Mid-1995 to Mid-1996)

The third-generation hangtag is fatter than the previous two generations, which is why it's often called the "bubble ty." The tag itself has put on a few pounds—it's a little bigger and less "squished"-looking than generations one and two, but the "ty" is still white and outlined in gold on a red background.

Here are more details on the third-generation hangtag:

➤ On the inner front of the tag, once again you'll find the words "The Beanie Babies Collection."

➤ On most tags, the corporate addresses also appear on the inner front (others may have similar information that had been found on the inner front of the second-generation tags).

➤ The Beanie's name and style number as well as the "To/From/With Love" lines appear on the inner back (but may be in italics).

➤ A few Beanies have their name in lowercase letters.

➤ The back of the tag may be the same as the second generation, or it may include notes about removing the tag, laundering information, and the bar code.

The third-generation hangtag.

The Fourth-Generation Hangtag (Mid-1996 to Late 1997)

Big changes came along with the fourth-generation hangtags. Gone is the gold outline around the "ty," although the gold foil still outlines the heart.

Get the Scoop

Bumble is the only Beanie whose fourth-generation tag is actually more valuable than the third generation, since Bumble was retired just as the fourth-generation tags came out.

Here are the other changes:

➤ A big yellow star appears just above the right side of the "y," with the words "BEANIE," "ORIGINAL," and "BABY" printed in block letters inside the star.

➤ The inner back of the tag now carries not just the Beanie's name and style number, but also a date of birth! The birthday is in mm-dd-yy format. Every current Beanie also has a short four-line poem.

➤ The back of the tag carries the removal warning and "Surface Wash."

The fourth-generation hangtag.

The Fifth-Generation Hangtag (Early 1998 to Present)

Apparently getting bored with the status quo,
Ty changed the font in the printing on the fifth-
generation tags for a more whimsical look. Other than
the font change, the only other major changes are:

➤ The style number from the inner back by is the
Beanie name is dropped (although it still
appears as the last four digits of the bar code on
the back of the tag).

➤ The date of birth is spelled out completely. (That
means that Beanies are Year 2000-compatible!)

Get the Scoop

A few of the December 31, 1997
retired Beanies, like Cubbie, Nip,
and Lizzy, were shipped with fifth-
generation tags early in 1998.

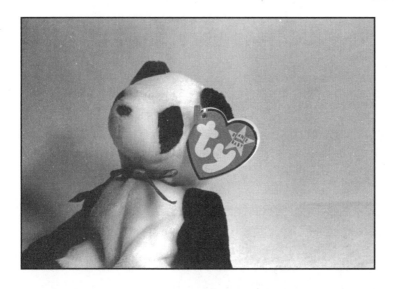

*The fifth-generation
hangtag.*

Tush Tags

Bringing up the rear on the Beanie Babies is what is known as the "tush tag," normally
found on (you guessed it!)—a Beanie's rump. Tush tags are made of cloth, not paper,
and are printed just one side only and then folded over before being sewn into the
seam. The terms "tush tag" and "sewn-in tag" are synonymous, and both refer to the
smaller tag sewn into a Beanie's end seam.

Technically, a few Beanies don't even have tushes at all, so in those cases the tush tag
may appear on a side or a leg—but the term "tush tag" persists. The tush tag is the
other means of helping identify a genuine Beanie Baby as opposed to a knock-off or
counterfeit. The difference between a "knock-off" and a "counterfeit" is that knock-offs
don't pretend to be a Beanie Baby. A counterfeit Beanie, however, is a deliberate
attempt to hoodwink a buyer into thinking they are getting the real thing: a Beanie
Baby with real Ty hangtags and tush tags.

Beanie Tails

You may run across a Beanie with a second tush tag printed in black ink on white, with one side written in English and the other in French. This extra tag appears on Beanies destined for resale in Canada. The code "MW3T" and "MW3MT" refer to Beanies with the extra Canadian tush tag and stand for "Mint with 3 tags" and "Mint with 3 mint tags."

The First-Generation Tush Tag (Pre-Beanie to Late 1995)

When tush tags started out, they were printed in black ink on white (although the white has typically faded over time). This tush tag is found on all Beanies with a first- or second-generation hangtag. Here's how to distinguish a first-generation tush tag:

➤ Unlike subsequent generations, there are no graphics on the black-and-white tush tag other than the copyright symbol.

➤ Five lines of printing on each side (but some of the very earliest Beanies may only have four lines).

The first-generation tush tag.

First-generation tush tag

The Second-Generation Tush Tag (Early 1996 to Mid-1996)

Are you ready for some real mind-boggling confusion? The second-generation tush tags appear only on Beanies with third-generation hangtags. Go figure. These second-generation tags have:

➤ Red ink on white tags

➤ Ty's heart logo (with "ty" in the middle of it) on one side of the tag

➤ Country of origin, corporate, instructions, and composition information on the other side

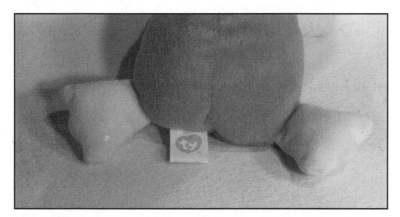

The second-generation tush tag.

The Third-Generation Tush Tag (Mid-1996 to Mid-1997)

As the tush tags evolved from the second to the third generation, the Beanie's name was added, which led to a new problem: mistagged Beanies. Even swing tags were rarely incorrect on earlier Beanies, but with the Beanie's name on the tush, mistakes are cropping up more often.

Other new details on the third-generation tush tags are:

➤ "The Beanie Babies Collection" notation (previously found only on the hangtag)

➤ A smaller heart logo (in order to fit in the new information)

➤ Country of origin, corporate, legal, and instructional information on the other side of the tag

253

*The third-generation
tush tag.*

The Fourth-Generation Tush Tag (Mid-1997 to Mid-1998)

During the summer of 1997, clear stickers started appearing over the heart logo on the tush tags. Each sticker had a little red star in the upper left-hand corner, and before long the star was added to the actual tag.

*The fourth-generation
tush tag.*

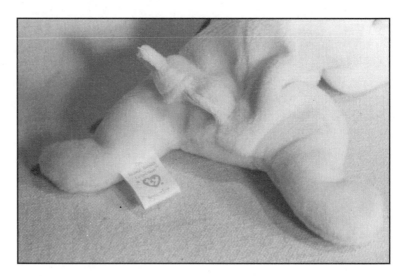

Beanie Tails

If you're holding a "stickered" Beanie, you may be disappointed to learn they're not worth a lot, even though the stickers appeared for only a short time. The stickers do give you an indication that the particular Beanie was produced mid-1997, making them a little older than those with the printed star.

The Fifth-Generation Tush Tag (Mid-1998 to Present)

Fifth-generation tush tags are still very new and may be nothing more than an anomaly, not a "true" fifth generation. The tags are the same as the fourth-generation tags, but inside of the tag fold you'll find a red stamp of concentric ovals. In the inner oval is a number, and in between the inner and outer ovals are a series of Chinese characters. Although the meaning behind these stamps is unknown, the Chinese characters seem to identify the factory at which the Beanie was manufactured. These stamps may be a quality control measure.

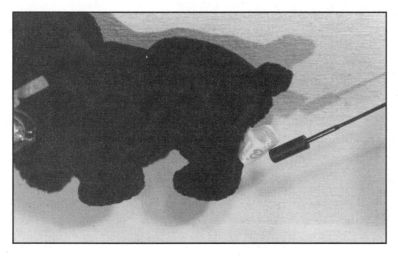

The fifth-generation tush tag.

Missing in Action

When it comes to missing tush tags, you're more likely to find a Beanie Baby whose tush tag has been removed than one that never had a tag to start with. You can usually see the ragged edges where the tag was cut, since it's nearly impossible to remove the tush tag close enough to the seam. If you're lucky, you may stumble upon a legitimate Beanie Baby whose tush tag was overlooked during the manufacturing process.

Tush Tag Details

The information on the tush tags isn't as consistent as some of the information on the hangtags, but all of them should have these references:

➤ Copyright symbol followed by the year of copyright for that particular Beanie

➤ The name "TY INC" (punctuation varies slightly)

➤ A reference to "Oakbrook, IL, USA" (punctuation varies slightly)

➤ The term "all new material"

➤ The term "polyester fiber"

➤ The words either "PVC pellets" (polyvinylchloride) or "PE pellets" (polyethylene)

On the Sly

Dishonest collectors can counterfeit not just the Beanie Babies, but their tags as well—so having a Beanie Baby hangtag alone doesn't guarantee that what you really have is a genuine Ty Beanie Baby.

Baby Talk

Mint condition means that a Beanie has never been played with; their plush body is shiny and in perfect condition.

What's in a Tag?

The tags are the only way you'll know for sure that you have an original Beanie Baby from the Beanie Babies Collection, rather than one of the many "knock-off" beanbag toys now flooding stores in the hopes of capturing some of the market. (See Chapter 21 for more on counterfeits.)

Unfortunately, not all Beanie Babies still have their hangtags—especially older Beanies. After all, long before Beanies became a collector's item, they were just a cute children's toy. Like most toys, parents removed the tags before giving them to their kids to play with. Even if the hangtag wasn't removed, it may have been squashed, chewed on, crinkled up, or written on. That's one of the reasons that the older Beanies—pretty much any Beanie retired before January 1, 1997—cost so much in *mint condition* with mint tags (or even with non-mint tags).

"Mint" doesn't necessarily mean the hangtag is intact—so if you're in doubt, ask. Often the term "mint with mint tags" is used instead of just "mint" to indicate the tags are in place and in perfect condition as well. These meanings are often abbreviated as "MWMT" (mint with mint tags) or "MWBMT" (mint with both mint tags). "MWCT" (mint with creased tag) refers to a Beanie with a creased tag. (It's okay if your tush tag was folded or creased, but it shouldn't be torn or frayed!)

To Tag or Not to Tag

A Beanie without a hangtag will be less valuable—but for many collectors, it may be the opportunity for you to get a Beanie that you wouldn't be able to afford otherwise. Unless you're intent in having only pristine Beanies in absolutely "mint" condition in your collection (and some collectors are), don't necessarily pass on a deal for a Beanie without a hangtag: It could be an intermediate step to getting the Beanie of your dreams. You can always upgrade later if you want to do so. In the meantime, you can enjoy the company of the tagless Beanie at about half the cost of a tagged Beanie!

It's not that hard to find Beanies in mint condition with mint tags. On the Internet, try **http:// www.beaniemom.com**, which is updated weekly. Or check out a magazine like *The Beanie Mania Newsletter* (published biweekly), which includes an updated pricing guide and pricing references for all generations of hangtags. (See Appendixes B and C for more on Beanie books and magazines and Beanie Web sites, respectively.)

On the Sly

When shopping for a Beanie, don't just grab one off the shelf and race to the checkout counter. Find one with an expression you like. Check the seams and tags to make sure they're in good condition with the right name. (Mistagged Beanies usually won't hold their value.)

Don't Mutilate That Tag!

It's not so easy to gauge the price of Beanies with bent, creased, or otherwise less-than-perfect tags. More recently retired Beanies are plentiful and easily found in mint condition with mint tags for a low price. Older Beanies may be harder to locate no matter what kind of tag you're talking about, let alone a tag in mint condition. A creased tag on a rare Beanie may not affect the price as much as one on a recently retired toy.

The effect of creasing also depends on whether the crease is on the front of the tag (more noticeable), the back of the tag, or (horrors!) both sides. Creases on the front of the tag lower the value of the Beanie more than those on the back of the tag (except on first-generation hangtags that aren't folded at all). A "lightly" creased tag will show some surface damage, but there shouldn't be any white showing through the red ink on the front of the heart. A single crease may decrease the value up to 25 percent, depending on the length and depth of the crease.

Get the Scoop

If your Beanie tag is only slightly bent, try correcting the damage by placing it under a heavy book, slipping it into a plastic tag protector, or ironing it under a cloth on low heat (don't use steam!) Even if the bend remains, the value may only be decreased by as little as 5 percent.

How does a mutilated tag affect the price?

➤ A heavily creased tag can take as much as 40 percent off your Beanie.

➤ Mangled tags (with rips or holes) on all but the oldest Beanies is just as bad as not having a tag at all, and may cut the value in half.

➤ Very old Beanies (such as a Spotless Spot or one of the old-faced Teddies) may lose 45 percent.

➤ A missing hangtag cuts the values by 50 percent.

➤ A missing tush tag *and* hangtag takes off 75 percent.

Don't Lose the Price Tag

A hangtag with a price tag on it may seem like a bad idea, but in the world of collectibles price tags are a GOOD thing. As long as the price sticker is also in mint condition and found on the back of the tag, its presence shouldn't bother your Beanie. However, if the price sticker is on the front of the tag or covers the Beanie's name—or if it's obvious you've tried to rip it off with your nail file—it may lower the value.

Sticker Shock

Some price stickers hang onto the tags tighter than a tick on a mule, so go carefully if you want to remove the sticker. Try aiming your hair dryer (on low heat) at the sticker for a few minutes, and then *slowly* try peeling off the sticker. Remember: A price tag may not affect the value of your Beanie, but a botched removal job can ruin its value! A Beanie tag with sticker residue is less valuable.

If you've removed the tag and now there's a mess of sticker "goo" left over, cheer up! You can buy products to remove it. However, these products are often oil-based, which may cause the ink on the tag to smear. Use these products sparingly.

Classic Beanie Mistags and Errors

Nobody promised us a perfect world, and even in Beaniedom, our beloved Beanies are not immune to errors. Some of these errors are considered "classic," meaning they affect shipments or production runs of Beanies.

Contrary to popular belief, just because you have a Beanie with an incorrect tag doesn't mean you can put yourself through college with the proceeds from its sale. Oddly enough, these mistagged Beanies aren't usually more valuable, although there are a few "classic" tag errors that may be exceptions to this rule (see Chapter 19 for more on tag errors). The reason: Hangtags can be changed too easily to be considered a legitimate mistag.

Tush tags with the wrong name (although not easily changed) shouldn't misidentify the Beanie. Let's say a Bumble was wearing Scoop's tush tag. He's still a Bumble, but he's not worth that much more. As with everything Beanie, there are a few collectors who think mistagged Beanies are interesting, but "interesting" doesn't necessarily mean "valuable."

The Least You Need to Know

➤ All Beanie Babies have a heart-shaped red tag outlined in gold foil with the name "ty" in white on the front and the "Beanie Babies Collection" phrase.

➤ Hangtags and tush tags can help you pinpoint the age of your Beanie.

➤ Check out the hangtags and tush tags to make sure you have a genuine Beanie.

➤ A badly mutilated tag can cut your Beanie's value in half.

Chapter 19

Ally-Oops

In This Chapter

➤ Read about which Beanies had typographical errors on their tags

➤ Discover which Beanies have had multiple identities

➤ Learn about designed and redesigned Beanies

➤ Find out which Beanies have had trademark problems

➤ Unravel the mystery of Rainbow and Iggy

➤ Find out if errors mean big bucks

It's not a perfect world, and even our beloved Beanies are not immune to errors. But some errors are more significant than others; some are considered "classic" in that they have affected entire shipments or production runs, not just an occasional Beanie hither or thither.

Gathering information on errors and mistags can be difficult, since Ty doesn't generally confirm when an error has been made. The only way we can really tell is by observing what happens over time and making educated guesses based on what we see.

I remember during the summer of 1997 when I hit the Beanie jackpot one day at a store while on vacation in Michigan. (Okay, actually my sister found them.) I managed to get a whole slew of currents I was still missing, including some of the then-new Mother's Day releases like Doodle. Among the new acquisitions were a black-and-white whale and a steel-blue dolphin, both of whom sat upright rather than lying down like Flash and Splash.

When we returned home, we started going through our treasures, reading the poems out loud and learning the names of each Beanie. We read the tags on the dolphin and started calling him Waves. Then we got to the whale—but it seemed strange that the whale's name was Echo. Dolphins are the ones who use a kind of sonar echo to investigate their surroundings, not whales.

It wasn't until we got back from vacation (and back to the computer) that we realized that our Echo and our Waves were mistagged, as were all the first shipments. Boy, was that confusing!! Little did we know that less than a year later, we'd be even more confused when Ty came out with Iggy and Rainbow!

What's in a Name?

There have been a few Beanies over time who have been subjected to either typographical errors or name changes. Trying to tell whether a Beanie has been the victim of an errant typesetter during production is anybody's guess for the most part. Oh, there are some that are more obvious than others—especially if the error is in the middle of the name (like "Tusk" and "Tuck"), but who can really tell whether a missing "S" at the end of a name was just an oversight or intentional? It's just about impossible, if there's no other way to confirm it (such as by a poem or tush tag). After all, Beanies retired before June 1996 never had poems or names on their tush tags.

Of course, now Ty has a checklist as part of the Beanie Babies Official Club, and that's helped a lot. It doesn't answer the questions about *why* Punchers became Pinchers or Nana became Bongo, but it does tell us which Beanies Ty recognizes as being distinct and unique. Every little bit helps!

Get the Scoop

When referring to a Beanie mistag error, most collectors call the Beanie by its true name followed by the mistag name. Therefore, Maples with "Pride" tush tags are known as "Maple/Pride," Echos with Waves tags are known as "Echo/Waves," and so on.

Typical Typos

Here's a rundown of some of the more common typographical errors you may run across in your search for Beanies.

Quackers

Both wingless and winged Quackers were released with the "s" missing from the name on his hangtag. We have to assume this was an oversight, since both were also released with the "s," and Quackers regained and kept the "s" until his retirement in May 1998. This particular error occurred only on the hangtag, since the tush tags didn't have the Beanie's name on them at the time.

Spooky

Another "only Ty knows for sure" error occurred with Spooky the ghost. The first (and until October 1997, the only) non-animal Beanie's name was "Spook" without the "y," but even now we don't really know if his name was initially supposed to be "Spook" or "Spooky." Like Quackers, this "classic" Beanie was released during a time where the Beanie's name didn't appear on the tush tag, so we don't have a way to confirm it as a true error as opposed to a renaming. "Spook" Beanies have been growing in value as collectors have begun to realize just how rare this error is.

Tusk

One Beanie that we know came with a typographical error in his name is Tusk. Some fourth-generation Tusks had the name printed as "Tuck" on their hangtags, while the tush tags (which by then did have the name on them) still called this charming walrus "Tusk." Although "Tuck" Beanies are rare, the price difference between Tusk and "Tuck" is minimal.

Get the Scoop

Third-generation Spookys were the only Beanies who actually list a designer's name on the tag. Spooky was designed by Jenna Boldebeck. A funny thing happened on the way to the printer, though: The word "designed" got spelled as "desined" on some of the tags.

Libearty

Libearty's error didn't involve his name, but rather a typographical error on his tush tag where the word "Beanie" in "The Beanie Babies Collection" was actually printed as "Beanine." Unlike the other classics, the "Beanine Libearty" is actually the more common find. Remember that Libearty was only out for about six months before he was retired, so there wasn't much time to correct this error.

On the Surface...

Also found on the "Beanine" tush tags was another misspelling. The word "surface" in "surface wash" was spelled out as "sufrace" with the "f" and the "r" transposed. The "sufrace" misspelling also occurred on Righty and Lefty tush tags as well as some of the other mid-1996 releases.

For some reason, "surface" really gave Ty typesetters a migraine. In early 1998, "surface" was mistyped on the back of the hangtag as "suface." Some efforts were made to correct this error with a little sticker placed over the tag with the correct spelling.

The "suface" misspelling on Valentino.

Beanie Tails

When the fifth-generation hangtags came onto the scene, a number of Beanies (Curly, Valentino, Blackie, Peace, and the three pastel bunnies Floppity, Hippity, and Hoppity) all had typos in the star on the front of their hangtags. It's a little odd that this typo didn't appear on all the new Beanies. The word "Original" ended up with the second "i" doubled up and spelled as "Origiinal." There hasn't been any extra value associated with the double-i tags so far.

The "origiinal" typo.

Name Changes

Typos aren't the only problems cropping up from time to time in the world of Beanie Babies. Read on for more details on name changes.

Maple/Pride

Did you know that Maple's name probably wasn't Maple in the beginning? Nobody really knows for sure, but the popular guesstimate is that about 3,000 to 5,000 Maples were released with a tush tag advertising "Pride" instead of "Maple." Given the already enormous popularity of Maple, the Maple/Pride Beanies are highly desirable, quite rare, and very valuable.

Cubbie/Brownie

The little fellow we know as "Cubbie," retired since October 1, 1997, was originally released as "Brownie." The two bears are identical with the exception of the name on their first-generation hangtags. You need to know that because many people will try to sell a "tagless" Brownie for a great deal of money. Without a hangtag that actually says "Brownie" on it, consider that Beanie to be a Cubbie. Ty lists Cubbie on their Beanie Babies Official Club checklist as "formerly Brownie," but lost to history is whether or not Brownie became Cubbie before or after the Original Nine were introduced. For our purposes, we've considered Brownie as a "pre-Beanie" Beanie.

Pinchers/Punchers

Unlike Cubbie/Brownie, there *is* a difference between Pinchers and his predecessor Punchers—but the difference is slight, having to do with the spacing of segments on the tail. In fact, it's so slight that like Cubbie/Brownie, most people want to see the swing tag with "Punchers" on his first-generation swing tag before they'll pay the premium. Just for the record, though, the segments in Puncher's tail are evenly spaced. The middle two segments on Punchers' tail are smaller than the outer ones. Punchers is usually considered a "pre-Beanie" just like Brownie.

Get the Scoop

At the moment, Bongo's tail is tan again and brown-tailed Bongos go for a premium. Maybe Ty makes the tail out of whichever material they seem to have on hand!

Bongo/Nana

Bongo has a varied and slightly confusing history himself. His original name was Nana, but for some unknown reason, Ty opted for a name change. A few of the monkeys with a "Nana" hangtag swung out of the trees, however. Others had a sticker with the name "Bongo" pasted over the "Nana." (Remember that this was before Beanie names were included on the tush tag.)

Nana should have a third-generation hangtag, first-generation tush tag, and a tan tail that matches her face, but so does Bongo. In order to be sure the Beanie is "Nana," look for the name in the swing tag. Later, Bongo's tail changed to match the darker plush of his body—and it has alternated back and forth ever since.

Spinner/Creepy?

In the "who knows" category, some Spinners delivered to stores in the United Kingdom appeared with tags listing his name as "Creepy." Since there isn't a Beanie named Creepy (at least not yet), many collectors are speculating that Spinner/Creepy may well fall into the same category as Maple/Pride—that is, that "Creepy" may have been Spinner's original name.

Wrong Tags

Sometimes the wrong tags just seem to end up on the wrong Beanies. Read on for more.

Sparky/Dotty

Foretelling Sparky's long-rumored and imminent demise, the final litter of Sparkys appeared with Dotty tush tags. Sparky/Dotty Beanies are fairly rare, but, like Tuck/Tusk, the difference in value between the correctly tagged version and the mistag is pretty minimal, only about $5 difference between Sparky and Sparky/Dotty.

Echo/Waves and Waves/Echo

Echo and Waves were a double error. When first released in May 1997, both Echo's hang- and tush tags named him as Waves, and Waves' hang and tush tags named him as Echo. Many collectors didn't realize the error until the correctly tagged versions came out, or until they heard different from someone who had Internet access. Now that both are retired, the mistagged versions go for a little bit more money. They're usually referred to as "Echo/Waves" (Echo with Waves tags) and "Waves/Echo" (Waves with Echo tags).

Snort/Tabasco

Snort had a bit of an identity crisis himself in late summer 1997. Some of the Canadian versions of Snort were released with the name "Tabasco" in his poem. The name Snort appeared on hang- and tush tags, but the poem started out "Although Tabasco is not so tall..." Since this error only occurred on Canadian Snorts, look for the second tush tag on this rare Beanie. (We discuss Tabasco's trademark problem a little later in this chapter.)

Birthday Errors

Even birthdays aren't sacred! Scottie (now retired) has had two different birthdays on his swing tags: June 3, 1996, and June 15, 1996. Freckles can be found with some tags listing July 28, 1996, and others June 3, 1996, as his birthday.

Redesigns

Sometimes, things don't go wrong at the factory—variations happen because the company deliberately redesigns a Beanie Baby.

Bongo

When you're talking monkey designs, look for two different colors of tails on Bongo. Some of the tails are tan and match Bongo's face and paws. Others are a darker brown that matches Bongo's body. The tan tail is current, but the color has gone back and forth several times during Bongo's lifetime.

Derby

The original Derby had a mane and tail of fine brown yarn, about the same weight as the yarn used in baby booties. The fine-maned Derby has about 40 strands of yarn in his mane. No matter how much you "yarn" for him, he is one of the rarest Beanies around. Not long after his release, designers went from fine to coarse yarn because it was less likely to fray. In early 1998, Derby earned a white star on his forehead, but kept the coarse mane and tail.

Get the Scoop

While the red version of Digger is much more common and quite reasonably priced, you'll need to break the piggy bank for the orange Digger.

Digger

Digger comes in two colors, and both of them are beautiful. The first Digger looked like an ad for Sunkist—the color of a bright orange and the same color as Goldie the goldfish. Although the orange was stunning, about a year after his release Ty changed him to red (like Pinchers).

Happy

Maybe Happy didn't look so engaging when he was gray, but many collectors prefer the businessman-gray version (especially if they were lucky enough to get him at $5). Ty may have changed the color to make the kids happier. In any case, Happy turned a lovely lilac color and remained that way until he was retired in May 1998.

Inch

Inch's redesign was very subtle. Originally wearing felt antennae, the "felt-tipped" Inch gave way to one bearing black yarn antennae in the latter half of 1996. The felt-tipped Inch isn't difficult to find if you've got a source for retired Beanies, but you can expect to pay about $150 for him while the more recently retired version can be had for about $15.

Inky

A light taupe Inky was the first on the Beanie scene. The first version didn't have a mouth at all, but the second smiled through a thread V-shaped smile. Maybe the smile wasn't enough to cheer Inky up, because he turned bright pink later in life. The tan versions are pretty pricey, and the pink version is one of the more expensive of the May 1, 1998, retireds.

Lizzy

Lizzy's original beautiful jewel and earth tone tie-dyed plush will leave you dizzy. But not one to rest on its laurels, Ty redesigned her with black spots on blue fabric on top and orange spots on yellow fabric on her tummy. The tie-dyed version is very hard to find and will cost about $1,100 in mint condition.

Lucky

You can easily spot the three different designs of Lucky. They're known as the 7-spot, 11-spot, and 21-spot versions, though the exact number of spots may vary slightly from these numbers. The 7-spot version's spots were actually made of black felt—but sometimes the spots fell off. You can't really have a ladybug without her spots, so Ty started using plush with the spots printed into the fabric. For a short time in 1996, small black spots dotted Lucky's back, but the spots grew in size and decreased in number to about 11. The 21-spot version is the rarest of the three and may run you as much as $600.

Mystic

Mystic's mane and tail started out with baby-fine yarn, but the fine-maned version has been in stores longer than Derby's fine-maned self, so it's not nearly as pricey. The coarse mane is current. The fine-maned version will cost about $200. In fall 1997, the long-rumored Mystic with an iridescent horn started appearing in stores. Until then, Mystic's horn had been golden tan.

> **Get the Scoop**
>
> Don't worry if you see horns of different lengths—it's just a slight variation in the manufacturing process.

Nip

Nip and Zip live in parallel universes; each has had three distinct designs since their creation. (Zip is featured a little later in this chapter.)

➤ Nip number 1: A very large head with a triangle of white from the middle of his forehead down over his belly.

➤ Nip number 2: This version featured a much smaller head. The second version had no white on his face or body, so he's known as the "all-gold Nip." The solid version wasn't on sale long, so it's the most valuable of the three (around $1,000 in mint condition).

➤ Nip number 3 (most common): White paws and white on the insides of his ears instead of pink, like his forerunners.

Patti

Officially, there are only two different Pattis, according to Ty: "maroon" and "magenta." Maybe it's only a dye lot difference in the fabric, but I've seen at least four different colors—and I own three of them. (Take a look at the pictures in the color section to see these differences.)

Peanut

The original Peanut is probably the most sought-after of all the Beanies. Though it's assumed the original color plush was a mistake, we don't know for sure. Maybe Ty really did intend this Queen of the pachyderms to be adorned in royal blue. What we do know for sure is that she didn't stay that way for long. Soon after her release, she appeared with light baby blue plush in place of the royal robe. Another thing we know for sure is that if you decide you really must have the Royal Blue Peanut in your castle, you will have to shell out between $4,500 and $5,000 for her in mint condition with mint tags.

Quackers

Whoever thought up Quackers' original design must have been having a bad day! A wingless duck? But that's exactly the way Quackers was first released. Sadly, the little guy was unbalanced and tended to lean. It wasn't long, though, before the folks at Ty took pity on him and Quackers got his wings. Some rumors claim there were less than 1,000 of the wingless Quackers produced, but I find that a little hard to swallow. What isn't rumor is the $1,900 to $2,100 price tag on a mint wingless Quackers.

Get the Scoop

Amazingly, the brown–bellied version of Sly still is reasonably priced (the $125 to $150 range), but I don't expect it to stay that way—especially now that Sly is retired.

Sly

I vote for the first Sly as the most undervalued out-of-production Beanie! The original fox had a belly made of the same brown plush as the rest of him, but someone must have pointed out that real foxes have white stomachs, not brown. Ty, wanting to be true to life, released a white-bellied version within just a month or two.

Spot

It must have been a joke. That's the only reason I can think of for a dog named "Spot" not to have even one blotch. Well, actually, he does—but it was on his face, more like a "patch" than a "spot." The original Spot is known by several names:

➤ Spot without a Spot

➤ Spotless Spot

➤ Spot no Spot

➤ Spot-less

Whatever-you-call-him-Spot was missing the little black half-circle spot on his back that most collectors know him by today. The spotless version will cost you a fair bit, around $1,900 to $2,100 in mint condition.

Stripes

Dark or light, thin or wide, the older, darker version of Stripes is the Beanie to have. It's easy to tell the difference, especially if you've seen the more recent Stripes "light."

The darker version has black stripes on a dark golden orange fabric, and the stripes are fairly close together (about 16 stripes on his tail). The "light" Stripes has a background of lighter yellow tan plush with about eight stripes on his tail.

Tank

It took Ty three tries to get Tank anatomically correct—or at least closer to being anatomically correct. When Tank first meandered onto the Beanie scene, he had seven lines. (By "line," we mean a line of stitching, not the fabric in between the stitching.) The seven lines were okay, but he was missing his shell—and everyone knows an armadillo needs a shell.

Get the Scoop

If you want a truly rare version, some of the dark Stripes had bellies made from a longer, fuzzier plush. These fuzzy-bellied versions command about $800 to $1,000 on the secondary market. You're better off with the plain dark version at around $250 if you're counting your pennies.

In his second incarnation, Tank was longer but not more rounded, and had added another couple of rows of stitching. But he still didn't have a shell. The nine-line version made a pretty good football for kids to toss around, but he looked a bit funny.

Not one to give up until getting it right, Ty's last version of Tank has a row of stitching along the bottom edge of his body that forms a quasi-shell, making him look a bit more normal—well, at least as normal as an armadillo can look. But the last version was shorter, more rounded and he lost the embroidered nostrils that were found on the previous versions.

Zip

Zippity-doo-dah! Zip and his buddy Nip went through similar changes as they worked their way through their nine—well, actually three— lives. The first Zip had a head as round as a tennis ball, with a triangle of white plush running from the middle of his forehead down his stomach.

White-faced Zip lasted about a year before being remodeled, with a downsized head and an all-black color (exception: pink plush in his inner ears). The all-black version of Zip was only available for a few months in the beginning of 1996, making him one of the most valuable Beanies around. (He'll set you back about $1,500 to $1,700.)

Even the third and last version of Zip has some value—he's one of the most difficult to find from the May 1, 1998, retirement group. He differs from his previous incarnation by virtue of his white paws and his white inner ears.

Name Conflicts

From time to time, Ty has had a problem with name conflicts, leading to preternaturally early retirements for a few Beanies. Rumors of any name conflict always run rampant; people seem to thrive on the hint of a potential retirement. Among rumored name-related retirements have been these Beanies.

Blizzard

This little guy was dogged from the beginning by retirement rumors because he shares his name with a brand of car tire and an ice cream concoction from a national fast-food chain. Blizzard did indeed retire, but not due to any actual known lawsuit.

Chops

Almost everyone (young and old) is familiar with the late ventriloquist Shari Lewis and her puppet pal, Lamb Chop. Chops was retired after just a year and replaced by another little lamb (Fleece), so many collectors think her demise was due in large part to a tie with Shari's little lamb.

Get the Scoop

Surprisingly, Doodle has not (yet!) followed in the footsteps of some of the other short-lived Beanies, and a year later is still relatively inexpensive as retired Beanies go—commanding less than other more aged Beanies like Seamore and Bessie.

Crunch

These rumors were swirling around the candy bar by the same name—but Crunch was still alive and swimming for 18 months until his September 1998 retirement.

Doodle

Released on Mother's Day in 1997, it didn't take long for rumors of Doodle's conflict with a fast-food chain (Chick-Fil-A) that used a trademarked rooster mascot named Doodles. Sure enough, very quietly, on August 15 Doodle disappeared from Ty's Web site checklist and was replaced by an identical twin named Strut.

Garcia

The tie-dyed tribute to the late Grateful Dead singer Jerry Garcia apparently ran into problems with Garcia's estate. Rumored to be a last-minute retirement on Mother's Day 1997, Garcia came back to life as the very similar and popular Peace the bear. The only difference (besides the name, obviously) is that Peace carries a multi-colored embroidered peace sign on his chest. Being bears, of course, both are extremely popular, and even now, Peace is one of the hardest Beanies to find.

Sparky

Not surprisingly, a Dalmatian named Sparky has long been used by the National Fire Protection Association. They took polite exception to Ty's Beanie Baby with the same name, and Ty retired Sparky after just nine months. News of Sparky's pending retirement leaked out of the bag when he started showing up with tush tags emblazoned with the name "Dotty." The Sparky/Dotty Beanie Babies are considered a classic Beanie error.

Tabasco

Tabasco became hot stuff after his January 1997 retirement due to the hot sauce of the same name. Accordingly, his price skyrocketed and by mid-summer that year was already being snapped up by any collector who could find him, for $150 and up.

Today, he's still popular, but his price has leveled off to the $175 to $200 range. Tabasco was replaced as he retired by Snort, who seems to be identical at first glance—but with cream-colored paws instead of Tabasco's all-red feet.

Wise

This chip off the block is the latest Beanie to carry the brunt of retirement rumors, because a potato chip company with the same name uses an owl as their symbol. However, Wise's days were always numbered right from the start, because of the number on his mortar board (Class of 1998). He's most likely destined to retire quickly regardless of any name conflict.

All of the Above—Rainbow and Iggy

The saga of Rainbow and Iggy is enough to drive a collector to madness. Though originally thought to have been a question of reversed tags the same way Echo and Waves were, collectors soon began to realize that the body style of the pastel tie-dyed Beanie tagged Iggy really did look like an iguana, not a chameleon, and that the blue tie-dyed Rainbow looked like a chameleon.

However, the poems didn't match because Rainbow's poem talked about, well, the rainbow colors of a chameleon, even though his plush was blue. Collectors waited to see if these January 1998 releases would carry "correct" tags or whether the plush would be switched to make the poems and style match the tags.

Instead, the Beanie tagged "Iggy" with the felt spine and pastel tie-dye appeared with a short pinkish velveteen tongue, but still maintained his Iggy tags. This version, too, appeared to be short-lived.

Recently, the felt-spiked Iggy with blue tie-dye and the hooded Rainbow with pastel tie-dye have started to surface, so it appears that collectors figured it out long before the factories!

On the Sly

If you want to buy one of these exceptional errors, look carefully to make sure that someone hasn't just ripped off a leg or taken a leg from another similar Beanie and stitched it on.

Sorry, Wrong Number

There are some Beanies who are notorious for popping up with an extra or missing leg. Since these go for a premium, it may pay you well to start counting the legs on Beanies like Inky, Digger, Claude, and Stinger.

Blank Stares

It pays to check those Beanie tags, because sometimes a glitch in the printing process causes problems. More and more of these errors have been showing up lately. You may be able to find a tag that's missing the printing of "Original Beanie Baby" in the yellow star on the front of the fourth-generation hangtag. (Some of the original Jolly shipments were known for that.) You might also get lucky and find a tag that missed getting printed inside, so not only is the company information missing, but so is the Beanie's name, birthday, and poem!

Upside Down and Missing in Action

Any Beanie with a patch or embroidery on its chest is a potential victim of a unique error. Sometimes (as with Valentino and Maple, or Garcia and Peace), the only way to know what Beanie you actually have is by checking the hang- and tush tags. Princess has been spotted without her rose; Erin without her shamrock. Glory, though newly released, seems to have suffered more than his share of missing and upside-down flags. Less common is to find a Lefty, Righty or Libearty missing theirs.

These Beanies do bring a high price on the secondary market, but make sure if you're looking into one of these that the tags match each other and that someone hasn't removed the embroidery or patch by hand.

The Value of an Error

Are Beanies with errors more valuable than those who are correct? There's no easy answer to that question. Classic errors do tend to bring slightly more. The exception is in those cases where the error is actually more common than the correct Beanie (as is in the case of Libearty). But you may find that a seller will try to convince you that it's worth more. Just remember the primary rule: A Beanie is only worth what someone is willing to pay for it. If you *really* want that Righty with the upside-down flag and the seller wants more than the current $450 to $500 value, only you can decide if it's worth it to you.

Just remember that a Beanie with an incorrect swing tag really isn't worth any more. Swing tags can be switched by hand easily. A Beanie with a wrong hangtag really might as well not have any swing tag unless, by some chance, that's a third-generation mint Rex hangtag on your fifth-generation Crunch. But even then, lots of counterfeit hangtags are running around, too, so you have to study and know those tags pretty well.

Tush tags are another story. Getting those tiny stitches back through the same holes is pretty tricky. But ask yourself this question if you are tempted to buy a "casual" mistag: If this was Princess with a Snort tush tag, would you still want it? I think you'll find the answer is "No."

Get the Scoop

There are some collectors who think these errors are interesting and find them very desirable. If you can find one of them when you're looking to sell your mistagged Beanie, all the better for you!

The Least You Need to Know

➤ You can find typographical errors on names for Quackers, Spooky, Libearty, and Tusk.

➤ Maple, Cubbie, Pinchers, Bongo, and maybe Spinner have had other names.

➤ Echo and Waves were shipped originally with reversed tags.

➤ Some Beanies have been retired because of naming conflicts.

➤ Any Beanie with a patch or embroidery may end up with it missing or upside down.

➤ "Classic" mistags and errors may increase your Beanie's value (but not always); "casual" mistags usually decrease the value of your Beanie.

Chapter 20

Extras for the Beanie Mom (or Dad)

In This Chapter

➤ Discover all kinds of accessories to dress, decorate, and entertain your Beanies

➤ Have fun outfitting your Beanie for every occasion

➤ Learn how to join Ty's Beanie Baby Official Club and get a Clubby bear

I know, I know—all you collectors out there are hoarding Beanies in Ziploc bags to keep them in mint condition—and that's fine! But there are also tons of kids who just love playing with these cuddly toys, and that's really what Ty intended all along.

In fact, kids seem to glom onto their Beanie Babies quicker than a pit bull with a pork chop. And if you'll notice, when you see a bunch of kids with Beanies, odds are they aren't just sitting around leafing through collectible magazines and jotting down the cash value. They really *play* with their Beanies, which is just what Ty had in mind when he created the reasonably priced, well-made stuffed toys.

What do kids do with their Beanies? Just about anything you can think of:

➤ Put on Beanie Baby "puppet" shows

➤ Stage Beanie Baby tea parties

➤ Have special Beanie Baby birthday parties

➤ Play school with Beanie Baby classes

➤ Organize a Beanie Olympics, with medals for winners

➤ Have Beanie sled races

➤ Set up Beanie Baby hospitals

In fact, kids were having so much fun playing with these little critters that soon lots of grownups began to take notice—and an entire new accessory market was born. It didn't take long before Beanie Baby magazines and Web sites were filled with ads offering a wide range of accessories for Beanies to dress in, sit on, sleep in, and eat from!

While these products are widely available, almost none of them are authorized by the Ty company. Ty does bring legal action against those companies it feels are violating its trademarks.

Get the Scoop

Odds are you won't find a big sign on any of these products trumpeting: "Hey! This stuff is designed for Beanie Babies!" Instead, products are usually offered for sale next to Beanie displays.

Furniture and Accessories

There's nothing sadder than a Beanie without a place to sit or sleep. Solution: Beanie Baby furniture, most of it very well made and surprisingly low-priced. Read on to get the lowdown on all these special gadgets and gizmos for your Beanie.

Who's Been Sleeping in MY Bed?

If it's sleeping accommodations you're after, you'll likely find lots to choose from in this department. Check out what's available:

➤ Wooden four-poster beds

➤ Bunk beds

➤ Cradles

➤ Cribs

➤ Sofa hide-a-beds

➤ Cots

Covers and Blankets and Quilts, Oh My!

There's nothing Beanie Babies like better than a nice cozy place to curl up. Fortunately, there are plenty of accessories for the dedicated Beanie mom and dad to provide. Available in all sorts of styles and colors, miniature bedspreads and pillows can be found in just about any specialty shop that carries Beanies, not to mention through mail order (magazine and online—see Appendixes B and C). Personalization is everywhere in the linens department: You can find handmade patchwork quilts with designs to match individual Beanies, matching monogrammed linen sets (with the Beanie name, not your name!), and monogrammed blankets. Just so your Beanies don't get mixed up!

Musical Chairs

If you're looking for a special place for your special Beanie to sit, you won't have to search very far—and they're just the right size, no matter how big or small your Beanie may be. Lots of stores and mail-order catalogs are offering:

➤ Beach chairs

➤ Beanbag chairs

➤ Benches (wooden or cast-iron)

➤ Hassocks

➤ High chairs

➤ Lairs

➤ Stools

➤ Twig chairs

Table-and-Chair Sets

For those Beanies who like to have someplace for a bite to eat while they're sitting around, you can provide a combination table-and-chair set:

➤ Wooden picnic tables

➤ Wooden table and chairs

➤ Wicker table and chairs

➤ Cast-iron table and chairs

Get the Scoop

Toy furniture designed for Beanies is fun to play with if you're a kid—but lots of the furniture also makes an ideal display arrangement for more serious collectors.

L.L. Beanies

Everybody needs a little fresh air, and Beanies are no exception! If you'd like to offer your collection some outdoor fun, you can find a range of outdoorsy equipment, such as:

➤ Tents

➤ Hammocks

➤ Teeter-totters

➤ Ladders

➤ Sleeping bags (sleeping from one to four Beanies)

279

Travelin' Around

Life can be boring if you're just sitting around on a shelf—so to solve that problem, why not buy something that can make your special Beanies more mobile, something they would enjoy riding in on pleasant days? There's lots to choose from, including:

Get the Scoop

If you're into collecting clothing for your Beanie Baby, why not buy some tiny hangers to keep their closets in order? You can find these at doll and toy stores and Beanie displays.

➤ Arks (as in the one Noah built)

➤ Backpacks (for Beanies to ride in)

➤ Carry aprons (carry 'em around!)

➤ Fishing boats (seats two Beanies—and they really float!)

➤ Pet carriers (they're pets—so carry 'em in this!)

➤ Sleds (for snowy days)

➤ Trains (good for display and playing, too)

➤ Wagons (hay wagons or kids' wagons)

➤ Wheelbarrows (makes it easy to push a bunch of Beanies!)

Clothes That Make the Beanie

If you can sew, there's no reason why you can't whip up a variety of smashing outfits for your Beanies. Patterns are available to cut out and make clothes for your Beanie. If you can't sew, never fear! There are many enterprising folks out there sewing little accouterments sized just for style-conscious Beanies.

So what are your options if you'd like to buy a few Beanie outfits? We've seen it all:

➤ Angel outfits

➤ Backpacks

➤ Ballet tutus and slippers

➤ Ballgowns

➤ Bandannas (with embroidered names)

➤ Bathing suits

➤ Berets

➤ Black tie and tails

➤ Blanket sleepers

➤ Bridal gowns and veils

➤ Cheerleader outfits

➤ Clown suits

➤ Cowboy outfits

➤ Detective outfits

➤ Dress and hairbows

➤ Exercise outfits

➤ Feather boas

➤ Fishing outfits

➤ Flower hair wreaths

➤ Glasses/sunglasses

➤ Golf outfits

➤ Graduation caps and gowns

➤ Hats (summer, straw, Victorian, baseball caps)

➤ Headbands

➤ Holiday outfits: Easter Egg costumes and bunny suits, Santa outfits, Valentine heart dresses, Halloween costumes

➤ Hula skirts and bikini tops

➤ Jeans

➤ Jogging outfits

➤ Leather jackets

➤ Martial arts outfits

➤ Overalls

➤ Party dresses

➤ Pilot outfits

➤ Ponchos

➤ School uniforms

➤ Raincoats and boots

➤ Robe and slippers

➤ Scarves

➤ Sheriff outfits

➤ Shoes

➤ Space suits

➤ Sports uniforms and jerseys: baseball, basketball, football, soccer

➤ Sun visors

➤ Sweaters (handknit cardigan, pullover, and turtleneck styles)

➤ Sweatshirts (hooded)

➤ Sweatsuits

➤ Tee shirts

➤ Tennis outfits

➤ Underwear

➤ Vests

Diamonds: A Beanie's Best Friend!

No Beanie can feel fully dressed without her jewelry. You can choose:

➤ A sparkly tiara

➤ Pearls and earrings

➤ Gemstone jewels

➤ A crown and scepter

➤ Brass name tags

➤ Make-your-own plastic bead necklaces (some come with initials to spell out the Beanie's name)

➤ Name tags fashioned after military-issue "dog tags" engraved with the Beanie's name and hung on a keychain

You can also buy jewelry for yourself featuring your favorite Beanies:

➤ Charms of individual Beanies

➤ Necklaces featuring Beanie Baby photos

On the Sly

When buying Beanie clothes, keep in mind whether your animals are boys or girls, and also whether the clothes have a "tail slit" so those Beanies so equipped can fit into them.

➤ Necklaces with Beanie Baby likenesses and the appropriate birth stone from the Beanie's "birth" month

➤ Keychains with individual plush Beanies (moveable arms and legs)

The Best of the Rest

There are so many different types of Beanie Baby paraphernalia it's hard to fit it all into one book. Here's a roundup of some miscellaneous Beanie-related stuff:

➤ Layettes, complete with baby bottle

➤ Beanie Baby biographies, complete with photos and bound and printed in color

➤ Bowls and foods (made of clay)

➤ Collars/harnesses and leashes

➤ Coloring books featuring your favorite Beanies

➤ Personalized Beanie Baby pillows and pillowcases

➤ Magnets

➤ Trading cards

➤ Diaries (to keep an inventory of your Beanies)

➤ Pouches to carry Beanies inside

➤ Bumper stickers

➤ "Parking for Beanie Baby collectors" signs

➤ Stationery

Electronic Beanies

I suspected it wouldn't take long for Beanie Baby lore to make it onto videotapes and CD-ROMS, and I was right. Today you can buy videos to help you learn how to buy, sell, and trade Beanies (check out Chapter 23 of this book also!). There's info on Beanie conventions, how to spot counterfeits, and all the details about tags that can be so confusing! There are videos to help you organize and keep track of your collection. In addition, various CD-ROM programs help you monitor the changing Beanie market and give you access to online auctions where you can buy, sell, or trade.

Join Ty's Beanie Babies Official Club

One of the special products that *has* been endorsed by the Ty company is the Beanie Babies Official Club (BBOC). You can join by buying the membership kit (it's usually sold for around $10) at specialty retailers who carry the Ty line of products. The club began in March 1998 and so far has attracted more than a million members. When you join the club, you get:

➤ An official club certificate of authenticity recognizing you as a member in good standing, with your name laser-printed onto the certificate

➤ A colorful matte suitable for framing the certificate

➤ A wall poster with 136 Beanie Baby stickers to decorate the poster

➤ A charter member gold card with your own special number

➤ A "Do not disturb—Beanie Babies meeting in progress" doorknob sign

➤ Official newsletter filled with games, puzzles, Beanie news, and coloring pictures

➤ Beanie Baby checklist

➤ Clubby the bear (see below)

Beanie Tails

The BBOC was invented by Ty, Inc., but is produced and marketed by Cyrk, Inc.—although Ty has officially endorsed the club. Cyrk is a full-service promotional marketing company, whose stock has skyrocketed since the partnership began.

"Members-Only": Ty Web Site

Once you've joined the BBOC, you can get special access to the BBOC section of the Ty Web site (**http://www.ty.com**) by using your club membership number. Once you're in the Web site, you can play "tic tac ty" with Quackers, print out and color a special Beanie Babies coloring page, do a Clubhouse crossword, or play photo frame riddles. Lots of other fun stuff will most likely be added to this BBOC Web site in the near future, so visit it often!

Clubby the Bear

One of the most special things about joining the Beanie Babies Official Club is the special Beanie Baby you can buy when you join. Clubby was introduced to the world July 10 on television's *Today* show, when Cyrk President Pat Brady brought him onstage. His big unveiling was the next day (July 11) at the Atlanta International Gift and Home Furnishings Show.

Clubby is a deep royal-blue bear wearing a tie-dyed ribbon and the official BBOC logo on his chest, with the numbers "00" in the upper-right of the red heart hang tag. (No one knows what those numbers mean, but there they are.)

He's an exclusive sort of bear, available only to those folks who join the club and then go on to follow the directions. Once you join the club, you must:

1. Send in the official reply card in order to receive the personalized certificate and order form for Clubby.
2. Fill out the Clubby order form.
3. Send it back together with $5.99 plus state sales tax, shipping, and handling.

Remember: You can only get one Clubby per membership card number (this is so Ty can cut down on the hoarding and high secondary prices).

The Least You Need to Know

➤ You'll find lots of accessories that fit your Beanie: jewelry, clothes, furniture, and more.

➤ Ty's Beanie Babies Official Club offers members a special certificate, newsletter, wall poster, and many other goodies.

➤ The only way you can get a Clubby bear is to join the Beanie Babies Official Club and send in the application.

➤ You can only get one Clubby per membership card number.

October 1997 releases: Spinner, Batty, Gobbles, Snowball, and 1997 Teddy.

January 1997 releases: Snort, Doby, Snip, Mel, Crunch, Bernie, Fleece, Hippity, Pouch, Gracie, Hoppity, Nuts, Floppity, and Maple.

Mid-1996 releases: Rover, Wrinkles, Sparky, Freckles, Righty, Lefty, Scottie, Spike, Scoop, Libearty, Curly, Congo, and brown-bellied Sly.

May 1997 releases: (dark) Claude, Chip, Dotty, Roary, Nanook, Tuffy, Blizzard, Pugsly, Baldy, Jolly, Echo, Waves, Doodle, and Peace.

Early 1996 releases: Flutter, Sting, Ziggy, Stinky, red Digger, pink Inky, tie-dye Lizzy, Bubbles, Steg, Waddle, Kiwi, Caw, fine-mane Derby, royal blue Peanut, dark Stripes, lilac Happy, Rex, Tabasco, Bronty, Bessie, Bongo, Magic, and Velvet.

Early 1995 releases: light blue Peanut, black and blue Lizzy, Inch, Ringo, Tusk, Bucky, Flip, Tank, Radar, Derby, Grunt, Mystic, Manny, Bumble, Weenie, Patti, Twigs, Coral, Ears, Seaweed, Garcia, Spooky, white-paw Nip, white-paw Zip, Hooty, and Pinky.

January 1998 releases: Prance, Spunky, Pounce, Bruno, Rainbow-Iggy, Iggy-Rainbow, Hissy, Puffer, Stretch, and Smoochy.

Mid-1998 releases: Stinger, Gigi, Fetch, Early, Whisper, Tracker, Ants, Jabber, Jake, Rocket, Wise, Glory, Fortune, and Kuku.

In the limo: Whisper, Stinger, Tracker, Fetch, Kuku, Glory, Ants, Fortune, Gigi, Jake, Early, Jabber, Wise, and Rocket.

Hissy wraps up Smoochy.

Coral, Bubbles, and Goldie in a bowl.

Legs, Hissy in costume, Hissy on Legs, Ally, and Smoochy.

Crunch 'n' Munch.

Spike the green iguana shares carrots with Iggy and Rainbow.

Derby star, fine-mane Derby, and coarse-mane Derby.

Royal blue Peanut and light blue Peanut.

Wingless and winged Quackers.

Tan-tail and dark-tail Bongo.

Clubby swing tag.

No writing in yellow star.

Patriots with problems: No-flag Lefty and upside-down-flag Glory.

Glory in distress.

Clubby and Beanie Babies Official Club kit.

Orange and red Digger.

The kitty-cat chorus line: white-paw Zip and Nip, all-black Zip, all-gold Nip, and white-face Zip and Nip.

Zip: white face, all black, and white paw.

Nip: white face, all gold, and white paw.

Mystic: coarse, iridescent, and fine-mane.

Black-and-blue Lizzy and tie-dye Lizzy.

7-, 21-, and 11-spot Lucky.

Inky: tan–no mouth, pink, and tan with mouth.

White- and brown-belly Sly.

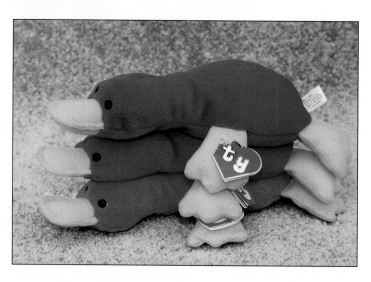

Patti: raspberry, magenta, and fuchsia.

The most recent Patti matches Inch's tail color.

Yarn and felt Inch.

Stripes: dark and light.

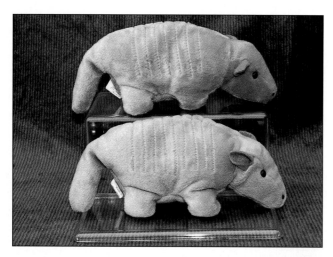

Tank: 7-line and 9-line.

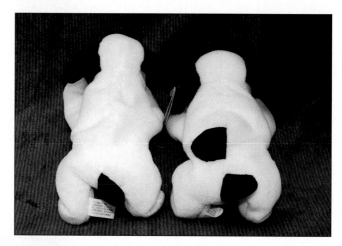

Spotless and spotted Spot.

Lilac and gray Happy.

Part 5

Keeping an Eye on Things

Whether you're bullish or bearish about Beanies, most financial experts agree that investing in Beanie Babies—as purely a long-term investment—is probably not a good idea. But there's lots more to know about collecting for now and the future, and we'll tell you how to keep them safe just in case they should accrue in value.

You'll also want to know how to clean your Beanies should they get dirty (and unless you keep them under Ziplock protection, they probably will!). We'll give you some innovative ideas on how to display your pals to their best advantage. We'll also tell you how to tell the counterfeits from the real thing.

Bee-Nee Babies

Chapter 21

Buyer Beware!

In This Chapter

➤ Discover the difference between other bean toys, "wannaBeanies," and Original Beanie Babies

➤ Read about the China connection for counterfeits

➤ Find out what questions to ask yourself (and the seller!) when buying retired Beanies to help determine if they're authentic

➤ Discover some hints and tips on successfully tracking down the Beanie of your dreams (not your nightmares)

As with all good things in life, there's always someone who comes along who wants to make a quick buck and ruin it for everybody else. I'm sad to say that Beanies have not been immune to scam artists and thieves. I wish it was different, but it's not. It's a rough world out there, folks, even in Beanie Land.

This is the chapter that will scare you. Don't let it scare you TOO much, but do let it arm you with facts and concepts that will help you become confident in your Beanie collecting. If you want to be an educated and dedicated collector, there's just some stuff you need to know.

"WannaBeanies"

I guess you can't blame them for wanting to hop on the money train. I'm talking, of course, about companies who produce other beanbag toys (also known as "beanies"—with a lowercase "b"). Beanbag toys of all kinds have ended up riding on the little tiny coattails of Ty's real Beanie Babies. Oh, some companies manage to come up with something completely different, like the "Meanie Beanies" or the line of Puffkins. Some companies have come to use bean toys to promote their primary products, such as the Disney collection that includes beanies of lots (and LOTS!) of their animated movie characters, or the Coke collection starring their polar spokesbear.

These toys are priced in the same range as Beanies, and many collectors decide to collect many different kinds of the toys. Nothing wrong in that! Why, Ty himself offers other lines of stuffed toys: the Pillow Pals, Attic Treasures, and the wonderful plush line. These products have also ridden the waves of Beanie Baby passion.

Unfortunately, there are other companies (who shall here remain nameless) whose primary goal seems to be to create a beanbag toy that comes close enough to an authentic Ty Beanie Baby to fool some of the people some of the time, but just not quite close enough to get a cease-and-desist order from Ty's lawyers. That's why it will really help you in the long run to educate yourself about Beanie Babies and learn to spot the differences between the imitators and the real thing. If you happen to walk past a store that has a pile of bean toys that look strikingly similar to authentic Beanie Babies, nobody will blame you for walking in to check them out. Even I've had to do a double-take on occasion. But when you get up close and personal—when you go nose to nose with those little creatures—I think you'll find that they just don't have the same magic that Beanies have. There's no sparkle, no plush pizzazz. (It's hard to understand, but there you are.) Take a strong grip of your wallet, and march out of the store! Save your money for the real deal.

Danger, Will Robinson!

Unfortunately, it seems to be the way of the world that whenever something incredibly popular and potentially valuable comes along, there's always people who want to line their own pockets at the expense of others. Beanie Babies are no exception. Counterfeit Beanies started appearing almost as soon as the first collectors started lining up at dawn for the first Original Nine Beanie Babies. Lucky for us that, at least so far, the counterfeits haven't quite gotten it right—yet. The bad news is that they are getting better over time. Of course, collectors are becoming more aware of counterfeits and educating themselves in order to protect themselves.

The fact is, it doesn't take much for the counterfeiters to make a profit (even a small one) and make it worth their while to continue churning out those fakes. If it ends up costing them $1.25 to make a fake Beanie, they can find a market to unload it onto an unsuspecting reseller at $2.50—and you don't need a mathematician to interpret those numbers: They've just doubled their money!

Resellers then sell the toys for $5, thereby doubling *their* money. Often (but not always), these are counterfeits of the more valuable retired toys. Who wouldn't jump at a chance to pick up what might just be a wingless Quackers for $5? The educated Beanie collector, that's who! It *is* possible for you to find a great deal. It does happen. I know of a woman who picked up a tagless Rex at a garage sale for $35 when that same Rex should have been selling for $200. I know of someone who found a mint Caw at a flea market for $5 (valued at the time around $500). But these were collectors who knew what they were looking at and for. There are just as many egg-on-the-face Beanie losers. That's why it really pays to be a savvy shopper when you're looking for Beanie bargains to add to your collection.

Beanie Tails

I know of a woman who bought what she thought to be a mint magenta new-faced Teddy at auction for $1,000 (valued at around $2,000) and thought she'd gotten a great bargain, planning to resell it for its market value. The only problem was that that "magenta" plush was the color of the fuschia Patti. When placed side by side with a real magenta Teddy, the difference became obvious, but a lot of Beanie-educated people had looked at it and not caught the problem before I spotted it. (Fortunately, she was able to get her money back, although it took a lot of time and trouble.)

The Chinese Connection

Most of the counterfeit Beanies come from China, shipped directly to the United States or Canada. Huge shipments of counterfeits have been confiscated at O'Hare International in Chicago. You have to wonder how many have made it through.

Sold in the Russian market in Beijing, they are often touted as being "factory seconds." Ty is a company that prides itself on the quality of its products, and it's highly unlikely that the company would allow manufacturing defects to be sold. Be cautious if someone tells you a tale about a Beanie born in China. Even though it's illegal to sell Beanie Babies in China, some legitimate ones can be found—but probably up to at least 90 percent of the toys found there are not.

However, some of the counterfeits are good—very good. For a novice collector (and often even a more advanced collector), detecting a counterfeit among the genuine articles can be a matter of educated guessing.

Get the Scoop

Fortunately, some of the counterfeits streaming out of China are almost laughingly obvious. Quackers does not come with mint-green plush. Wingless Quackers does not come with a red-and-white tush tag. Tie-dyed Lizzy is not made with the same plush as Beanie roosters Strut and Doodle. You get the idea. If the color looks goofy, you may be looking at a counterfeit.

Making a List and Checking It Twice

So now that you know that there are counterfeits out there, you'll need to know what kinds of things to look for to try to help you determine whether or not you've got a fake on your hands.

Naturally, it helps if you have an authentic Beanie to compare it with, but obviously that's not always possible. So here's what to do:

Get the Scoop

The difference between a "fake" and a "wannaBeanie": A fake is deliberately created to convince the buyer they are buying a legitimate Beanie Baby, including tags. A "wanna-Beanie" may be created to look like a legitimate Beanie, but the tags will give the actual company name that created it, and there should be obvious differences in the styling.

➤ Go to as many Beanie shows as possible.

➤ Frequent stores that deal in a secondary market for retireds where you can get your hands on the real thing as much as possible. (The more familiar you are with Beanies, the better.)

➤ Don't be afraid to use a current or more common retired to help compare with a rarer Beanie: Use the light blue Peanut to compare size and shape to Righty. Derby and Lefty have the same body style. Peking and Chilly are similar to the more common Cubbie and Blackie. You get the picture!

➤ One warning-buzzer indicator alone is probably not enough to determine whether or not you've got a counterfeit. Most fakes have multiple problems. On one fake Britannia, I counted 15 distinct problems.

In Search of Body Style

One of the best ways to sniff out a suspect Beanie is by checking out the body style: size, shape, fabric, color, and stitching.

Size

Is the Beanie-in-question the right size? Most Beanies are about the same length, so if the Righty you've got in your hand is larger or smaller than, say, Peanut (who has the same body style), be suspicious.

Shape

Study pictures of real Beanies. Know the shape of heads and fins and snouts as best you can from the pictures. If a head is supposed to be conical—we're talking a real conehead here—make sure it comes to a point at the nose rather than having a rounded nose. If an ear is supposed to be rounded, make sure it's not squared off.

If a fin is supposed to be V-shaped, make sure that it's not C-shaped. Keep the pictures close by if you know you're going to be looking at Beanies.

Fabric

The plush on Beanie Babies is really very soft, whether you stroke it with or against the nap. Fakes often have "rougher" plush, especially if you rub it the wrong direction. It may not have the same shine a real Beanie's plush has—or it may have too much shine. Some of the white plush fakes almost sparkle.

Color

They don't waste stuff at the Ty company: Most Beanies are made from plush that's used on other Beanies. Try to find a Beanie with the same plush and use it as a color gauge. Even the royal blue in the Royal Blue Peanut is used on Kiwi's beak. Compare and beware!

Stitching

Authentic Ty Beanie Babies are very well made. The stitching is tight and tidy, and the spacing of the stitches is fairly small. You will always find one part of the Beanie (usually on the back) where the Beanie has been hand-sewn because they're created inside-out and then turned inside-in to be filled, so there's always about an inch or two that's obviously not machine sewn. If you suspect "counterfeit," check out the stitching. If it varies from short to long stitches, or looks sloppy and uneven, as if a preschooler did the sewing, watch out!

On the Sly

The size, color, and quality of the patches and embroidery on Beanies such as Maple, Erin, Princess, Righty, Lefty, Valentino, and Libearty can also tell you if the toy is the real thing or a counterfeit. Check it carefully!

Eyes

The eyes are the windows of the soul, and they are also a dead giveaway when you're dealing with counterfeits. Read on for an eyeful on Beanie fakes:

➤ *Placement.* Is the placement of the eyes correct? You can often check against other Beanies with similar body styles.

➤ *Pointy eye backs.* This sounds icky, but you need to feel the back of the toy's plastic eye. (It's easier to do on some lightly-stuffed Beanie heads, such as Ants.) Just grab the toy firmly, and with one hand pinch its little head. You should be able to feel the post of the eye. Many fakes have long posts on the back inside the Beanie's head; these posts are more pointed rather than having a flat end like authentic eyes.

➤ *Shine*. Real Beanie eyeballs are very shiny. Fakes are often dull, with an almost matte appearance—kind of like a Beanie who's short on sleep.

➤ *Shape*. Are the eyes too round? (You can check this by comparing with almost any other Beanie Baby.) Real Beanies have flatter eyes than many of the counterfeits.

➤ *Material*. Is the Beanie *supposed* to have plastic eyes? Some fake Flutters have plastic eyes, but the genuine Flutter's eyes are French knots. We're talking thread.

Beans: The Magical Fruit

No, we're not talking limas and string. We mean those plastic pellets inside your Beanies that give them that adorable heft and wobble. The PVC or PE "beans" used inside real Beanies are small and round. Some fakes use larger pellets or pellets that aren't completely spherical. They may be cylindrical with either rounded or flat ends. Start scrunching your Beanies and try to feel the difference.

All Stuffed Up

There's more than beans in them thar Beanies! Many parts of them are also filled with fiberfill (like the bear's heads), so feel the stuffing closely. While the fiberfilled parts should be less soft, they shouldn't be hard as a rock, either. Nor should the Beanie have more stuffing than beans. These are BEANies, after all.

Take the squish test! While some parts of some Beanies don't have a lot of pellets (like Flutter's body or the pointed tips of Flutter's wings), most of them should feel fairly full even though understuffed. (Kind of like the way you do after Thanksgiving dinner.) But they shouldn't lie totally flat. If you squish all the pellets toward the head of the Beanie, they shouldn't really squish down more than halfway.

Ribbons

Ribbons can be a common giveaway. Check out these aspects:

➤ *Shininess*. The real ribbons on a Beanie are two-sided, meaning they're shiny on both sides. That way, they look good no matter which side is up. (We told you Ty had quality stuff here!) Often the ribbons on counterfeits are dull on the back side.

➤ *Weave*. It will be obvious if the weave isn't as tight as it should be. The weave on the front of the ribbon should be the same on the back.

➤ *Width*. The real ribbons are also usually more narrow than those found on counterfeit Beanies.

In addition, not all the Beanie bears have ribbons; Erin, Glory, and Peace are ribbon-free. So if you see an Erin with a ribbon on it, you know it's a fake!

Ears to You!

Are the ears the right shape for this Beanie? Too small? Too large? (If the Beanie is starting to look a bit like Prince Charles, you know you may have a problem....) Are they placed too high or too low? Again, with many Beanies sharing similar body styles, it's fairly easy to bring along a sample with which to compare.

Get the Scoop

When you check out ribbons, take a beribboned Beanie with you (like Princess or Fortune) to compare. Is the ribbon tied correctly (and tightly)? Is it sewn to the Beanie's neck? (It shouldn't be.)

The Nose Knows

Here's where you can really sniff out a counterfeit. Some of the bears (Libearty, Maple, and Valentino) have brown oval noses, not black. Check the color of the nose. Check to make sure that the nose isn't too wide or too big. Some of the fake Britannias have a nose that looks more like Bones' eyes rather than a Beanie bear nose. Some of the fake Pekings have a big triangular nose rather than the size of the one that's also found on more common bears like Blackie and Cubbie.

Wag the Tail

Many Beanies (especially the jungle cats) come with flat or round tails. But is the tail sewn too high or too low on the body? If it's knotted, is there a little bit sticking out the end of the knot? There usually is, so this might be one indicator.

Get the Scoop

Flat tails have the seam on the outside. Round ones have a seam on the inside. They were sewn inside out and then turned inside-in.

Thread Accents

Many Beanies have a bit of thread about the face as a decoration or to define an expression. If this particular Beanie has thread accents—say, whiskers—are they the right color? The right weight?

In Search of Counterfeit Tags

Now, here's where things get REALLY confusing: tags! As you may know, there are enough legitimate mistakes on the tags to give every collector nightmares. Counterfeits just add to the angst.

Tush Tag

Make sure the tush tag matches the swing tag (if there is one), or even if it matches that Beanie at all. If you're looking at a Beanie that only had a first- or second-generation swing tag, you know it shouldn't have a second-generation (or later) tush tag.

Likewise, match the width and length of the tush tag with one you know is real. (They're not so hard to find as to not be able to locate one to check it against.)

If this is a Canadian Beanie, like Maple, does it have its Canadian tush tag? It should! If it does have one, look to make sure all the English writing is on the English side and all the French is on the French side, especially the last line "Fabrique en Chine."

Ask yourself if the tush tag looks *too* good, too clean, too white. This is especially true with the first-generation black-and-white tush tags. A suspect Beanie *could* have been owned by Mr. Clean—or it could be a fake.

Hangtag

You can really get a hang-up about hangtags. Here's the skinny:

➤ *Color.* Is the color of the red the right shade of red? (Mind you, some tags may have faded a bit over time. But if the color looks fresh, are you sure it's the right color?)

➤ *Outline.* Is the gold outlining on the heart and on the Ty (on fourth- and fifth-generation hangtags) too wide? Is it shiny? The real tags use gold foil, but often fakes use gold ink or a more "rubbed" gold. Does the outline match up with the "Ty," or can you see white outside the gold?

➤ *Inside.* On the inside of the tag, can you see the edge of where the gold is pressed against the tag? (Although it's not out of the question that you might see an "edge" inside the tag, it might be an indicator of a fake.)

Baby Talk

A **font** is a complete assortment of type in one size and style.

Font

Check the font used in printing the swing tags. Is it the right font for the generation of swing tag? The fifth-generation tags use a *font* called MS Comic Sans—It's kind of a fun-looking font.

Before Ty got so whimsical, most of the fonts looked like what you might find in a book, except for the printing in the yellow star which is just a very plain font (called sans serif). Is the size of the font correct? (Check the tush tags, too! There are fake Britannias where her name on the tush tag is in a smaller font than it should be.)

Poem

Check the poem. Does it match the known poems? Is the right Beanie name used in the poem? At least one set of counterfeit Garcias stole Spike's poem, even though the name on the tag said "Garcia." But remember: Canadian Snorts from the fall of 1997 sometimes had Tabasco's name in the poem, so that one's legit. (Do you have a headache yet?)

Birthday

For those Beanies with birthdays, is the birthday correct (or in the case of Scottie and Freckles, one of their two known birthdays)? Is the birthday formatted correctly for the generation of hangtag? Fourth-generation hangtags showed the birthday in a mm-dd-yy format (for example, 10-31-93). Fifth-generation birthdays have the birthday spelled out completely (October 31, 1993).

Style Number

Does the style number inside the tag match the one on the bar code (for those hangtags that have bar codes)? Does it match the style number for that particular Beanie? Even though the style number was removed from the inside of the hangtag when the fifth-generation tags came out, the style number is still part of the bar code on the back. It's the last four digits.

Printing

Is the printing too dark? Too bold? The printing on the hang- and tush tags should be clear, but not necessarily thick and overly dark. Look at the copyright mark (©) on the tush tag. The "C" in the middle should be distinct from the circle surrounding it. Is the printing on the tush tag red and not orange-red?

Typos

Are there words spelled incorrectly that aren't known tag errors? If you happen to be looking at a Peking with a mint third-generation tag, does the city Nürnberg have an umlaut (that funny little mark that looks like a colon on its side) over the "u"? If so, are the dots over each "tip" of the u, or more centered? (They should be centered.) Are the commas and the periods in the right place, especially on the tush tag around "Ty, Inc." and "Oakbrook, IL"? If your Beanie has a Canadian tush tag, don't forget to check it for typographical errors, too!

On the Sly

Fake Jakes have been found without this mark (concentric ovals with the number in the middle and Chinese characters in between the two ovals). Jake was released May 30, 1998. He should have it.

Markings

If this Beanie is known to need a fifth-generation tush tag, as far as you can tell, it should also have the marks on the *inside* of the tush tag, the concentric ovals with the number in the middle, and Chinese characters in between the two ovals. (Assuming that the fifth-generation tush tag really is a distinct generation, any Beanie manufactured and shipped from mid-1998 should have this mark.)

Spacing

Look at the spacing of the words on the tags. Do they correspond with known tags? Does the (trademark) symbol appear after the Beanie's name, not above one of the letters in the Beanie's name? Is the name on the tush tag spaced properly?

Forewarned Is Forearmed

Now that you know some of the things to look for, you may be feeling so hesitant that you're afraid to stick your nose into the next Beanie Baby show. Don't be! Just remember: Never let your guard down when it comes to buying Beanies, because not even current toys are immune. Counterfeits of some of the May 30, 1998 releases were coming out just about the same time the new ones were shipping!

As our friends in the Pentagon know so well, the best defense is a good offense. Arm yourself by educating yourself as much as possible. This needn't (and shouldn't) be the only book on Beanies that you buy. (Besides, I'm sure that if you become as enamored of these sweet critters as so many other people, you will want to learn as much as you can!)

Just keep in mind two things:

1. If it sounds too good to be true, it probably is.
2. P.T. Barnum said that there's a sucker born every minute. You don't have to be one of them!

The following tips will help you make sure that you're buying what you really want: original and authentic Beanie Babies!

➤ Shop for your Beanies at authorized Ty retailers. These are the folks who can help make sure that you get the real thing. Many retailers also sell retired Beanies on the secondary market.

➤ Really study the tags of any bean toy that you're thinking about buying, whether it be current or retired. Don't just grab something you think is a Beanie Baby because it has a similar tag.

➤ Take a reference book with you so you can compare pictures of authentic Beanie Babies, especially if you're a new collector.

➤ Go to Beanie shows. Even if you're not buying, you'll get a chance to see loads of Beanie Babies. The more you see, the better you'll be able to spot "wannaBeanies" and counterfeits. (And be careful when you're leaving a show, especially if you've been picking up some of those rarer Beanies you've been wanting. Try to leave with a group. Don't go out to a parking lot alone, especially at night. Keep your eyes open to make sure you're not followed. Don't ever compromise your own safety for your Beanies.)

➤ Network! Network! Network! You'll meet lots of people at your local Beanie hangout and at Beanie shows. Almost all of them will be thrilled to death to talk Beanies and will be more than happy to share any information (and rumors!) they have. Just remember to try to keep the rumors separated from the facts. You'll hear lots of rumors presented as facts, so it may take you some time to learn to distinguish the two. Treat pretty much anything anyone (including me!) says about what Beanie is going to retire next as a rumor. Sure, some people will hit some of them right, but as far as I know, nobody has ever gotten them *all* right. Ty doesn't even retire the same number of Beanies every time!

➤ And, last, but not least…have fun!!

The Least You Need to Know

➤ Not all bean toys are created equal. Knock-offs may look like authentic Beanie Babies, but may be of inferior quality.

➤ Many counterfeit Beanies come from China.

➤ Counterfeit Beanies will almost always have multiple indications that they are, indeed, counterfeits.

➤ Learning the right questions to ask can save you a lot of money, hassle, and time.

Chapter 22

Buying, Selling, and Trading

> ## In This Chapter
>
> ➤ Learn how to obtain your dream Beanie
>
> ➤ Get the skinny on "investing" in plush
>
> ➤ Find out the best places to buy
>
> ➤ Discover the ins and outs of shows—buying and selling

It's not as tricky as it seems it might be. Most of what you need to know to buy, sell, or trade Beanies is pretty much common sense. You *can* make money, but it shouldn't be your primary goal. (It would be easier if this was a Rod Serling TV show, and you could time-warp back a couple years and pick up those colored bears and a few Royal Blue Peanuts for a song and a dance...)

Like any true collectible or antique, if there aren't many of them, they'll be more valuable. If you could buy Faberge eggs in your local Kmart, you can bet your Michelangelo they wouldn't be fighting over them at Sothebys. The sad fact is, the more recently retired Beanies (say, since October 1997) have been better cared for, and there are more of them around, so they'll just never become as valuable as their ancestor Beanies.

But that doesn't mean you can't obtain your dream Beanie. The one really amazing thing about Beanie Baby collecting is that both buyer and seller (or two traders, if that's what you're up to) can come out as winners. You may be able to obtain your Royal Blue Peanut without having to shell out that cool $5,000. (But it's doubtful you'll be able to get it for $5, even after multiple times of trading up and up and *up*.)

Read on for tips about making the most of your investment, but don't put all of your Beanies in one basket!

Investments: Yes or No?

If you ask a financial adviser if you should plow the egg money into Beanie Babies, you can pretty much count on a negative reaction.

Beanie Babies as fun toys? Terrific! Beanie Babies as a hedge against inflation, a down payment on your future security, or your child's college tuition in 15 years? Not on your life. Betting on Beanies is a gamble, just as if you were plunking down a pile of blue Peanuts on a Las Vegas blackjack table. It's a *fun* gamble, sure! But it's a gamble nonetheless.

If it's investing you've a hankering for, take your money and put it into a financial instrument that has proven its worth over the long haul—such as a no-load stock mutual fund. Even given the volatility of the stock market, over the long run (no cheating and removing your money every two weeks!) you'll earn good money and be reasonably safe.

Of course, if you can afford to sink a few dollars into some Beanies, and you won't miss the money if your gamble doesn't pay off—that's fine. Or if you just like the little fellows and you just want to collect something and have some fun doing it, that's okay, too. Just don't get involved in spending more money than you can afford in an investment that may be bust two weeks from tomorrow. Take a page from the diary of Edsel Ford.

Go out and buy Beanies because you like them…because you collect donkeys…because Radar looks like your Uncle Fred—but *not* because you want to make a killing. There are a whole raft of reasons why the bottom may fall out of the Beanie market—and if it does, you don't want to be riding it all the way down. (Not with your last dime, anyway.)

Financial analysts (such as the folks over at *Forbes* magazine who should know) have been advising wealthy clients for some time that the Beanie craze is beginning to die down. Some collectible price guides don't include Beanies at all, dismissing them as an evanescent fad destined to roll away into the mists of time, like yesterday's hula hoop.

When you peer into the Beanie crystal ball, you're likely to see and hear gloom and doom on every corner. Maybe it's justified—maybe it's not. We just don't know *what* the Beanie fad will do in two weeks, two months, or two years from now, which is why we're advising you *not* to bet the ranch on a bunch of Beanies. It's also quite possible that the Beanie craze will continue for months and even years to come, given Ty Warner's uncanny talent for marketing and whetting the public's appetite. Part of the fun lies in the unpredictability!

Unique Fad

It's clear that some critics have already been a bit too quick to dismiss the Beanie phenomenon. Unlike earlier toy fads (such as Tickle Me Elmo), the Beanie Babies may indeed have "legs." After all, Beanies have triggered an incredible secondary market in which prospectors buy a toy for $5 to $7 and then sell it the next day for five, 10, 100—sometimes 1,000 percent more.

Evidence of their strength as a genuine phenomenon, and not a momentary flash in the bean pot, is the fact that Beanies also have spawned an incredibly diverse accessory market, with clothes, furniture, related toys, CDs, books, and magazines all related to the Beanie phenomenon (see Chapter 20). The risk—and the thrill—for many people is that the bubble *might* burst at any moment, leaving an awful lot of people with soap on their faces—but then again, it might not!

On the Sly

There are some experts in the collectibles world who question the authenticity of some of the prices said to be received on the secondary market—especially trading done over the Internet, but other experts insist that by and large, the Internet is legit. As always: Buyer beware.

Location! Location! Location!

Whether the fad is boom or bust, one thing is fairly certain: Beanie prices vary with geographic location. One part of the country may be a seller's dream and a buyer's nightmare while in another, it's a buyer's market. On the whole, prices on the east coast, California, and the Chicago area seem to be higher. Folks *love* to sell Beanies there. But if you're looking to buy? Head to the Midwest. Although the market is by no means soft, collectors in the middle of the country seem to be able to pick up their desired treasures for 10 to 15 percent less than the prime areas.

Get the Scoop

Experts believe collectors may be able to make more money by actively trading their Beanies, not hoarding them and hoping they will continue to appreciate in value.

Patience Is a Virtue

Don't feel like you have to be the first on your block to get new releases. I've seen it happen time and time again. Every time Ty begins shipping their latest Beanie Babies, collectors flock to the stores. Unfortunately, the secondary market dealers are flocking right along with them. (That's why it gets so crowded in there!)

Secondary market dealers start snatching up as many of the new releases as they can and reselling them for four times their retail prices. Some of the more popular styles (like Glory the bear) may cost 50 times the recommended $5 price tag at the beginning of a shipping cycle.

Why do they do this? In a word: greed. They know there are people who are willing to pay the price, whether it stems from needing to be "first" or a fear that Ty will retire a Beanie quickly, leaving them eating Beanie dust.

Truth is, if people didn't patronize secondary dealers, the dealers wouldn't have the incentive to grab up new releases—leaving more of the new releases for collectors. Don't worry about a particular Beanie retiring quickly. You'll still be able to get one, and you may have to pay a little more for it, but chances are you will have saved more than enough by paying only the recommended price for the others.

Get the Scoop

Don't trade retired Beanies for new releases. The value of the retireds is most likely going to increase (perhaps significantly) over the same time that the value of the new release will drop toward its $5 retail price.

Now You See It, Now You Don't: Price Fluctuations

The Beanie Baby market is a little bit like hog futures and the state of the world's finances: they fluctuate. They're volatile. Sure, the stock market lost a ton of points in October 1987. But then it came right back up again.

That's sort of how most experts see Beanie Baby prices. They're normal. They don't worry the experts, because the market needed to settle down from its initial wild swing. It's just as well, since collectors couldn't participate at the inflated prices. A slow and steady rise is a good thing.

I Dream of Beanies

Okay, so let's say you want Garcia, but you don't have the cash for the going price of $150. What you do have are some duplicates of other retired Beanies. How do you go about getting your dream Garcia?

First and most importantly, know the current value of each of the Beanies you have. You can find this out by checking some of the pricing guides in magazines, the *Beanie Mania Bulletin,* or one of the tons of Internet sites (see Appendix C). Go to local stores and Beanie shows to check up on the prices as well.

For the sake of this example, let's say you have extras of Bessie, Teddy, Tank, Flip, and Zip, all of which you bought at $6. That's about a $30 investment. Now, let's say Bessie is currently selling for about $50, Teddy for $75, Tank for $60, Flip for $30, and Zip for $25. Right there you have about $230 in value. "Easy!" I hear you saying.

Well, hang on just a second. The chances are pretty good that the person from whom you want to get this particular Garcia, whose colors you adore, insists on $160 instead of $150. You'll need to make the choice as to whether you *must* have *this* Garcia or whether you want to wait and find one you like as much for a better price. Only you can make that choice.

"Okay," you say, "I *really* like this one. It's worth the extra $10."

The next thing to realize is that this seller will want to resell the Beanies you want to trade, so they aren't going to give you the full value. They may decide they want anywhere from 10 to 50 percent to count as "profit." Most people are pretty reasonable, but some stores will stick to that 50 percent mark. You can do better. Honest! In reality, 25 percent is reasonable (and of course, 10 percent is great!).

At 25 percent, your $230 worth of Beanies should get you about $172.50 in trade. Hey! That dream Garcia is *yours!* And you get $12.50 back in the process. That means that you really only spent $17.50 for Garcia! The seller is happy because he or she should be able to get about $230 out of what had been Garcia instead of $160. You're happy (no, you're *thrilled*!) because you got your Garcia for $17.50. Everyone wins!

The tricks are:

➤ Know what you want and know what you're willing to spend on it. You don't have to make it a hard and fast rule, but you should know a fairly close range of price.

➤ Know the value of the Beanies you have that you're willing to trade.

➤ Know what kind of percentage profit you're willing to give the seller.

➤ It's hard, but you must be willing to walk away from the deal and look for a better one. Don't let yourself be intimidated.

And, best of all, you can repeat this win-win process until you turn blue—Royal Blue if you want!

On the Sly

You can trade commons for retireds, but you probably won't be able to make as good a deal, and you'll find far fewer takers, especially if you want a Beanie that's more popular.

Auctions

It's possible to buy Beanies by attending a live auction, or by bidding in an online auction. The key to coming out ahead in an auction is to set yourself a pre-bidding frenzy limit, and to *never* go above it.

For more information, check out this Web site: **www.frii.com/~afs/ebay//**. Though this page refers to just one online auction site, the basic principles can be applied to all of them.

On with the Show

Arm yourself before attending a Beanie show. Don't be afraid to take printouts of price lists, books to check facts and, certainly, references to make sure that what you're getting is the real thing and not a counterfeit. (You can read more about questions to ask yourself about a Beanie to help determine its authenticity in Chapter 21.)

If you're taking Beanies to trade, carry them in something sturdy and protective. Make sure they're wearing tag protectors. If a dealer (or a fellow trader) knows that you take care of your Beanies, you're more likely to get some respect.

Decide what you have that you are absolutely willing to trade. You don't want to get hit with a case of nerves in the middle of a trade or buyer's remorse after a trade by wishing you hadn't traded that 1997 Teddy because it was your last one.

Some of your duplicate retireds are tagless? No problem. It's usually not too difficult to find people who want a Beanie but don't want to spend the money for one with tags. You can still do just fine. But be aware that a tagless Happy may not get you much even though he's retired. He's not terribly expensive even with mint tags and for a small sum of money, collectors can easily get one.

Go early. Stay late. Go early to catch deals that are so good they won't be around more than just a few minutes. Stay late because dealers would rather walk out with money than Beanies. You may be able to negotiate a better price.

Unless you bump into an absolute heart-stopping price (and maybe not even then), take your time to go through the entire exhibit. Look to see what each dealer offers. Some may only have currents with a smattering of new or hard-to-find Beanies. Some dealers may have a plethora of older retireds. More than likely the pricing will be similar (not always), but some dealers may be more willing to negotiate (or trade) than others.

Don't be afraid to ask questions! Whether you're inquiring about a Beanie you don't see or if they can offer a better price, the worst thing that can happen is that the dealer says "No." Well, okay, I suppose they could laugh and say "No way!" but so what? They may just as easily say, "Well, I've had that one for a while and I'd like to move it." Make them an offer. Cross your fingers. Wear your lucky Beanie keychain.

If you're interested in several Beanies a dealer has, ask if you can get a discount for a multiple Beanie purchase. While individually priced, you may be able to find them for less at several other dealers' tables, but a combo buy from a single dealer may end up costing you less in the long run.

Rumors run rampant at shows. Even though most dealers will be straightforward, you may well run into someone who will tell you anything to get you to buy a particular Beanie at an inflated price. Be a skeptic, and take everything you hear with a grain of salt. Take the really ridiculous statements with an entire box of Morton's.

After you've looked around and talked with a number of the dealers, you'll probably find that there are several with whom you made a "connection." Those are the dealers you want to go back and talk to again. It helps to develop a relationship, even if it's only for a day. Keep going back if they have something you want. You may find the price coming down just because you're persistent.

Beanie Tails

If you're trading, don't be afraid to trade up even within a single show. Take that $17.50 Garcia you got earlier, combine it with a 1997 set of Teenie Beanies that cost you about $25 in Happy Meals and a million calories, and for $42.50, you can find yourself with a Dark Stripes or an absolutely mint Libearty.

If you brought trades with you, don't ignore a trading table where other collectors come with their extras. These folks are less likely to need some kind of profit, and you may be able to find something you want and trade off less for it.

Don't be afraid to say "no" yourself. If you don't think the prices (or trades) are reasonable, there's always the next show.

Talk to other buyers! Share with them where you found great deals and who's willing to trade. They'll return the favor.

The Other Side of the Beanie

Now that you've read all the hints and tips about buying (and trading) Beanies, what if you want to be the seller. It's easy!! Well, part of it is. Everything said about buying Beanies is true here, too. Know the going rates on Beanies. Know what you need to make a profit. Don't be afraid to walk away from a deal.

Be honest. Be fair. Be open. Treat your buyers as you would want to be treated. (The "Golden Rule" really does apply.) Buyers will flock to you. There will be some who want to pay unrealistic prices, but saying "No, thank you" politely is just as easy as saying "Buzz off!" and it won't lose you a potential customer. (Remember that buyer can turn around and talk to other buyers!)

Allow people to just look if they want to, but don't let them stand there without asking if there's a question you can answer for them.

Don't be afraid to trade. You can come out ahead easily. People know you're there to make a profit (and pay for any table space!).

Be kind to children, but you don't have to agree to a bad sale or trade because of a sob story. Unfortunately, many people will use hard-luck stories (or

Get the Scoop

Share your gossip and rumors, but don't do it just to sell a Beanie. Do it because it's fun!

send children with hard-luck stories) to try to get a better price. A friend of mine was approached at a show last summer by a woman who said that her son was in the hospital and she wanted to get him a Beanie to cheer him up. She wanted my friend to sell her Red Digger (then going for $35) for $10. My friend explained she really couldn't do that, but if she wanted a crab, she would sell her Claude (then new and going for about $15) for $10. The woman tried again with Flash and then Splash (also going for $35), wanting to buy them at $10. Smell the rat here? If the woman really just wanted a Beanie to cheer up her son, it really didn't matter what Beanie it was. But the woman was only interested in retired Beanies. The woman finally moved on to the next table to try her luck there.

Showtime!

As a seller, you will need to prepare for a show. The following tips should help:

➤ Find out if tables are provided as part of the vendor fee. If not, make arrangements to bring a table of a suitable size. Don't forget a chair! You won't want to stand the entire day.

➤ If tablecloths aren't provided, bring one. It will make your display look neater and cleaner.

➤ Figure out how you're going to transport your Beanies. Plastic storage cases work well, but don't make them so heavy you can't carry them. Check to see if dollies will be available or try to bring your own if not. You'll be happy at the end of the day if you do.

➤ Plan how you want to display your Beanies. Haphazard displays won't attract too many people. If you can, display your prices so they're visible even when you have people stacked up in front of the table. Higher is better.

➤ Have a business card ready. You'll be asked for one.

➤ Plan on having two people to work. At some point, you'll need to take a break. You won't want to leave your table unattended. Also, two sets of eyes are better if there's a crowd milling around, and much easier to break down your display at the end of a long day. Unless you have a large area, three people may be a bit crowded, but it never hurts to have a "spare" person wandering around checking out the competition and coming in as a relief pitcher.

➤ Use a work apron (or at least big pockets) to keep things like pens, notepads, scissors, tape, paper towels, and even money. Unless the area is protected so someone can't reach it, you won't want to leave a money box around.

➤ Make sure you have plenty of change, including $1 bills.

➤ Scout out the other dealers. Make sure your prices are in line (or at least not noticeably higher). Be able to point out dealers who seem honest and fair who might have what they need to buyers whom you can't service.

➤ Keep water on hand. You'll need it! But make sure it's not spillable.

➤ Know how much your bottom line is on each Beanie (at least until the end of the show). Don't tell one customer one price and the next one another. It will make it easier on you if you don't have to remember what you told someone, and you won't hear "Fifteen dollars? You told me $14 ten minutes ago!" Have a price sheet available if you can—if not for handing out, at least posted for reference.

➤ Take the time to put tag protectors on your Beanies. It tells the customer that you're a dealer who knows the tags are important and you care that they're getting a good product.

➤ Wear comfortable shoes with good support. (Trust me on this.)

➤ Take a sweater if it's cool out, but dress lightly. You can always put the sweater on, but with all the people and lights, rooms tend to warm up quickly.

➤ Take your smile with you and wear it!! Even if you're having a lousy day, you want buyers to think you're the best person in the world.

Get the Scoop

When you're selling Beanies at a show, have some secondary items available for sale (clothes, furniture, books). They'll bring in more people.

The Least You Need to Know

➤ Invest in mutual funds, not Beanie Babies. Don't use money you can't afford to lose to buy plush.

➤ No one knows where the Beanie craze will go, so hang on and enjoy the ride.

➤ Don't patronize secondary dealers for current Beanies. Have patience and trust that you *will* find them in a store.

➤ Don't pay exorbitant prices to get the "first" Beanie new releases.

➤ Beanie prices vary with location.

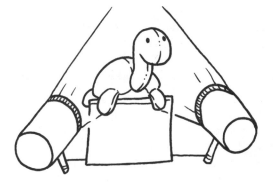

Beanies on Display

If you love Beanies—or you live with someone who does—odds are you've got them tumbling onto the floor, falling off bureaus, and rolling under the bed. If you're the parent of an 8-year-old Beanie fanatic, you've probably picked up and tripped over your share of the cuddly little creatures and wondered, "Where on Earth are we going to put the next one?"

Because, of course, there is ALWAYS a next one.

Serious collectors have more complex concerns, faced with the need to preserve in mint condition not just the Beanie but its tags, commemorative cards, bags, and so on.

But whether you're a serious collector or a novice, odds are you're going to be interested in the best way to display your Beanies. In this chapter we'll discuss all the methods people have found to display and protect their collections. You may find a few ideas for yourself, whether you've got one or 1,001 Beanies to call your own!

Corralling a Kids' Collection

Let's face it—Beanies were born to be played with. Ty originally designed these toys for elementary-age kids, which is why they're priced so kids can afford them. Word on the street is, Ty wanted kids to be able to buy a beautifully made, quality toy with their allowances—a toy that wouldn't break, didn't look cheap, and had lots of play value.

And boy, do kids love to play with their Beanies! The key to a good kids' display system is to make the Beanies accessible without having them actually falling onto your head or getting under your feet every time you enter your child's room. You want to display the creatures in some fairly neat fashion, while giving a child easy access. Who has time to unlock a bank safety deposit box every time a child wants to play Beanies?

In the next few pages, we'll be discussing innovative ways to showcase and organize your Beanies, for those of you more interested in play than posterity.

Wooden Circus Trains

What could be more appropriate to display a collection of animal Beanies than a wooden circus train! With this colorful home-on-wheels, your Beanies can fit inside the cars and engine, hanging out the windows for the ultimate in display potential.

At the same time, kids will enjoy playing with the train itself, which comes in several different sizes to fit all Beanie collection dimensions. While a display opportunity such as this train may not offer serious collectors the protection they desire, it's just the thing for younger Beanie enthusiasts.

Bean Stalk

This clever design features a wooden pole appropriately created as a little bean stalk (get it?), tall enough to accommodate 52 Beanies with loops to stick their little heads through so they can dangle neatly off the floor. (You may need two if your child is seriously into Beanies—don't say we didn't warn you!)

This upright approach keeps Beanies off the floor and eliminates their annoying tendency of flowing up and out of drawers or baskets like some great plush tidal wave.

Those of you who also have Teenie Beanies (and who doesn't?) may be pleased to know there's also a special "Teenie Stalk" with space for 12 Teenies. If you're a real McDonald's hound and you've got both Teenie sets, get yourself two trees. You'll be glad you did!

Hanging Chain

Here's a lightweight plastic, chain-link version of the Beanie stalk. Suspended from the ceiling, the plastic chain includes lots of little plastic clips (similar to spring-loaded clothespins) that clip each Beanie onto the chain.

Most chains allow you to attach a huge number of Beanies (and you may be able to get two lightweight Beanies on one clip if you're very good with your teeth)—and what's even better, most kids can handle the clips themselves.

If you're handy with a screwdriver or a drill, you can install the chains in a matter of minutes. Voilà—a vertical vortex of Beanies!

Corner Hammock

Another good way to sweep up those errant plush play pals is by installing a wall hammock (this usually works best in a corner). Once it's installed, you can simply toss all your Beanies into the hammock to get them out of the way. The hammocks tend to expand and can hold quite a number of Beanies.

This is a good system if you don't have the time to clip or noose a Beanie, and you have large numbers of the plush playthings to keep in order. (It's an especially effective tidying method when company's coming over at the last minute.)

On the other hand, while the hammock does keep the Beanies off the floor, it's a more haphazard system, looks messier, and isn't as effective a display. It's hard to appreciate the individual personality and charm of each Beanie Baby when they are mashed together in the corner like a Waldorf salad.

On the Sly

Keep your Beanie Babies away from direct sunlight so they don't fade from the strong rays.

Beanie Ark

Now here's a fun way to store your Beanies—and what could be more appropriate than Noah's ark, where all the animals march in two by two? Arks come in several different sizes and may store as many as 40 Beanie Babies at a time. This is another one of those display ideas that also makes a good toy in itself.

Hang 'Em High!

There are several different varieties of wall hangings available, so you can really get creative and explore options. If you like to keep things simple, you can just go out and buy a plastic shoe organizer bag designed to hang behind a door or in a closet. Each Beanie is then inserted into a pocket. These shoe organizers come in many different colors and materials (from cloth to plastic), and they're fairly inexpensive.

A cousin to the shoe organizer is the cloth banner display with individual pockets for each Beanie. You can buy (or make) the colorful Beanie "banner" and then stuff a Beanie into each pocket. If the banners are colorful enough, you may want to consider decorating your child's room with a series of banners, displaying them in the same way you'd display a prized painting or photograph. As the collection grows, you can simply add extra banners around the wall. You can find these pocket banners for sale in 12-, 20-, and 30-pocket sizes.

Buckle Up Your Beanies

Now here's a fascinating display idea: Buckle each Beanie into a small, belt-like device attached to a suction cup, and stick 'em on a mirror or window. Any child is guaranteed to have fun sticking those Beanies all over the glass, although the buckles may be hard for some tiny fingers to manipulate. If your child has trouble with the buckles, try attaching a suction cup to a Velcro belt tied around the Beanie's waist.

L.L. Beanie Pet Beds

We've all seen those soft, round cedar pet beds offered by well-known Maine sportsmen catalogs. Don't your Beanies deserve the same royal treatment? Soft pillows in a variety of sizes and colors are available to do just that.

While perhaps not a sensible choice for large collections, smaller groupings of Beanies might be very happy to rest on these display cushions.

Top Drawer!

In the interest of space and neatness, some folks have chosen to just stuff their Beanies in a drawer and be done with it. This has the added benefit of not costing anything extra—although you *will* need to find some place to put the extra clothes that your Beanies have evicted.

Drawer storage has the added benefit of being easily accessible to a child, while keeping the bean toys out of reach of marauding pets and away from dirt and dust.

Underbed Storage

They come in a host of styles, sizes, and materials, but just about every home furnishing mail-order catalog offers some type of underbed storage boxes.

When you stash your Beanies in this type of box and roll them out of sight, they stay neat and clean—but you don't have the enjoyment of putting them on display for all your friends to admire.

Still, the underbed storage option is inexpensive and doesn't take up extra room. Most kids can pull the boxes out by themselves, and there's plenty of room in there for most collections.

For Serious Collectors

There are collectors, and there are collectors. If you're more interested in keeping your Beanies pristine for later resale, or you're daydreaming that they will appreciate in value and someday pay your way to Paris, you're going to need to make sure they stay in mint condition. Here are a wide variety of display possibilities that can help you do just that.

Display Boxes

All you have to do is pick up a collector's magazine (we list several in Appendix B) and you'll find more types of clear plastic or acrylic boxes than you can shake a Beanie Baby at. These boxes are popular because you can see through them—thereby enjoying your Beanies—while keeping out the dust bunnies, dirt specks, heat, and humidity—not to mention your beagle Georgette, who's just looking for something to shred.

They're called boxes, cubes, tubes, coffins, display cases—and they come in all shapes and sizes. One Beanie (Clubby bear) comes with his own acrylic case, right to your door. No matter what the size or shape, however, these acrylic boxes make good display sense.

Various Beanie display boxes.

Display Accessories

You can buy everything from leashes to clay corn flakes for your Beanies, so you shouldn't be surprised to find out that you can buy accessories for your display boxes as well. To make sure your Beanies are resting comfortably inside their little plastic homes, you can buy special fluffy cushions for the bottom in a variety of colors.

313

If you want to announce to the world which Beanie is which, you can also get name plates for each of your display cases, engraved with your Beanie's names (as if you'd forget!)

Beanie Motels and Barns

These "the-more-the-merrier" display shelves may come in a wide variety of sizes and shapes—some are actually designed to look like small houses, hotels, and barns. They all feature a clear acrylic door that locks in your Beanies to keep them as clean as possible.

Crowd on In!

Another display option is long rectangular display boxes in various lengths, so that a long line of Beanies can nestle next to each other and yet still be safe from dust and dirt.

Shelf Life

One of the simplest ways to display a Beanie is on a wooden bookshelf. Of course, an open bookshelf leaves your Beanies open to the elements, so you may want to consider those special Beanie bookshelves with clear plastic doors in front.

Stackable Acrylic

Other display boxes are stackable, so that you can arrange your Beanies in a variety of interesting ways, taking advantage of the different Beanie body styles.

On the Sly

Airtight plastic bags and acrylic containers can lead to condensation, mildew, fabric deterioration, and fading from sunlight. So—no storing your Beanies in bread bags!

Cardboard Storage

While many folks prefer the clear acrylic cases—after all, these Beanies are *cute*, and you want to be able to look at them—some truly finicky collectors prefer to store their Beanies out of the damaging UV sunlight, wrapped in acid-free archival tissue paper and placed in special boxes made of archival board.

These work well, and if you've got the room to stack them, they will surely survive the elements and the years intact. The down side is—well, you can't see your Beanies. This system would work well for those folks who buy two Beanies—one to play with, and one to store away.

Tag Protectors

We've talked about displaying your Beanies, and how to protect them from getting damaged if you're a serious collector. The next thing to think about is how to protect the heart of your Beanie—the hangtag.

You'll be glad to know that there are as many tag protectors as there are Beanies to put them in, and it pays to shop around. There are some tag protector basics you might like to keep in mind when pushing around that shopping cart. Your tag protectors should:

➤ Be made of archival, PVC-free plastic (so it won't yellow your tags)

➤ Have an easy-on, easy-off design

➤ Make your tags be easily visible

➤ Be acid- and wax-free

A-Round the Corner Tags

The rounded corner tags allow the hangtag to slip snugly into its plastic case. Its square top design allows the tag to be removed and reinserted without a problem.

Heart Tags: Clips and Sleeves

A heart-shaped tag makes a lot of sense—it fits the hangtag so well. The clip has the advantage over a plastic sleeve in that because it opens with a hinge, you can gently place the hangtag inside the protector without risking damage by trying to shove it into a thin sleeve.

Protecting Your Tush

In the beginning, collectors were most concerned about protecting their hangtags. With the advent of "tush-tag protectors," collectors have taken that concern one step further. The protectors lock onto the tush tags, smoothing out creases while protecting the tags.

Beanie Tails

If you're a serious collector—and even if you're not—it's a good idea to keep an inventory of what you own, where you bought it, how much you paid, and—if you sell—what you received. Those of you who are serious about your collection will want to fill out this collection inventory checklist included in the middle of the book (see Part 3). You can also keep track of your Beanies by product number or by birthdate.

Clean Your Bean

It's the first day of spring. You're dreaming of clean wet sheets snapping in the breeze, of sparkling windows shining in the sun, of your collection of Beanie Babies...wait! Hold that thought! Do you really need to grab your entire collection of Beanie Babies and stuff them into your washer?

Dirt and grime may not be a problem if you're a serious collector and your entire collection is safely resting in glass, acrylic, or a bomb-proof wall safe. But if your collection is out in the atmosphere, it's going to get a bit dusty after a while. Your Beanies are probably too new to have attracted much in the way of insects, but dust is almost inevitable.

While some folks have tossed a dirty Beanie into the washer, cleaning experts (and you know who you are!) insist that a Beanie Baby should never be subjected to the rough-and-tumble world of the washer-dryer. So what do you do when your beautiful Valentino is wearing more condiments than the takeout counter at McDonald's?

We have just two words to say about that: spot clean.

This means no washer, no dryer, and no dunking into a pail of water. To clean a small spot on the plush:

1. Dampen a cloth or a toothbrush with cold water.
2. Rub the spot gently.

It's not rocket science, folks, but it should be effective. (That is, unless your nephew has just taken an indelible black marker to your Special Olympics Maple's plush...)

If you need to de-matt a much-loved Beanie, try a toothbrush dipped in cool water. Some enterprising folks do like to pop their Beanies into the wash for a couple of minutes on "delicate"—but if you do this, you must first remove the hangtag. You can do this by taking a #7 crochet hook and guiding the tag connector through the hole to remove the tag.

If you don't think that spot cleaning will do the trick, try vacuuming. (What works really well is the tiny vacuum attachment you can use to suck the dust off of computer keyboards and other small electrical devices.) The important thing when vacuuming a Beanie is to be careful that the suction isn't so strong that a stray plastic eye or nose disappears into the guts of your Electrolux.

On the Sly

Beware of stain removers! The chemicals in some of these products may stain fur or plush. If it's imperative to use a chemical, try it first on some out-of-the-way spot on the Beanie.

Get the Scoop

If you notice a stubborn spot on your Beanie, try sprinkling cornmeal directly on the stain and let it set for 24 hours. Then vacuum up the cornmeal.

Queasy about cleaning collectibles? Don't worry. We'll bet even Martha Stewart uses a professional for those times when plush collectibles need that little something extra.

Now that your collection is all spiffed up, safe and sound—it's time to think about how to make sure they *stay* that way. We're talking insurance—and you'd better have some if you're building a nice collection. There have been reports of Beanie-napping all across the country, and your town could be next.

Insurance from A to Z

If you're a collector, you may have been paying top dollar for some of your Beanies and you'll want to make sure they're insured, in the most painless way possible. Read on for details!

Finding an Agent

The first thing to do when you're thinking about buying insurance to cover your collection is to get references from family and friends so that you can work with a broker who's knowledgeable about the insurance industry—and about collectibles.

Collectibles insurance is *not* something that every agent fully understands. Try to find several different agents or companies and compare prices and policy options.

"WHAT Fine Print?"

Once you find an agent you can trust, make sure that you understand everything in the insurance policy before you sign. You want to avoid unpleasant shocks should something ever happen to your collection. Chances are, if you sit down with an agent to talk insurance, you'll hear the following buzzwords fly:

➤ *Actual cash value.* If you have this type of policy, you'll be paid the actual replacement cost of your item MINUS depreciation. Unless you have lots of money to beef up your insurance payout in case of an emergency, this is probably *not* the way to go.

➤ *Replacement cost guarantee.* With this option, you're guaranteed to be insured for the full current value of the Beanie. You won't have to factor in depreciation.

Baby Talk

Replacement cost refers to how much money it will take to replace the lost item the day you lost it.

The Standard Deal

If you've got a standard homeowner's policy, you've insured the contents of your home. With such a policy, you're usually limited in your ability to collect for a specific item, and most policies outline those limits (for example, $1,000 for jewelry or $200 for coins). That's why you may need to buy a "rider" (extra insurance) to cover high-priced collectibles.

Be sure to check out what exactly the policy will pay you if you need to collect because something has happened to your Beanies. Some policies pay for replacement at current value—that is, if you lost your Princess bear, they would pay you the current cost to replace it. Other policies pay you what Princess costs minus wear and tear (this is called "depreciation"). Obviously, the first example is the way to go. What good does it do to insure your Princess if you can't afford to replace her if she gets stolen or damaged?

It's important to remember that most standard homeowners' policies cover specific hazards—but not EVERYTHING that can happen. If lightning strikes your Beanie Baby collection, you're probably covered, but if your waterbed explodes and floods your display cabinets, you may well find that "water damage" is not included in the covered hazards. Read your policy carefully! You'll be glad you did.

If you have a particularly valuable collection—let's say you have five examples each of the top 10 rarest Beanies, in super-mint condition—you should probably buy a special insurance policy to cover these irreplaceable collectibles in addition to your regular homeowner's policy. On the other hand, you may find that it costs more to insure your collection than the Beanies are worth. If that's the case, think about insuring just the rarest plush animals in your collection.

For More Information

For information about insuring your Beanies, check first with your current homeowner's or renter's policy agent. If your own insurance company doesn't offer adequate coverage for Beanies, try contacting a specialist such as the Collectibles Insurance Agency, Inc., P.O. Box 1200, Westminster, MD 21158; (410) 876-8833.

The Least You Need to Know

➤ There are lots of ways to display just-for-fun Beanie collections.

➤ Serious collectors need to protect their Beanies from mold, mildew, dust, and direct sunlight.

➤ You can spot-clean a Beanie with a damp cloth or a toothbrush dipped in cold water, but don't throw them in the washer for long cycles.

➤ Extensive Beanie collections should be properly insured (perhaps with a rider covering them specifically).

Catalog
of Beanies

By Birthday

Name	Style#	Birthday	Issued	Retired	HT Gen
Spot the dog (with a spot)	4000	1-3-93	4-13-94	10-1-97	2-4
Patti the fuchsia platypus	4025	1-6-93	2-28-95	5-1-98	3-5
Squealer the pig	4005	4-23-93	1-8-94	5-1-98	1-5
Legs the frog	4020	4-25-93	1-8-94	10-1-97	1-4
Chocolate the moose	4015	4-27-93	1-8-94		1-5
Flash the dolphin	4021	5-13-93	1-8-94	5-11-97	1-4
Pinchers the lobster	4026	6-19-93	1-8-94	5-1-98	1-5
Splash the whale	4022	7-8-93	1-8-94	5-11-97	1-4
Cubbie the bear	4010	11-14-93	1-8-94	12-31-97	1-4
Bones the dog	4001	1-18-94	6-25-94	5-1-98	1-5
Valentino the bear	4058	2-14-94	1-7-95		2-5
Happy the lavender hippo	4061	2-25-94	6-3-95	5-1-98	3-5
Nip the gold cat (white paws)	4003	3-6-94	3-10-96	12-31-97	3-4
Ally the alligator	4032	3-14-94	6-25-94	10-1-97	1-4
Zip the black cat (white paws)	4004	3-28-94	3-10-96	5-1-98	3-5

continues

continued

Name	Style#	Birthday	Issued	Retired	HT Gen
Quackers the duck (with wings)	4024	4-19-94	1-7-95	5-1-98	2-5
Daisy the cow	4006	5-10-94	6-25-94	9-15-98	1-5
Mystic the unicorn (brown horn)	4007	5-21-94	early 1996	10-23-97	3-4
Mystic the unicorn (iridescent horn)	4007	5-21-94	10-23-97		4-5
Blackie the bear	4011	7-15-94	6-25-94	9-15-98	1-5
Speedy the turtle	4030	8-14-94	6-25-94	10-1-97	1-4
Goldie the goldfish	4023	11-14-94	6-25-94	12-31-97	1-4
Inky the pink octopus	4028	11-29-94	6-3-95	5-1-98	3-5
Peanut the light blue elephant	4062	1-25-95	10-2-95	5-1-98	3-5
Stinky the skunk	4017	2-13-95	6-3-95	9-28-98	3-5
Pinky the flamingo	4072	2-13-95	6-3-95		3-5
Tank the armadillo (9 lines, without shell)	4031	2-22-95	6-3-96	Fall 1996	4
Tank the armadillo (with shell)	4031	2-22-95	Fall 1996	10-31-97	4
Flip the white cat	4012	2-28-95	1-7-96	10-1-97	3-4
Coral the fish	4079	3-2-95	6-3-95	1-1-97	3-4
Ears the brown rabbit	4018	4-18-95	1-7-96	5-1-98	3-5
Lucky the ladybug (11 spots)	4040	5-1-95	6-15-96	5-1-98	4-5
Lucky the ladybug (21 spots)	4040	5-1-95	2-25-96		4
Lizzy the blue lizard	4033	5-11-95	1-7-96	12-31-97	3-4
Snort the bull	4002	5-15-95	1-1-97	9-15-98	4-5
Tabasco the bull	4002	5-15-95	6-3-95	1-1-97	3-4
Twigs the giraffe	4068	5-19-95	1-7-96	5-1-98	3-5
Bucky the beaver	4016	6-8-95	1-7-96	12-31-97	3-4

Name	Style#	Birthday	Issued	Retired	HT Gen
Manny the manatee	4081	6-8-95	1-7-96	5-11-97	3-4
Magic the dragon	4088	6-8-95	6-3-95	12-31-97	3-4
Stripes the tiger (light)	4065	6-11-95	6-3-96	5-1-98	4-5
Bessie the cow	4009	6-27-95	6-3-95	10-1-97	2-4
Bubbles the fish	4078	7-2-95	6-3-95	5-11-97	3-4
Ringo the raccoon	4014	7-14-95	1-7-96	9-16-98	3-5
Grunt the razorback	4092	7-19-95	1-7-96	5-11-97	3-4
Weenie the Dachshund	4013	7-20-95	1-7-96	5-1-98	3-5
Garcia the bear	4051	8-1-95	1-7-96	5-11-97	3-4
Hoot the owl	4073	8-9-95	1-7-96	10-1-97	3-4
Bongo (brown tail)	4067	8-17-95	2-6-96	6-29-96	3-4
Bongo (tan tail)	4067	8-17-95	6-3-95		3-5
Digger the red crab	4027	8-23-95	6-25-94	5-11-97	3-4
Sting the stingray	4077	8-27-95	6-3-95	1-1-97	3-4
Inch the inchworm (felt antennae)	4044	9-3-95	6-3-95	10-15-96	3-4
Inch the inchworm (yarn antennae)	4044	9-3-95	10-15-96	5-1-98	4-5
Derby the horse (coarse mane)	4008	9-16-95	late 1995	12-15-97	3-5
Derby the horse (star)	4008	9-16-95	12-15-97		5
Kiwi the toucan	4070	9-16-95	6-3-95	1-1-97	3-4
Tusk the walrus	4076	9-18-95	1-7-95	1-1-97	3-4
Radar the bat	4091	10-30-95	9-1-95	5-11-97	3-4
Spooky the ghost	4090	10-31-95	9-1-95	12-31-97	3-4
Teddy the new-faced brown bear	4050	11-28-95	1-7-95	10-1-97	2-4
Velvet the panther	4064	12-16-95	6-3-95	10-1-97	3-4
Waddle the penguin	4075	12-19-95	6-3-95	5-1-98	3-5
Ziggy the zebra	4063	12-24-95	6-3-95	5-1-98	3-5

continues

continued

Name	Style#	Birthday	Issued	Retired	HT Gen
Crunch the shark	4130	1-13-96	1-1-97	9-24-98	4-5
Mel the koala	4162	1-15-96	1-1-97		4-5
Nuts the squirrel	4114	1-21-96	1-1-97		4-5
Chip the cat	4121	1-26-96	5-1-97		4-5
Peace the bear	4053	2-1-96	5-11-97		4-5
Baldy the eagle	4074	2-17-96	5-11-97	5-1-98	4-5
Roary the lion	4069	2-20-96	5-11-97		4-5
Sparky the Dalmatian	4100	2-27-96	6-15-96	5-11-97	4
Doodle the rooster	4171	3-8-96	5-11-97	7-12-97	4
Strut the rooster	4171	3-8-96	7-12-97		4-5
Seaweed the otter	4080	3-19-96	1-7-96	9-19-98	3-5
Fleece the lamb	4125	3-21-96	1-1-97		4-5
Hoppity the rose bunny	4117	4-3-96	1-1-97	5-1-98	4-5
Curly the bear	4052	4-12-96	6-15-96		4-5
Wrinkles the Bulldog	4103	5-1-96	6-15-96	9-22-98	4-5
Pugsly the Pug dog	4106	5-2-96	5-11-97		4-5
Chops the lamb	4019	5-3-96	1-7-96	1-1-97	3-4
Floppity the lilac bunny	4118	5-28-96	1-1-97	5-1-98	4-5
Rover the dog	4101	5-30-96	6-15-96	5-1-98	4-5
Hippity the mint bunny	4119	6-1-96	1-1-97	5-1-98	4-5
Freckles the leopard	4066	6-3-96	6-15-96		4-5
Scottie the Scottish Terrier	4102	6-15-96	6-15-96	5-1-98	4-5
Gracie the swan	4126	6-17-96	1-1-97	5-1-98	4-5
Scoop the pelican	4107	7-1-96	6-15-96		4-5
Maple the bear	4600	7-1-96	1-1-97		4-5
Righty the elephant	4085	7-4-96	6-15-96	1-1-97	4
Lefty the donkey	4086	7-4-96	6-15-96	1-1-97	4

Name	Style#	Birthday	Issued	Retired	HT Gen
Libearty the bear	4057	Summer 96	6-15-96	1-1-97	4
Spike the rhinoceros	4060	8-13-96	6-15-96		4-5
Claude the crab	4083	9-3-96	5-11-97		4-5
Sly the brown-bellied fox	4115	9-12-96	6-15-96	8-6-96	4
Sly the white-bellied fox	4115	9-12-96	8-6-96	9-22-98	4-5
Bernie the St. Bernard	4109	10-3-96	1-1-97	9-22-98	4-5
Doby the Doberman	4110	10-9-96	1-1-97		4-5
Tuffy the terrier	4108	10-12-96	5-11-97		4-5
Dotty the Dalmatian	4100	10-17-96	5-11-97		4-5
Snip the Siamese cat	4120	10-22-96	1-1-97		4-5
Spinner the spider	4026	10-28-96	10-1-97	9-19-98	4-5
Batty the bat	4035	10-29-96	10-1-97		4-5
Pouch the kangaroo	4161	11-6-96	1-1-97		4-5
Congo the gorilla	4160	11-9-96	6-15-96		4-5
Nanook the husky	4104	11-21-96	5-11-97		4-5
Gobbles the turkey	4023	11-27-96	10-1-97		4-5
Jolly the walrus	4082	12-2-96	5-11-97	5-1-98	4-5
Waves the whale	4084	12-8-96	5-11-97	5-1-98	4-5
Blizzard the tiger	4163	12-12-96	5-11-97	5-1-98	4-5
Seamore the seal	4029	12-14-96	6-25-94	10-1-97	1-4
Echo the dolphin	4180	12-21-96	5-11-97	5-1-98	4-5
Snowball the snowman	4201	12-22-96	10-1-97	12-31-97	4
"Teddy, 1997"	4200	12-25-96	10-1-97	12-31-97	4
Kuku the cockatoo	4192	1-5-97	5-30-98		5
Spunky the Cocker Spaniel	4184	1-14-97	12-31-97		5
Fetch the Golden Retriever	4189	2-4-97	5-30-98		5

continues

323

continued

Name	Style#	Birthday	Issued	Retired	HT Gen
Rocket the blue jay	4202	3-12-97	5-30-98		5
Erin the bear	4186	3-17-97	1-31-98		5
Early the robin	4190	3-20-97	5-30-98		5
Hissy the snake	4185	4-4-97	12-31-98		5
Whisper the deer	4194	4-5-97	5-30-98		5
Jake the mallard duck	4199	4-16-97	5-30-98		5
Wise the owl	4194	5-31-97	5-30-98		5
Tracker the Bassett Hound	4198	6-5-97	5-30-98		5
Glory the bear	4188	7-4-97	5-30-98		5
Iggy the iguana	4038	8-12-97	12-31-97		5
Pounce the cat	4122	8-28-97	12-31-97		5
Bruno the terrier	4183	9-9-97	12-31-97	9-18-98	5
Stretch the ostrich	4182	9-21-97	12-31-97		5
Stinger the scorpion	4193	9-29-97	5-30-98		5
Smoochy the frog	4039	10-1-97	12-31-97		5
Jabber the parrot	4197	10-10-97	5-30-98		5
Rainbow the chameleon	4037	10-14-97	12-31-97		5
Puffer the puffin	4181	11-3-97	12-31-97	9-18-98	5
Ants the anteater	4195	11-7-97	5-30-98		5
Prance the cat	4123	11-20-97	12-31-97		5
Fortune the panda	4196	12-6-97	5-30-98		5
Britannia the bear	4601	12-15-97	12-31-97		5
Gigi the Poodle	4191	4-7-98	5-30-98		5
Spot the dog (without a spot)	4000		1-8-94	4-13-94	1-2
Nip the gold cat	4003		1-7-96	3-10-96	3
Nip the gold cat (white face)	4003		1-7-95	1-7-96	2-3
Zip the all-black cat	4004		1-7-96	3-10-96	3

Name	Style#	Birthday	Issued	Retired	HT Gen
Zip the black cat (white face)	4004		1-7-95	1-7-96	2-3
Mystic the unicorn (fine mane)	4007		6-25-94	early 1996	1-3
Derby the horse (fine mane)	4008		6-3-95	late 1995	3
Brownie the bear	4010		1993	1993	1
Chilly the polar bear	4012		6-25-94	1-7-96	1-3
Peking the panda	4013		6-25-94	1-7-96	1-3
Quackers the duck (wingless)	4024		6-25-94	1-7-95	1-2
Patti the maroon platypus	4025		1-8-94	2-28-95	1-3
Punchers the lobster	4026		1993	1993	1
Digger the orange crab	4027		6-25-94	6-3-95	1-3
Inky the octopus (tan—mouth)	4028		9-12-94	6-3-95	3
Inky the octopus (tan—no mouth)	4028		6-25-94	9-12-94	1-2
Slither the snake	4031		6-25-94	6-15-95	1-3
Tank the armadillo (7 lines, without shell)	4031		1-7-95	1-7-96	3
Lizzy the tie-dyed lizard	4033		6-3-95	1-7-96	3
Lucky the ladybug (7 spots)	4040		6-25-94	2-27-96	1-3
Web the spider	4041		6-25-94	1-7-96	1-3
Trap the mouse	4042		6-25-94	6-15-95	1-3
Flutter the butterfly	4043		6-3-95	6-15-96	3
Bumble the bee	4045		6-3-95	6-15-96	3-4
Teddy the old-faced brown bear	4050		6-25-94	1-7-95	1-2

continues

325

continued

Name	Style#	Birthday	Issued	Retired	HT Gen
Teddy the new-faced teal bear	4051		1-7-95	1-7-96	2-3
Teddy the old-faced teal bear	4051		6-25-94	1-7-95	1-2
Teddy the new-faced cranberry bear	4052		1-7-95	1-7-96	2-3
Teddy the old-faced cranberry bear	4052		6-25-94	1-7-95	1-2
Teddy the new-faced violet bear	4055		1-7-95	1-7-96	2-3
Teddy the old-faced violet bear	4055		6-25-94	1-7-95	1-2
Teddy the new-faced magenta bear	4056		1-7-95	1-7-96	2-3
Teddy the old-faced magenta bear	4056		6-25-94	1-7-95	1-2
Teddy the new-faced jade bear	4057		1-7-95	1-7-96	2-3
Teddy the old-faced jade bear	4057		6-25-94	1-7-95	1-2
Humphrey the camel	4060		6-25-94	6-15-95	1-3
Happy the gray hippo	4061		6-25-94	6-3-95	1-3
Peanut the royal blue elephant	4062		6-3-95	10-2-95	3
Stripes the tiger (dark)	4065		1-7-96	6-3-96	3
Nana the tan-tailed monkey	4067		6-3-95		3
Caw the crow	4071		6-3-95	6-15-96	3
Bronty the brontosaurus	4085		6-3-95	6-15-96	3
Rex the tyrannosaurus	4086		6-3-95	6-15-96	3
Steg the stegosaurus	4087		6-3-95	6-15-96	3
Princess the bear	4300		10-29-97		special

By Style Number

Name	Style#	Birthday	Issued	Retired	HT Gen
Spot the dog (with a spot)	4000	1-3-93	4-13-94	10-1-97	2-4
Spot the dog (without a spot)	4000		1-8-94	4-13-94	1-2
Bones the dog	4001	1-18-94	6-25-94	5-1-98	1-5
Snort the bull	4002	5-15-95	1-1-97	9-15-98	4-5
Tabasco the bull	4002	5-15-95	6-3-95	1-1-97	3-4
Nip the gold cat	4003		1-7-96	3-10-96	3
Nip the gold cat (white face)	4003		1-7-95	1-7-96	2-3
Nip the gold cat (white paws)	4003	3-6-94	3-10-96	12-31-97	3-4
Zip the all-black cat	4004		1-7-96	3-10-96	3
Zip the black cat (white face)	4004		1-7-95	1-7-96	2-3
Zip the black cat (white paws)	4004	3-28-94	3-10-96	5-1-98	3-5
Squealer the pig	4005	4-23-93	1-8-94	5-1-98	1-5
Daisy the cow	4006	5-10-94	6-25-94	9-15-98	1-5
Mystic the unicorn (fine mane)	4007		6-25-94	early 1996	1-3
Mystic the unicorn (brown horn)	4007	5-21-94	early 1996	10-23-97	3-4
Mystic the unicorn (iridescent horn)	4007	5-21-94	10-23-97		4-5
Derby the horse (fine mane)	4008		6-3-95	late 1995	3
Derby the horse (coarse mane)	4008	9-16-95	late 1995	12-15-97	3-5
Derby the horse (star)	4008	9-16-95	12-15-97		5
Bessie the cow	4009	6-27-95	6-3-95	10-1-97	2-4

continues

continued

Name	Style#	Birthday	Issued	Retired	HT Gen
Brownie the bear	4010		1993	1993	1
Cubbie the bear	4010	11-14-93	1-8-94	12-31-97	1-4
Blackie the bear	4011	7-15-94	6-25-94	9-15-98	1-5
Chilly the polar bear	4012		6-25-94	1-7-96	1-3
Flip the white cat	4012	2-28-95	1-7-96	10-1-97	3-4
Peking the panda	4013		6-25-94	1-7-96	1-3
Weenie the Dachshund	4013	7-20-95	1-7-96	5-1-98	3-5
Ringo the raccoon	4014	7-14-95	1-7-96	9-16-98	3-5
Chocolate the moose	4015	4-27-93	1-8-94		1-5
Bucky the beaver	4016	6-8-95	1-7-96	12-31-97	3-4
Stinky the skunk	4017	2-13-95	6-3-95	9-28-98	3-5
Ears the brown rabbit	4018	4-18-95	1-7-96	5-1-98	3-5
Chops the lamb	4019	5-3-96	1-7-96	1-1-97	3-4
Legs the frog	4020	4-25-93	1-8-94	10-1-97	1-4
Flash the dolphin	4021	5-13-93	1-8-94	5-11-97	1-4
Splash the whale	4022	7-8-93	1-8-94	5-11-97	1-4
Gobbles the turkey	4023	11-27-96	10-1-97		4-5
Goldie the goldfish	4023	11-14-94	6-25-94	12-31-97	1-4
Quackers the duck (with wings)	4024	4-19-94	1-7-95	5-1-98	2-5
Quackers the duck (wingless)	4024		6-25-94	1-7-95	1-2
Patti the fuchsia platypus	4025	1-6-93	2-28-95	5-1-98	3-5
Patti the maroon platypus	4025		1-8-94	2-28-95	1-3
Pinchers the lobster	4026	6-19-93	1-8-94	5-1-98	1-5
Punchers the lobster	4026		1993	1993	1
Spinner the spider	4026	10-28-96	10-1-97	9-19-98	4-5
Digger the orange crab	4027		6-25-94	6-3-95	1-3

Name	Style#	Birthday	Issued	Retired	HT Gen
Digger the red crab	4027	8-23-95	6-25-94	5-11-97	3-4
Inky the octopus (tan—mouth)	4028		9-12-94	6-3-95	3
Inky the octopus (tan—no mouth)	4028		6-25-94	9-12-94	1-2
Inky the pink octopus	4028	11-29-94	6-3-95	5-1-98	3-5
Seamore the seal	4029	12-14-96	6-25-94	10-1-97	1-4
Speedy the turtle	4030	8-14-94	6-25-94	10-1-97	1-4
Slither the snake	4031		6-25-94	6-15-95	1-3
Tank the armadillo (7 lines, without shell)	4031		1-7-95	1-7-96	3
Tank the armadillo (9 lines, without shell)	4031	2-22-95	6-3-96	Fall 1996	4
Tank the armadillo (with shell)	4031	2-22-95	Fall 1996	10-31-97	4
Ally the alligator	4032	3-14-94	6-25-94	10-1-97	1-4
Lizzy the blue lizard	4033	5-11-95	1-7-96	12-31-97	3-4
Lizzy the tie-dyed lizard	4033		6-3-95	1-7-96	3
Batty the bat	4035	10-29-96	10-1-97		4-5
Rainbow the chameleon	4037	10-14-97	12-31-97		5
Iggy the iguana	4038	8-12-97	12-31-97		5
Smoochy the frog	4039	10-1-97	12-31-97		5
Lucky the ladybug (11 spots)	4040	5-1-95	6-15-96	5-1-98	4-5
Lucky the ladybug (21 spots)	4040	5-1-95	2-25-96		4
Lucky the ladybug (7 spots)	4040		6-25-94	2-27-96	1-3
Web the spider	4041		6-25-94	1-7-96	1-3
Trap the mouse	4042		6-25-94	6-15-95	1-3

continues

continued

Name	Style#	Birthday	Issued	Retired	HT Gen
Flutter the butterfly	4043		6-3-95	6-15-96	3
Inch the inchworm (felt antennae)	4044	9-3-95	6-3-95	10-15-96	3-4
Inch the inchworm (yarn antennae)	4044	9-3-95	10-15-96	5-1-98	4-5
Bumble the bee	4045		6-3-95	6-15-96	3-4
Teddy the new-faced brown bear	4050	11-28-95	1-7-95	10-1-97	2-4
Teddy the old-faced brown bear	4050		6-25-94	1-7-95	1-2
Garcia the bear	4051	8-1-95	1-7-96	5-11-97	3-4
Teddy the new-faced teal bear	4051		1-7-95	1-7-96	2-3
Teddy the old-faced teal bear	4051		6-25-94	1-7-95	1-2
Curly the bear	4052	4-12-96	6-15-96		4-5
Teddy the new-faced cranberry bear	4052		1-7-95	1-7-96	2-3
Teddy the old-faced cranberry bear	4052		6-25-94	1-7-95	1-2
Peace the bear	4053	2-1-96	5-11-97		4-5
Teddy the new-faced violet bear	4055		1-7-95	1-7-96	2-3
Teddy the old-faced violet bear	4055		6-25-94	1-7-95	1-2
Teddy the new-faced magenta bear	4056		1-7-95	1-7-96	2-3
Teddy the old-faced magenta bear	4056		6-25-94	1-7-95	1-2
Libearty the bear	4057	Summer 1996	6-15-96	1-1-97	4
Teddy the new-faced jade bear	4057		1-7-95	1-7-96	2-3

Name	Style#	Birthday	Issued	Retired	HT Gen
Teddy the old-faced jade bear	4057		6-25-94	1-7-95	1-2
Valentino the bear	4058	2-14-94	1-7-95		2-5
Humphrey the camel	4060		6-25-94	6-15-95	1-3
Spike the rhinoceros	4060	8-13-96	6-15-96		4-5
Happy the gray hippo	4061		6-25-94	6-3-95	1-3
Happy the lavender hippo	4061	2-25-94	6-3-95	5-1-98	3-5
Peanut the light blue elephant	4062	1-25-95	10-2-95	5-1-98	3-5
Peanut the royal blue elephant	4062		6-3-95	10-2-95	3
Ziggy the zebra	4063	12-24-95	6-3-95	5-1-98	3-5
Velvet the panther	4064	12-16-95	6-3-95	10-1-97	3-4
Stripes the tiger (dark)	4065		1-7-96	6-3-96	3
Stripes the tiger (light)	4065	6-11-95	6-3-96	5-1-98	4-5
Freckles the leopard	4066	6-3-96	6-15-96		4-5
Bongo (brown tail)	4067	8-17-95	2-6-96	6-29-96	3-4
Bongo (tan tail)	4067	8-17-95	6-3-95		3-5
Nana the tan-tailed monkey	4067		6-3-95		3
Twigs the giraffe	4068	5-19-95	1-7-96	5-1-98	3-5
Roary the lion	4069	2-20-96	5-11-97		4-5
Kiwi the toucan	4070	9-16-95	6-3-95	1-1-97	3-4
Caw the crow	4071		6-3-95	6-15-96	3
Pinky the flamingo	4072	2-13-95	6-3-95		3-5
Hoot the owl	4073	8-9-95	1-7-96	10-1-97	3-4
Baldy the eagle	4074	2-17-96	5-11-97	5-1-98	4-5
Waddle the penguin	4075	12-19-95	6-3-95	5-1-98	3-5
Tusk the walrus	4076	9-18-95	1-7-95	1-1-97	3-4

continues

continued

Name	Style#	Birthday	Issued	Retired	HT Gen
Sting the stingray	4077	8-27-95	6-3-95	1-1-97	3-4
Bubbles the fish	4078	7-2-95	6-3-95	5-11-97	3-4
Coral the fish	4079	3-2-95	6-3-95	1-1-97	3-4
Seaweed the otter	4080	3-19-96	1-7-96	9-19-98	3-5
Manny the manatee	4081	6-8-95	1-7-96	5-11-97	3-4
Jolly the walrus	4082	12-2-96	5-11-97	5-1-98	4-5
Claude the crab	4083	9-3-96	5-11-97		4-5
Waves the whale	4084	12-8-96	5-11-97	5-1-98	4-5
Bronty the brontosaurus	4085		6-3-95	6-15-96	3
Righty the elephant	4085	7-4-96	6-15-96	1-1-97	4
Lefty the donkey	4086	7-4-96	6-15-96	1-1-97	4
Rex the tyrannosaurus	4086		6-3-95	6-15-96	3
Steg the stegosaurus	4087		6-3-95	6-15-96	3
Magic the dragon	4088	6-8-95	6-3-95	12-31-97	3-4
Spooky the ghost	4090	10-31-95	9-1-95	12-31-97	3-4
Radar the bat	4091	10-30-95	9-1-95	5-11-97	3-4
Grunt the razorback	4092	7-19-95	1-7-96	5-11-97	3-4
Dotty the Dalmatian	4100	10-17-96	5-11-97		4-5
Sparky the Dalmatian	4100	2-27-96	6-15-96	5-11-97	4
Rover the dog	4101	5-30-96	6-15-96	5-1-98	4-5
Scottie the Scottish Terrier	4102	6-15-96	6-15-96	5-1-98	4-5
Wrinkles the Bulldog	4103	5-1-96	6-15-96	9-22-98	4-5
Nanook the husky	4104	11-21-96	5-11-97		4-5
Pugsly the Pug Dog	4106	5-2-96	5-11-97		4-5
Scoop the pelican	4107	7-1-96	6-15-96		4-5
Tuffy the terrier	4108	10-12-96	5-11-97		4-5
Bernie the St. Bernard	4109	10-3-96	1-1-97	9-22-98	4-5
Doby the Doberman	4110	10-9-96	1-1-97		4-5

Name	Style#	Birthday	Issued	Retired	HT Gen
Nuts the squirrel	4114	1-21-96	1-1-97		4-5
Sly the brown-bellied fox	4115	9-12-96	6-15-96	8-6-96	4
Sly the white-bellied fox	4115	9-12-96	8-6-96	9-22-98	4-5
Hoppity the rose bunny	4117	4-3-96	1-1-97	5-1-98	4-5
Floppity the lilac bunny	4118	5-28-96	1-1-97	5-1-98	4-5
Hippity the mint bunny	4119	6-1-96	1-1-97	5-1-98	4-5
Snip the Siamese cat	4120	10-22-96	1-1-97		4-5
Chip the cat	4121	1-26-96	5-1-97		4-5
Pounce the cat	4122	8-28-97	12-31-97		5
Prance the cat	4123	11-20-97	12-31-97		5
Fleece the lamb	4125	3-21-96	1-1-97		4-5
Gracie the swan	4126	6-17-96	1-1-97	5-1-98	4-5
Crunch the shark	4130	1-13-96	1-1-97	9-24-98	4-5
Congo the gorilla	4160	11-9-96	6-15-96		4-5
Pouch the kangaroo	4161	11-6-96	1-1-97		4-5
Mel the koala	4162	1-15-96	1-1-97		4-5
Blizzard the tiger	4163	12-12-96	5-11-97	5-1-98	4-5
Doodle the rooster	4171	3-8-96	5-11-97	7-12-97	4
Strut the rooster	4171	3-8-96	7-12-97		4-5
Echo the dolphin	4180	12-21-96	5-11-97	5-1-98	4-5
Puffer the puffin	4181	11-3-97	12-31-97	9-18-98	5
Stretch the ostrich	4182	9-21-97	12-31-97		5
Bruno the terrier	4183	9-9-97	12-31-97	9-18-98	5
Spunky the Cocker Spaniel	4184	1-14-97	12-31-97		5
Hissy the snake	4185	4-4-97	12-31-98		5
Erin the bear	4186	3-17-97	1-31-98		5
Glory the bear	4188	7-4-97	5-30-98		5

continues

continued

Name	Style#	Birthday	Issued	Retired	HT Gen
Fetch the Golden Retriever	4189	2-4-97	5-30-98		5
Early the robin	4190	3-20-97	5-30-98		5
Gigi the Poodle	4191	4-7-98	5-30-98		5
Kuku the cockatoo	4192	1-5-97	5-30-98		5
Stinger the scorpion	4193	9-29-97	5-30-98		5
Whisper the deer	4194	4-5-97	5-30-98		5
Wise the owl	4194	5-31-97	5-30-98		5
Ants the anteater	4195	11-7-97	5-30-98		5
Fortune the panda	4196	12-6-97	5-30-98		5
Jabber the parrot	4197	10-10-97	5-30-98		5
Tracker the Bassett Hound	4198	6-5-97	5-30-98		5
Jake the mallard duck	4199	4-16-97	5-30-98		5
"Teddy, 1997"	4200	12-25-96	10-1-97	12-31-97	4
Snowball the snowman	4201	12-22-96	10-1-97	12-31-97	4
Rocket the blue jay	4202	3-12-97	5-30-98		5
Princess the bear	4300		10-29-97		special
Maple the bear	4600	7-1-96	1-1-97		4-5
Britannia the bear	4601	12-15-97	12-31-97		5

By Release

Name	Style#	Birthday	Issued	Retired	HT Gen
Brownie the bear	4010		1993	1993	1
Punchers the lobster	4026		1993	1993	1
Squealer the pig	4005	4-23-93	1-8-94	5-1-98	1-5
Legs the frog	4020	4-25-93	1-8-94	10-1-97	1-4
Chocolate the moose	4015	4-27-93	1-8-94		1-5
Flash the dolphin	4021	5-13-93	1-8-94	5-11-97	1-4

Name	Style#	Birthday	Issued	Retired	HT Gen
Pinchers the lobster	4026	6-19-93	1-8-94	5-1-98	1-5
Splash the whale	4022	7-8-93	1-8-94	5-11-97	1-4
Cubbie the bear	4010	11-14-93	1-8-94	12-31-97	1-4
Spot the dog (without a spot)	4000		1-8-94	4-13-94	1-2
Patti the maroon platypus	4025		1-8-94	2-28-95	1-3
Spot the dog (with a spot)	4000	1-3-93	4-13-94	10-1-97	2-4
Bones the dog	4001	1-18-94	6-25-94	5-1-98	1-5
Ally the alligator	4032	3-14-94	6-25-94	10-1-97	1-4
Daisy the cow	4006	5-10-94	6-25-94	9-15-98	1-5
Blackie the bear	4011	7-15-94	6-25-94	9-15-98	1-5
Speedy the turtle	4030	8-14-94	6-25-94	10-1-97	1-4
Goldie the goldfish	4023	11-14-94	6-25-94	12-31-97	1-4
Digger the red crab	4027	8-23-95	6-25-94	5-11-97	3-4
Seamore the seal	4029	12-14-96	6-25-94	10-1-97	1-4
Mystic the unicorn (fine mane)	4007		6-25-94	early 1996	1-3
Chilly the polar bear	4012		6-25-94	1-7-96	1-3
Peking the panda	4013		6-25-94	1-7-96	1-3
Quackers the duck (wingless)	4024		6-25-94	1-7-95	1-2
Digger the orange crab	4027		6-25-94	6-3-95	1-3
Inky the octopus (tan—no mouth)	4028		6-25-94	9-12-94	1-2
Slither the snake	4031		6-25-94	6-15-95	1-3
Lucky the ladybug (7 spots)	4040		6-25-94	2-27-96	1-3
Web the spider	4041		6-25-94	1-7-96	1-3
Trap the mouse	4042		6-25-94	6-15-95	1-3

continues

335

continued

Name	Style#	Birthday	Issued	Retired	HT Gen
Teddy the old-faced brown bear	4050		6-25-94	1-7-95	1-2
Teddy the old-faced teal bear	4051		6-25-94	1-7-95	1-2
Teddy the old-faced cranberry bear	4052		6-25-94	1-7-95	1-2
Teddy the old-faced violet bear	4055		6-25-94	1-7-95	1-2
Teddy the old-faced magenta bear	4056		6-25-94	1-7-95	1-2
Teddy the old-faced jade bear	4057		6-25-94	1-7-95	1-2
Humphrey the camel	4060		6-25-94	6-15-95	1-3
Happy the gray hippo	4061		6-25-94	6-3-95	1-3
Inky the octopus (tan—mouth)	4028		9-12-94	6-3-95	3
Valentino the bear	4058	2-14-94	1-7-95		2-5
Quackers the duck (with wings)	4024	4-19-94	1-7-95	5-1-98	2-5
Tusk the walrus	4076	9-18-95	1-7-95	1-1-97	3-4
Teddy the new-faced brown bear	4050	11-28-95	1-7-95	10-1-97	2-4
Nip the gold cat (white face)	4003		1-7-95	1-7-96	2-3
Zip the black cat (white face)	4004		1-7-95	1-7-96	2-3
Tank the armadillo (7 lines, without shell)	4031		1-7-95	1-7-96	3
Teddy the new-faced teal bear	4051		1-7-95	1-7-96	2-3
Teddy the new-faced cranberry bear	4052		1-7-95	1-7-96	2-3
Teddy the new-faced violet bear	4055		1-7-95	1-7-96	2-3

Name	Style#	Birthday	Issued	Retired	HT Gen
Teddy the new-faced magenta bear	4056		1-7-95	1-7-96	2-3
Teddy the new-faced jade bear	4057		1-7-95	1-7-96	2-3
Patti the fuchsia platypus	4025	1-6-93	2-28-95	5-1-98	3-5
Happy the lavender hippo	4061	2-25-94	6-3-95	5-1-98	3-5
Inky the pink octopus	4028	11-29-94	6-3-95	5-1-98	3-5
Stinky the skunk	4017	2-13-95	6-3-95	9-28-98	3-5
Pinky the flamingo	4072	2-13-95	6-3-95		3-5
Coral the fish	4079	3-2-95	6-3-95	1-1-97	3-4
Tabasco the bull	4002	5-15-95	6-3-95	1-1-97	3-4
Magic the dragon	4088	6-8-95	6-3-95	12-31-97	3-4
Bessie the cow	4009	6-27-95	6-3-95	10-1-97	2-4
Bubbles the fish	4078	7-2-95	6-3-95	5-11-97	3-4
Bongo (tan tail)	4067	8-17-95	6-3-95		3-5
Sting the stingray	4077	8-27-95	6-3-95	1-1-97	3-4
Inch the inchworm (felt antennae)	4044	9-3-95	6-3-95	10-15-96	3-4
Kiwi the toucan	4070	9-16-95	6-3-95	1-1-97	3-4
Velvet the panther	4064	12-16-95	6-3-95	10-1-97	3-4
Waddle the penguin	4075	12-19-95	6-3-95	5-1-98	3-5
Ziggy the zebra	4063	12-24-95	6-3-95	5-1-98	3-5
Derby the horse (fine mane)	4008		6-3-95	late 1995	3
Lizzy the tie-dyed lizard	4033		6-3-95	1-7-96	3
Flutter the butterfly	4043		6-3-95	6-15-96	3
Bumble the bee	4045		6-3-95	6-15-96	3-4
Peanut the royal blue elephant	4062		6-3-95	10-2-95	3

continues

337

continued

Name	Style#	Birthday	Issued	Retired	HT Gen
Nana the tan-tailed monkey	4067		6-3-95		3
Caw the crow	4071		6-3-95	6-15-96	3
Bronty the brontosaurus	4085		6-3-95	6-15-96	3
Rex the tyrannosaurus	4086		6-3-95	6-15-96	3
Steg the stegosaurus	4087		6-3-95	6-15-96	3
Radar the bat	4091	10-30-95	9-1-95	5-11-97	3-4
Spooky the ghost	4090	10-31-95	9-1-95	12-31-97	3-4
Peanut the light blue elephant	4062	1-25-95	10-2-95	5-1-98	3-5
Derby the horse (coarse mane)	4008	9-16-95	late 1995	12-15-97	3-5
Flip the white cat	4012	2-28-95	1-7-96	10-1-97	3-4
Ears the brown rabbit	4018	4-18-95	1-7-96	5-1-98	3-5
Lizzy the blue lizard	4033	5-11-95	1-7-96	12-31-97	3-4
Twigs the giraffe	4068	5-19-95	1-7-96	5-1-98	3-5
Bucky the beaver	4016	6-8-95	1-7-96	12-31-97	3-4
Manny the manatee	4081	6-8-95	1-7-96	5-11-97	3-4
Ringo the raccoon	4014	7-14-95	1-7-96	9-16-98	3-5
Grunt the razorback	4092	7-19-95	1-7-96	5-11-97	3-4
Weenie the Dachshund	4013	7-20-95	1-7-96	5-1-98	3-5
Garcia the bear	4051	8-1-95	1-7-96	5-11-97	3-4
Hoot the owl	4073	8-9-95	1-7-96	10-1-97	3-4
Seaweed the otter	4080	3-19-96	1-7-96	9-19-98	3-5
Chops the lamb	4019	5-3-96	1-7-96	1-1-97	3-4
Nip the gold cat	4003		1-7-96	3-10-96	3
Zip the all-black cat	4004		1-7-96	3-10-96	3
Stripes the tiger (dark)	4065		1-7-96	6-3-96	3
Mystic the unicorn (brown horn)	4007	5-21-94	early 1996	10-23-97	3-4

Name	Style#	Birthday	Issued	Retired	HT Gen
Bongo (brown tail)	4067	8-17-95	2-6-96	6-29-96	3-4
Lucky the ladybug (21 spots)	4040	5-1-95	2-25-96		4
Nip the gold cat (white paws)	4003	3-6-94	3-10-96	12-31-97	3-4
Zip the black cat (white paws)	4004	3-28-94	3-10-96	5-1-98	3-5
Tank the armadillo (9 lines, without shell)	4031	2-22-95	6-3-96	Fall 1996	4
Stripes the tiger (light)	4065	6-11-95	6-3-96	5-1-98	4-5
Lucky the ladybug (11 spots)	4040	5-1-95	6-15-96	5-1-98	4-5
Sparky the Dalmatian	4100	2-27-96	6-15-96	5-11-97	4
Curly the bear	4052	4-12-96	6-15-96		4-5
Wrinkles the Bulldog	4103	5-1-96	6-15-96	9-22-98	4-5
Rover the dog	4101	5-30-96	6-15-96	5-1-98	4-5
Freckles the leopard	4066	6-3-96	6-15-96		4-5
Scottie the Scottish Terrier	4102	6-15-96	6-15-96	5-1-98	4-5
Scoop the pelican	4107	7-1-96	6-15-96		4-5
Righty the elephant	4085	7-4-96	6-15-96	1-1-97	4
Lefty the donkey	4086	7-4-96	6-15-96	1-1-97	4
Spike the rhinoceros	4060	8-13-96	6-15-96		4-5
Sly the brown-bellied fox	4115	9-12-96	6-15-96	8-6-96	4
Congo the gorilla	4160	11-9-96	6-15-96		4-5
Libearty the bear	4057	Summer 1996	6-15-96	1-1-97	4
Sly the white-bellied fox	4115	9-12-96	8-6-96	9-22-98	4-5
Inch the inchworm (yarn antennae)	4044	9-3-95	10-15-96	5-1-98	4-5

continues

continued

Name	Style#	Birthday	Issued	Retired	HT Gen
Tank the armadillo (with shell)	4031	2-22-95	Fall 1996	10-31-97	4
Snort the bull	4002	5-15-95	1-1-97	9-15-98	4-5
Crunch the shark	4130	1-13-96	1-1-97	9-24-98	4-5
Mel the koala	4162	1-15-96	1-1-97		4-5
Nuts the squirrel	4114	1-21-96	1-1-97		4-5
Fleece the lamb	4125	3-21-96	1-1-97		4-5
Hoppity the rose bunny	4117	4-3-96	1-1-97	5-1-98	4-5
Floppity the lilac bunny	4118	5-28-96	1-1-97	5-1-98	4-5
Hippity the mint bunny	4119	6-1-96	1-1-97	5-1-98	4-5
Gracie the swan	4126	6-17-96	1-1-97	5-1-98	4-5
Maple the bear	4600	7-1-96	1-1-97		4-5
Bernie the St. Bernard	4109	10-3-96	1-1-97	9-22-98	4-5
Doby the Doberman	4110	10-9-96	1-1-97		4-5
Snip the Siamese cat	4120	10-22-96	1-1-97		4-5
Pouch the kangaroo	4161	11-6-96	1-1-97		4-5
Chip the cat	4121	1-26-96	5-1-97		4-5
Peace the bear	4053	2-1-96	5-11-97		4-5
Baldy the eagle	4074	2-17-96	5-11-97	5-1-98	4-5
Roary the lion	4069	2-20-96	5-11-97		4-5
Doodle the rooster	4171	3-8-96	5-11-97	7-12-97	4
Pugsly the Pug dog	4106	5-2-96	5-11-97		4-5
Claude the crab	4083	9-3-96	5-11-97		4-5
Tuffy the terrier	4108	10-12-96	5-11-97		4-5
Dotty the Dalmatian	4100	10-17-96	5-11-97		4-5
Nanook the husky	4104	11-21-96	5-11-97		4-5
Jolly the walrus	4082	12-2-96	5-11-97	5-1-98	4-5
Waves the whale	4084	12-8-96	5-11-97	5-1-98	4-5

Name	Style#	Birthday	Issued	Retired	HT Gen
Blizzard the tiger	4163	12-12-96	5-11-97	5-1-98	4-5
Echo the dolphin	4180	12-21-96	5-11-97	5-1-98	4-5
Strut the rooster	4171	3-8-96	7-12-97		4-5
Spinner the spider	4026	10-28-96	10-1-97	9-19-98	4-5
Batty the bat	4035	10-29-96	10-1-97		4-5
Gobbles the turkey	4023	11-27-96	10-1-97		4-5
Snowball the snowman	4201	12-22-96	10-1-97	12-31-97	4
"Teddy, 1997"	4200	12-25-96	10-1-97	12-31-97	4
Mystic the unicorn (iridescent horn)	4007	5-21-94	10-23-97		4-5
Princess the bear	4300		10-29-97		special
Derby the horse (star)	4008	9-16-95	12-15-97		5
Spunky the Cocker Spaniel	4184	1-14-97	12-31-97		5
Iggy the iguana	4038	8-12-97	12-31-97		5
Pounce the cat	4122	8-28-97	12-31-97		5
Bruno the terrier	4183	9-9-97	12-31-97	9-18-98	5
Stretch the ostrich	4182	9-21-97	12-31-97		5
Smoochy the frog	4039	10-1-97	12-31-97		5
Rainbow the chameleon	4037	10-14-97	12-31-97		5
Puffer the puffin	4181	11-3-97	12-31-97	9-18-98	5
Prance the cat	4123	11-20-97	12-31-97		5
Britannia the bear	4601	12-15-97	12-31-97		5
Erin the bear	4186	3-17-97	1-31-98		5
Kuku the cockatoo	4192	1-5-97	5-30-98		5
Fetch the Golden Retriever	4189	2-4-97	5-30-98		5
Rocket the blue jay	4202	3-12-97	5-30-98		5
Early the robin	4190	3-20-97	5-30-98		5

continues

continued

Name	Style#	Birthday	Issued	Retired	HT Gen
Whisper the deer	4194	4-5-97	5-30-98		5
Jake the mallard duck	4199	4-16-97	5-30-98		5
Wise the owl	4194	5-31-97	5-30-98		5
Tracker the Bassett Hound	4198	6-5-97	5-30-98		5
Glory the bear	4188	7-4-97	5-30-98		5
Stinger the scorpion	4193	9-29-97	5-30-98		5
Jabber the parrot	4197	10-10-97	5-30-98		5
Ants the anteater	4195	11-7-97	5-30-98		5
Fortune the panda	4196	12-6-97	5-30-98		5
Gigi the Poodle	4191	4-7-98	5-30-98		5
Hissy the snake	4185	4-4-97	12-31-98		5

By Retirement

Name	Style#	Birthday	Issued	Retired	HT Gen
Brownie the bear	4010		1993	1993	1
Punchers the lobster	4026		1993	1993	1
Spot the dog (without a spot)	4000		1-8-94	4-13-94	1-2
Inky the octopus (tan—no mouth)	4028		6-25-94	9-12-94	1-2
Quackers the duck (wingless)	4024		6-25-94	1-7-95	1-2
Teddy the old-faced brown bear	4050		6-25-94	1-7-95	1-2
Teddy the old-faced teal bear	4051		6-25-94	1-7-95	1-2
Teddy the old-faced cranberry bear	4052		6-25-94	1-7-95	1-2
Teddy the old-faced violet bear	4055		6-25-94	1-7-95	1-2

Name	Style#	Birthday	Issued	Retired	HT Gen
Teddy the old-faced magenta bear	4056		6-25-94	1-7-95	1-2
Teddy the old-faced jade bear	4057		6-25-94	1-7-95	1-2
Patti the maroon platypus	4025		1-8-94	2-28-95	1-3
Digger the orange crab	4027		6-25-94	6-3-95	1-3
Happy the gray hippo	4061		6-25-94	6-3-95	1-3
Inky the octopus (tan—mouth)	4028		9-12-94	6-3-95	3
Slither the snake	4031		6-25-94	6-15-95	1-3
Trap the mouse	4042		6-25-94	6-15-95	1-3
Humphrey the camel	4060		6-25-94	6-15-95	1-3
Peanut the royal blue elephant	4062		6-3-95	10-2-95	3
Derby the horse (fine mane)	4008		6-3-95	late 1995	3
Chilly the polar bear	4012		6-25-94	1-7-96	1-3
Peking the panda	4013		6-25-94	1-7-96	1-3
Web the spider	4041		6-25-94	1-7-96	1-3
Nip the gold cat (white face)	4003		1-7-95	1-7-96	2-3
Zip the black cat (white face)	4004		1-7-95	1-7-96	2-3
Tank the armadillo (7 lines, without shell)	4031		1-7-95	1-7-96	3
Teddy the new-faced teal bear	4051		1-7-95	1-7-96	2-3
Teddy the new-faced cranberry bear	4052		1-7-95	1-7-96	2-3
Teddy the new-faced violet bear	4055		1-7-95	1-7-96	2-3

continues

343

continued

Name	Style#	Birthday	Issued	Retired	HT Gen
Teddy the new-faced magenta bear	4056		1-7-95	1-7-96	2-3
Teddy the new-faced jade bear	4057		1-7-95	1-7-96	2-3
Lizzy the tie-dyed lizard	4033		6-3-95	1-7-96	3
Mystic the unicorn (fine mane)	4007		6-25-94	early 1996	1-3
Lucky the ladybug (7 spots)	4040		6-25-94	2-27-96	1-3
Nip the gold cat	4003		1-7-96	3-10-96	3
Zip the all-black cat	4004		1-7-96	3-10-96	3
Stripes the tiger (dark)	4065		1-7-96	6-3-96	3
Flutter the butterfly	4043		6-3-95	6-15-96	3
Bumble the bee	4045		6-3-95	6-15-96	3-4
Caw the crow	4071		6-3-95	6-15-96	3
Bronty the brontosaurus	4085		6-3-95	6-15-96	3
Rex the tyrannosaurus	4086		6-3-95	6-15-96	3
Steg the stegosaurus	4087		6-3-95	6-15-96	3
Bongo (brown tail)	4067	8-17-95	2-6-96	6-29-96	3-4
Sly the brown-bellied fox	4115	9-12-96	6-15-96	8-6-96	4
Inch the inchworm (felt antennae)	4044	9-3-95	6-3-95	10-15-96	3-4
Tank the armadillo (9 lines, without shell)	4031	2-22-95	6-3-96	Fall 1996	4
Tusk the walrus	4076	9-18-95	1-7-95	1-1-97	3-4
Coral the fish	4079	3-2-95	6-3-95	1-1-97	3-4
Tabasco the bull	4002	5-15-95	6-3-95	1-1-97	3-4
Sting the stingray	4077	8-27-95	6-3-95	1-1-97	3-4
Kiwi the toucan	4070	9-16-95	6-3-95	1-1-97	3-4

Name	Style#	Birthday	Issued	Retired	HT Gen
Chops the lamb	4019	5-3-96	1-7-96	1-1-97	3-4
Righty the elephant	4085	7-4-96	6-15-96	1-1-97	4
Lefty the donkey	4086	7-4-96	6-15-96	1-1-97	4
Libearty the bear	4057	Summer 1996	6-15-96	1-1-97	4
Flash the dolphin	4021	5-13-93	1-8-94	5-11-97	1-4
Splash the whale	4022	7-8-93	1-8-94	5-11-97	1-4
Digger the red crab	4027	8-23-95	6-25-94	5-11-97	3-4
Bubbles the fish	4078	7-2-95	6-3-95	5-11-97	3-4
Radar the bat	4091	10-30-95	9-1-95	5-11-97	3-4
Manny the manatee	4081	6-8-95	1-7-96	5-11-97	3-4
Grunt the razorback	4092	7-19-95	1-7-96	5-11-97	3-4
Garcia the bear	4051	8-1-95	1-7-96	5-11-97	3-4
Sparky the Dalmatian	4100	2-27-96	6-15-96	5-11-97	4
Doodle the rooster	4171	3-8-96	5-11-97	7-12-97	4
Legs the frog	4020	4-25-93	1-8-94	10-1-97	1-4
Spot the dog (with a spot)	4000	1-3-93	4-13-94	10-1-97	2-4
Ally the alligator	4032	3-14-94	6-25-94	10-1-97	1-4
Speedy the turtle	4030	8-14-94	6-25-94	10-1-97	1-4
Seamore the seal	4029	12-14-96	6-25-94	10-1-97	1-4
Teddy the new-faced brown bear	4050	11-28-95	1-7-95	10-1-97	2-4
Bessie the cow	4009	6-27-95	6-3-95	10-1-97	2-4
Velvet the panther	4064	12-16-95	6-3-95	10-1-97	3-4
Flip the white cat	4012	2-28-95	1-7-96	10-1-97	3-4
Hoot the owl	4073	8-9-95	1-7-96	10-1-97	3-4
Mystic the unicorn (brown horn)	4007	5-21-94	early 1996	10-23-97	3-4
Tank the armadillo (with shell)	4031	2-22-95	Fall 1996	10-31-97	4

continues

continued

Name	Style#	Birthday	Issued	Retired	HT Gen
Derby the horse (coarse mane)	4008	9-16-95	late 1995	12-15-97	3-5
Cubbie the bear	4010	11-14-93	1-8-94	12-31-97	1-4
Goldie the goldfish	4023	11-14-94	6-25-94	12-31-97	1-4
Magic the dragon	4088	6-8-95	6-3-95	12-31-97	3-4
Spooky the ghost	4090	10-31-95	9-1-95	12-31-97	3-4
Lizzy the blue lizard	4033	5-11-95	1-7-96	12-31-97	3-4
Bucky the beaver	4016	6-8-95	1-7-96	12-31-97	3-4
Nip the gold cat (white paws)	4003	3-6-94	3-10-96	12-31-97	3-4
Snowball the snowman	4201	12-22-96	10-1-97	12-31-97	4
"Teddy, 1997"	4200	12-25-96	10-1-97	12-31-97	4
Squealer the pig	4005	4-23-93	1-8-94	5-1-98	1-5
Pinchers the lobster	4026	6-19-93	1-8-94	5-1-98	1-5
Bones the dog	4001	1-18-94	6-25-94	5-1-98	1-5
Quackers the duck (with wings)	4024	4-19-94	1-7-95	5-1-98	2-5
Patti the fuchsia platypus	4025	1-6-93	2-28-95	5-1-98	3-5
Happy the lavender hippo	4061	2-25-94	6-3-95	5-1-98	3-5
Inky the pink octopus	4028	11-29-94	6-3-95	5-1-98	3-5
Waddle the penguin	4075	12-19-95	6-3-95	5-1-98	3-5
Ziggy the zebra	4063	12-24-95	6-3-95	5-1-98	3-5
Peanut the light blue elephant	4062	1-25-95	10-2-95	5-1-98	3-5
Ears the brown rabbit	4018	4-18-95	1-7-96	5-1-98	3-5
Twigs the giraffe	4068	5-19-95	1-7-96	5-1-98	3-5
Weenie the Dachshund	4013	7-20-95	1-7-96	5-1-98	3-5
Zip the black cat (white paws)	4004	3-28-94	3-10-96	5-1-98	3-5

Name	Style#	Birthday	Issued	Retired	HT Gen
Stripes the tiger (light)	4065	6-11-95	6-3-96	5-1-98	4-5
Lucky the ladybug (11 spots)	4040	5-1-95	6-15-96	5-1-98	4-5
Rover the dog	4101	5-30-96	6-15-96	5-1-98	4-5
Scottie the Scottish Terrier	4102	6-15-96	6-15-96	5-1-98	4-5
Inch the inchworm (yarn antennae)	4044	9-3-95	10-15-96	5-1-98	4-5
Hoppity the rose bunny	4117	4-3-96	1-1-97	5-1-98	4-5
Floppity the lilac bunny	4118	5-28-96	1-1-97	5-1-98	4-5
Hippity the mint bunny	4119	6-1-96	1-1-97	5-1-98	4-5
Gracie the swan	4126	6-17-96	1-1-97	5-1-98	4-5
Baldy the eagle	4074	2-17-96	5-11-97	5-1-98	4-5
Jolly the walrus	4082	12-2-96	5-11-97	5-1-98	4-5
Waves the whale	4084	12-8-96	5-11-97	5-1-98	4-5
Blizzard the tiger	4163	12-12-96	5-11-97	5-1-98	4-5
Echo the dolphin	4180	12-21-96	5-11-97	5-1-98	4-5
Daisy the cow	4006	5-10-94	6-25-94	9-15-98	1-5
Blackie the bear	4011	7-15-94	6-25-94	9-15-98	1-5
Snort the bull	4002	5-15-95	1-1-97	9-15-98	4-5
Ringo the raccoon	4014	7-14-95	1-7-96	9-16-98	3-5
Bruno the terrier	4183	9-9-97	12-31-97	9-18-98	5
Puffer the puffin	4181	11-3-97	12-31-97	9-18-98	5
Seaweed the otter	4080	3-19-96	1-7-96	9-19-98	3-5
Spinner the spider	4026	10-28-96	10-1-97	9-19-98	4-5
Bernie the St. Bernard	4109	10-3-96	1-1-97	9-22-98	4-5
Wrinkles the Bulldog	4103	5-1-96	6-15-96	9-22-98	4-5
Sly the white-bellied fox	4115	9-12-96	8-6-96	9-22-98	4-5
Crunch the shark	4130	1-13-96	1-1-97	9-24-98	4-5

continues

continued

Name	Style#	Birthday	Issued	Retired	HT Gen
Stinky the skunk	4017	2-13-95	6-3-95	9-28-98	3-5
Chocolate the moose	4015	4-27-93	1-8-94		1-5
Valentino the bear	4058	2-14-94	1-7-95		2-5
Pinky the flamingo	4072	2-13-95	6-3-95		3-5
Bongo (tan tail)	4067	8-17-95	6-3-95		3-5
Nana the tan-tailed monkey	4067		6-3-95		3
Lucky the ladybug (21 spots)	4040	5-1-95	2-25-96		4
Curly the bear	4052	4-12-96	6-15-96		4-5
Freckles the leopard	4066	6-3-96	6-15-96		4-5
Scoop the pelican	4107	7-1-96	6-15-96		4-5
Spike the rhinoceros	4060	8-13-96	6-15-96		4-5
Congo the gorilla	4160	11-9-96	6-15-96		4-5
Mel the koala	4162	1-15-96	1-1-97		4-5
Nuts the squirrel	4114	1-21-96	1-1-97		4-5
Fleece the lamb	4125	3-21-96	1-1-97		4-5
Maple the bear	4600	7-1-96	1-1-97		4-5
Doby the Doberman	4110	10-9-96	1-1-97		4-5
Snip the Siamese cat	4120	10-22-96	1-1-97		4-5
Pouch the kangaroo	4161	11-6-96	1-1-97		4-5
Chip the cat	4121	1-26-96	5-1-97		4-5
Peace the bear	4053	2-1-96	5-11-97		4-5
Roary the lion	4069	2-20-96	5-11-97		4-5
Pugsly the Pug dog	4106	5-2-96	5-11-97		4-5
Claude the crab	4083	9-3-96	5-11-97		4-5
Tuffy the terrier	4108	10-12-96	5-11-97		4-5
Dotty the Dalmatian	4100	10-17-96	5-11-97		4-5
Nanook the husky	4104	11-21-96	5-11-97		4-5
Strut the rooster	4171	3-8-96	7-12-97		4-5
Batty the bat	4035	10-29-96	10-1-97		4-5

Name	Style#	Birthday	Issued	Retired	HT Gen
Gobbles the turkey	4023	11-27-96	10-1-97		4-5
Mystic the unicorn (iridescent horn)	4007	5-21-94	10-23-97		4-5
Princess the bear	4300		10-29-97		special
Derby the horse (star)	4008	9-16-95	12-15-97		5
Spunky the Cocker Spaniel	4184	1-14-97	12-31-97		5
Iggy the iguana	4038	8-12-97	12-31-97		5
Pounce the cat	4122	8-28-97	12-31-97		5
Stretch the ostrich	4182	9-21-97	12-31-97		5
Smoochy the frog	4039	10-1-97	12-31-97		5
Rainbow the chameleon	4037	10-14-97	12-31-97		5
Prance the cat	4123	11-20-97	12-31-97		5
Britannia the bear	4601	12-15-97	12-31-97		5
Erin the bear	4186	3-17-97	1-31-98		5
Kuku the cockatoo	4192	1-5-97	5-30-98		5
Fetch the Golden Retriever	4189	2-4-97	5-30-98		5
Rocket the blue jay	4202	3-12-97	5-30-98		5
Early the robin	4190	3-20-97	5-30-98		5
Whisper the deer	4194	4-5-97	5-30-98		5
Jake the mallard duck	4199	4-16-97	5-30-98		5
Wise the owl	4194	5-31-97	5-30-98		5
Tracker the Bassett Hound	4198	6-5-97	5-30-98		5
Glory the bear	4188	7-4-97	5-30-98		5
Stinger the scorpion	4193	9-29-97	5-30-98		5
Jabber the parrot	4197	10-10-97	5-30-98		5
Ants the anteater	4195	11-7-97	5-30-98		5
Fortune the panda	4196	12-6-97	5-30-98		5
Gigi the Poodle	4191	4-7-98	5-30-98		5
Hissy the snake	4185	4-4-97	12-31-98		5

Promotional Beanies Checklist

MLB Beanies

Chicago Cubs	Cubbie	18 May 1997
Chicago Cubs	Cubbie	6 Sept 1997
Chicago Cubs (Convention)	Cubbie	15–18 Jan 1998
New York Yankees (Spring Training)	Bones	10 Mar 1998
Oakland A's (Spring Training)	Ears	15 Mar 1998
Chicago Cubs (Harry Caray)	Daisy	3 May 1998
New York Yankees (Perfect Game)	Valentino	17 May 1998
St. Louis Cardinals	Stretch	22 May 1998
Milwaukee Brewers	Batty	31 May 1998
Kansas City Royals	Roary	31 May 1998
Detroit Tigers	Stripes	31 May 1998
Arizona Diamondbacks	Hissy	14 June 1998
All-Star Game	Glory	7 July 1998
New York Mets	Batty	12 July 1998
Chicago White Sox	Blizzard	12 July 1998
Tampa Bay Devil Rays	Weenie	26 July 1998
Minnesota Twins	Lucky	31 July 1998
Oakland A's	Peanut	1 Aug 1998
Detroit Tigers	Stripes	8 Aug 1998
New York Yankees	Stretch	9 Aug 1998
St. Louis Cardinals	Smoochy	14 Aug 1998
San Diego Padres	Waves	14 Aug 1998
Houston Astros	Derby	16 Aug 1998
Atlanta Braves	Chip	19 Aug 1998
New York Mets	Curly	22 Aug 1998
Tampa Bay Devil Rays	Pinky	23 Aug 1998
Arizona Diamondbacks	Sly	27 Aug 1998
Atlanta Braves	Pugsly	2 Sept 1998
Seattle Mariners	Chocolate	5 Sept 1998

Oakland A's	Peanut	6 Sept 1998
Toronto Blue Jays	Rocket	6 Sept 1998
Chicago Cubs	Gracie	13 Sept 1998

NBA Beanies

Philadelphia 76ers	Baldy	17 Jan 1998
Indiana Pacers	Strut	2 April 1998
Cleveland Cavaliers	Bongo	5 April 1998
Denver Nuggets	Chocolate	17 April 1998
San Antonio Spurs	Curly	27 April 1998
San Antonio Spurs	Pinky	29 April 1998

WNBA Beanies

Charlotte Sting	Curly	15 June 1998
Washington Mystics	Mystic	11 July 1998
Detroit Shock	Mel	25 July 1998
Cleveland Rockers	Curly	15 Aug 1998

NFL Beanies

| Dallas Cowboys | Chocolate | 6 Sept 1998 |

NHL Beanies

Boston Bruins	Blackie	12 Oct 1998
St. Louis Blues	To be announced	24 Nov 1998
St. Louis Blues	To be announced	22 Mar 1999

Broadway Beanies

"Joseph and the Amazing Technicolor Dreamcoat" (rainbow-striped ribbon)	Garcia	
	Peace	
	Inch	
	Fleece	
"Candide" (violet-blue velvet ribbon stamped with show name in gold)	Roary	
	Fleece	

continues

continued

"Show Boat" (light blue ribbon
stamped with show name in gold)

Peace

Goldie

Scoop

"Phantom of the Opera" (red ribbon
stamped with show name in gold)

Congo

Velvet

Maple

Bongo

Peanut

"Ragtime" (maroon, ivory, or navy
ribbon stamped with show name
in gold)

Curly

Further Reading

Beanie Magazines

Beanie Collector
Published bi-monthly.
Beckett & Associates, publisher

Beanie Mania
Published bi-monthly.
Beanie Mania LLC, publisher

Beans!
Published monthly.
Tuff Stuff Publications

Mary Beth's Beanie World
Published monthly.
H & S Media, publisher

Mary Beth's Beanie World for Kids
Published quarterly.
H & S Media, publisher

Beanie Books

Brecka, Shawn. *The Bean Family Album.* Norfolk, VA: Antique Trader Books, 1998.

_____. *The Bean Family Pocket Guide.* Norfolk, VA: Antique Trader Books, 1998.

Carey, Susan S. and Ryan M. Carey. *The Beanie Encyclopedia: Identification and Values.* Paducah, KY: Collector Books, 1998.

Cook, Rachel, et.al. *Encyclo-Beanie-A: An Educational Reference Guide to Beanie Babies & the Animal Kingdom*. Seattle, WA: Buckaroo Books, 1998.

Fox, Les and Sue Fox. *The Beanie Baby Handbook: Fall 1998*. Midland Park, NJ: West Highland Publishing Co., 1998.

Neebascher, B. *The Official Beanie Basher Handbook*. Kansas City, MO: Andrews & McMeel, 1998.

Phillips, Becky and Becky Estenssoro. *Beanie Mania: A Comprehensive Collector's Guide*. Naperville, IL: Dinomates, Inc., 1997.

_____. *Beanie Mania II: A Comprehensive Collector's Guide*. Naperville, IL: Dinomates, Inc., 1998.

_____. *Beanie Mania II With Poster*. Naperville, IL: Dinomates, Inc., 1998.

_____. *Beanie Mania International*. Naperville, IL: Dinomates, Inc., 1998.

Stowe, Holly. *Beanie Babies Collector's Guide*. New York, NY: Penguin USA, 1998.

Wells, Rosie (ed). *Rosie's Price Guide for Ty's Beanie Babies*. Canton, IL: Rosie Wells Enterprises, Inc., 1998.

_____. *Beanie Digest*. Canton, IL: Rosie Wells Enterprises, Inc., 1998.

Beanie Web Sites

News, articles, and references to other links:

Ty, Inc.
www.ty.com

BeanieMom
www.beaniemom.com

Ctoys
www.ctoys.com

Beaniemonium
www.beaniemonium.com

Mary Beth's Beanie World
www.beanieworld.net

Beanie Mania LLC
www.beaniemania.net

The Beanie Philes
www.beaniephiles.com

Beanieholics
www.geocities.com/Heartland/Park/4116/

RJW Retail (Canada)
www.beaniemania.com

Ashley's Awesome Beanies
www.awesomebeanies.com

The Toy Box
www.the-toybox.com

Beanie Phenomenon
www.beaniephenomenon.com/

Janie Davis
www.netreach.net/people/rjones/beanie.html

K 'n K Collectibles
www.knkcollectibles.com

Swap meets and shows:

www.beaniemom.com/swaplinks.html

Pricing guides:

www.beaniemom.com/beaninfo.html

www.beaniephenomenon.com/checklist.html

www.ctoys.com/list/

Merchants links:

www.beaniemom.com/mercmain.html

www.beaniemania.com/ring/ring.html

Auctions, classifieds, and trading boards:

www.beaniemom.com/collcorn.html

cgi.ty.com/fastcgi/viewguest.fcgi

toys.ebay.com

up4sale.com/beaniebabies.html

jango.excite.com/xsh/query.dcg?cat=beanies&svc=&cobrand=xsh

Counterfeit info:

www.beaniemom.com/countermain.html

Links for accessories:

www.beaniemom.com/accessmain.html

http://www.netreach.net/people/rjones/beanie.html#Accessories

Beanbag-toy–related books:

www.amazon.com

www.barnesandnoble.com

www.borders.com

Beanie Babies— Approximate Market Values

Values approximated for October 15, 1998; retireds as of September 27, 1998. Currents valued $5–7 US, $8–15 Cdn, 10–15 pounds sterling.

Ally the alligator	$38–45
Ants the anteater	$5–7
Baldy the eagle	$11–15
Batty the bat	$5–7
Bernie the St. Bernard	$9–12
Bessie the cow	$55–62
Blackie the bear	$9–12
Blizzard the tiger	$11–15
Bones the dog	$11–15
Bongo (brown tail)	$48–55
Bongo (tan tail)	$5–7
Britannia the bear	10–15 pounds sterling
Bronty the brontosaurus	$800–950
Brownie the bear	$2,800–3,200
Bruno the terrier	$10–14
Bubbles the fish	$100–115
Bucky the beaver	$32–38
Bumble the bee	$475–525

Caw the crow	$500–550
Chilly the polar bear	$1,800–2,000
Chip the cat	$5–7
Chocolate the moose	$5–7
Chops the lamb	$135–160
Claude the crab	$5–7
Congo the gorilla	$5–7
Coral the fish	$160–175
Crunch the shark	$5–7
Cubbie the bear	$20–25
Curly the bear	$5–7
Daisy the cow	$9–12
Derby the horse (fine mane)	$2,750–3,250
Derby the horse (coarse mane)	$20–25
Derby the horse (star)	$5–7
Digger the orange crab	$700–800
Digger the red crab	$90–100
Doby the Doberman	$5–7
Doodle the rooster	$35–40
Dotty the Dalmatian	$5–7
Early the robin	$5–7
Ears the brown rabbit	$11–15
Echo the dolphin	$11–15
Erin the bear	$5–7
Fetch the Golden Retriever	$5–7
Flash the dolphin	$90–100
Fleece the lamb	$5–7
Flip the white cat	$30–35
Floppity the lilac bunny	$11–15
Flutter the butterfly	$900–1,000

Fortune the panda	$5–7
Freckles the leopard	$5–7
Garcia the bear	$140–160
Gigi the Poodle	$5–7
Glory the bear	$5–7
Gobbles the turkey	$5–7
Goldie the goldfish	$32–38
Gracie the swan	$11–15
Grunt the razorback	$140–160
Happy the gray hippo	$625–725
Happy the lavender hippo	$11–15
Hippity the mint bunny	$11–15
Hissy the snake	$5–7
Hoot the owl	$32–40
Hoppity the rose bunny	$11–15
Humphrey the camel	$1,600–1,850
Iggy the iguana (bright tie-dye, no tongue)	$10–15
Iggy the iguana (bright tie-dye, tongue)	$12–17
Iggy the iguana (blue tie-dye)	$5–7
Inch the inchworm (felt antennae)	$135–160
Inch the inchworm (yarn antennae)	$12–18
Inky the octopus (tan—mouth)	$650–750
Inky the octopus (tan—no mouth)	$750–850
Inky the pink octopus	$15–20
Jabber the parrot	$5–7
Jake the mallard duck	$5–7
Jolly the walrus	$11–15
Kiwi the toucan	$160–180
Kuku the cockatoo	$5–7
Lefty the donkey	$250–300

Legs the frog	$15–22
Libearty the bear	$325–375
Lizzy the blue lizard	$22–27
Lizzy the tie-dyed lizard	$900–1,000
Lucky the ladybug (11 spots)	$18–22
Lucky the ladybug (21 spots)	$500–600
Lucky the ladybug (7 spots)	$160–180
Magic the dragon	$40–50
Manny the manatee	$150–175
Maple the bear	$8–15 Cdn
Mel the koala	$5–7
Mystic the unicorn (fine mane)	$200–250
Mystic the unicorn (brown horn)	$28–35
Mystic the unicorn (iridescent horn)	$5–7
Nana the tan-tailed monkey	$3,500–4,000
Nanook the Husky	$5–7
Nip the gold cat	$850–900
Nip the gold cat (white face)	$500–550
Nip the gold cat (white paws)	$18–22
Nuts the squirrel	$5–7
Patti the fuchsia platypus	$15–20
Patti the maroon platypus	$700–1,000
Peace the bear	$5–7
Peanut the light blue elephant	$11–15
Peanut the royal blue elephant	$4,500–5,000
Peking the panda	$1,800–2,000
Pinchers the lobster	$11–15
Pinky the flamingo	$5–7
Pouch the kangaroo	$5–7
Pounce the cat	$5–7

Prance the cat	$5–7
Princess the bear	$5–7
Puffer the puffin	$10–14
Pugsly the Pug dog	$5–7
Punchers the lobster	$2,800–3,200
Quackers the duck (with wings)	$11–15
Quackers the duck (wingless)	$1,750–2,000
Radar the bat	$130–160
Rainbow the chameleon (blue tie-dye)	$10–15
Rainbow the chameleon (bright tie-dye)	$5–7
Rex the tyrannosaurus	$800–950
Righty the elephant	$250–300
Ringo the raccoon	$8–12
Roary the lion	$5–7
Rocket the blue jay	$5–7
Rover the dog	$15–20
Scoop the pelican	$5–7
Scottie the Scottish Terrier	$18–22
Seamore the seal	$125–150
Seaweed the otter	$15–20
Slither the snake	$1,800–2,000
Sly the brown-bellied fox	$125–150
Sly the white-bellied fox	$5–7
Smoochy the frog	$5–7
Snip the Siamese cat	$5–7
Snort the bull	$8–12
Snowball the snowman	$38–45
Sparky the Dalmatian	$100–125
Speedy the turtle	$28–35
Spike the rhinoceros	$5–7

Spinner the spider	$9–14
Splash the whale	$90–100
Spooky the ghost	$28–38
Spot the dog with a spot	$38–45
Spot the dog without a spot	$1,800–2,000
Spunky the Cocker Spaniel	$5–7
Squealer the pig	$20–25
Steg the stegosaurus	$800–900
Sting the stingray	$150–175
Stinger the scorpion	$5–7
Stinky the skunk	$8–12
Stretch the ostrich	$5–7
Stripes the tiger (dark)	$275–325
Stripes the tiger (light)	$11–15
Strut the rooster	$5–7
Tabasco the bull	$150–175
Tank the armadillo (7 lines without shell)	$165–180
Tank the armadillo (9 lines without shell)	$175–200
Tank the armadillo (with shell)	$60–70
Teddy the new-faced brown bear	$70–90
Teddy the new-faced cranberry bear	$1,750–1,950
Teddy the new-faced jade bear	$1,750–1,950
Teddy the new-faced magenta bear	$1,750–1,950
Teddy the new-faced teal bear	$1,750–1,950
Teddy the new-faced violet bear	$1,750–1,950
Teddy the old-faced brown bear	$2,750–3,250
Teddy the old-faced cranberry bear	$1,750–1,950
Teddy the old-faced jade bear	$1,750–1,950
Teddy the old-faced magenta bear	$1,750–1,950
Teddy the old-faced teal bear	$1,750–1,950

Teddy the old-faced violet bear	$1,750–1,950
Teddy, 1997	$40–60
Tracker the Bassett Hound	$5–7
Trap the mouse	$1,250–1,500
Tuffy the terrier	$5–7
Tusk the walrus	$120–140
Twigs the giraffe	$12–18
Valentino the bear	$5–7
Velvet the panther	$22–30
Waddle the penguin	$11–15
Waves the whale	$11–15
Web the spider	$1,250–1,500
Weenie the Dachshund	$18–25
Whisper the deer	$5–7
Wise the owl	$5–7
Wrinkles the Bulldog	$8–12
Ziggy the zebra	$15–20
Zip the all-black cat	$1,650–1,800
Zip the black cat (white face)	$625–675
Zip the black cat (white paws)	$32–40

Index

News Flash!

As this book was going to press, Ty announced 10 new Beanie Babies along with a new product line of larger Beanie-look-alikes called "Beanie Buddies"! Permit me to introduce you to the latest Beanie Babies!

Beak   Well, I'm having a tough time deciding whether Beak is a kiwi bird or an emu. His (her?) beak is much more kiwi-like than emu-ish, but kiwis only have the most rudimentary of wings. Beak's are more pronounced. His/her fur appears to be yet another new kind of plush, a longer napped fur. I can't wait to see Beak in person!

Canyon   Cougar is the best guess for this feline. It's light brown in color with ear fronts of white plush and backs of black plush. Its belly and snout are white plush, and the white plush on its snout is surrounded by a thin line of black plush. Purrrr-fect!

Halo   A white new-faced bear, Halo bears what looks like the retired Magic's wings of iridescent material filled with stuffing. S/he also has, what else, a halo made of the same material. Collectors will be dancing rings around this bear.

Loosy   Goosey! Joining Jake the mallard drake, Loosy is similar in style and coloring, but with the black head and white "chin strap" of the Canadian goose. Loosy also sports a red bow around his neck. You may have to migrate to find this bird in the stores anytime soon!

Pumkin   Only the third "thing" Beanie, following in the footsteps of Spooky and Snowball. Pumkin is a pumpkin, of course! This pumpkin has a topknot of dark green plush leaves and long, viney arms and legs. Not nearly as scary as the recently departed Halloween spider, Spinner.

Roam   Oh, give me a home for the buffalo, Roam! I've got to admit, of the non-holiday Beanies, Roam is probably going to be my favorite with his nappy fur on his head, shoulders, and front legs and smooth plush on his hindquarters. (Not to mention the little bit of nappy plush at the tip of his tail!)

Santa   A Beanie first—a "person" Beanie! Santa is… well… Santa! Complete with white, fluffy beard and Santa hat (one of three Beanies in this release with Santa-type caps!), the most distinguishing (and surprising) feature is Santa's Erin-green mittens! (Or maybe Santa is really Legs in disguise.)

Scorch   It took me a minute upon looking at the name of this new Beanie to realize what it was. It's a new dragon to replace our dearly departed Magic. Very similar in shape and size to the all-white Magic, Scorch appears to be the love child of Pounce and Fleece with what seems to be brown tie-dye nappy plush. His wings are iridescent gold, and is that a tongue or a little flame shooting from his mouth?

Zero   Think of Waddle, then put a Santa cap on him and you have Zero. It's hard to tell at this point if Zero is supposed to be a holiday Beanie (and perhaps intended to be short-lived) or just a winter Beanie. If you can find him in the store, check out his poem to see what you think!

1998 Holiday Teddy   All it takes is a glance at my given name to figure out which Beanie is my favorite among this set of new releases. If you replace the stars on Glory with holly leaves and holly berries, then stick a Santa-style cap (of the same plush) on her, add green and red ribbons around her neck (like the original pictures and rare version of the 1997 Teddy), and you'll have my "berry" favorite bear!

Give your Beanie Babies® a chance to camp-out in style! Send for your FREE sleeping bag today.

Each orange and blue sleeping bag is designed to keep your favorite Beanie snug and secure on those cold winter nights. To receive your free sleeping bag, please fill in the following information*:

Name: _____

Address:_____

City _____ State _____ ZIP _____

Had you heard of *The Complete Idiot's Guide*® series prior to your purchase of this book?
❏ yes   ❏ no

Have you purchased any other *Complete Idiot's Guides*? ❏ yes   ❏ no

If yes, what other titles?_____

What other topics would you like to see in this series?_____

Tell us more about yourself:
Age range: ❏ under 21 ❏ 21–35 ❏ 36–50 ❏ over 50
Education: ❏ high school ❏ college ❏ graduate school
Occupation: _____

Are you: Male ❏   Female ❏

Send coupon to:
Sleeping Bag Offer
Macmillan Publishing
1633 Broadway, 7th Floor
New York, NY 10019-6785

Allow 8–12 weeks for delivery. Only one sleeping bag per name or household. Offer expires 9/30/99.

Sleeping bags are made by GBS Sales.

*This information is solely for the use of Macmillan Publishing USA and will not be sold or given to any outside company.